CHARLES DICKENS AND THE FORM
OF THE NOVEL

CHARLES DICKENS
and the Form
of the Novel

Fiction and Narrative in Dickens' Work

GRAHAM DALDRY

BARNES AND NOBLE BOOKS
Totowa, New Jersey

© 1987 G. Daldry
First published in the USA 1986 by
Barnes & Noble Books
81 Adams Drive
Totowa, New Jersey, 07512
Printed in Great Britain

Library of Congress Cataloging-in-Publication Data

Daldry, Graham.
    Charles Dickens and the form of the novel.

    Bibliography: p.
    Includes index.
    1. Dickens, Charles, 1812-1870 — Technique.
2. Fiction — Technique.   3. Narration (Rhetoric)
4. Comic, The, in literature.   I. Title.
PR4591.D35 1986   823′.8   86-17315
ISBN 0-389-20675-X

CONTENTS

ACKNOWLEDGEMENTS

My thanks are due to all who have helped me in the preparation of this book. I would like to thank everybody at Liverpool University who has read and commented upon the typescript in various stages of preparation, but particularly Brian Nellist, who supervised my thesis, and without whose help, encouragement and enthusiasm everything would have been made very much more difficult.

I dedicate this book to Suzanne.

TEXTUAL NOTE

All pages references to works by Dickens are to the current Penguin editions except for those which refer to *Miscellaneous Papers* and *Sketches by Boz*. References for these are
to the 1870 Library Edition, published by Chapman and Hall.

INTRODUCTION

'Fiction' and 'Narrative'

My purpose in this book will be to trace the relation of two elusive and difficult aspects of literature, commonly described as those of genre and structure, within the novels of Charles Dickens. These two terms are notoriously problematic; within the novel, I want to show, they produce a deep division. This division, I will suggest, is so acute in Dickens' work that criticism has found itself effectively dividing the novelist into two writers, identifying Dickens either as a writer whose concerns are with language and the internal concerns of linguistic structure, or seeing him as a writer of 'social conscience'. The latter criticiam offers a writer concerned with the outer context of social reality, attempting to produce in the novel a realism for Victorian England, and to provide the novel as a social genre (1).

My concern is not primarily with either of these aspects alone, but with them both, and I have attempted to provide a study which is capable of drawing upon and integrating both approaches in order to understand the development of Dickens' works, and its importance in the evolution of the novel.

It has of course been necessary to be selective in the texts I have chosen to discuss, since it would simply not have been possible in a book of this length to examine the whole of Dickens' writing in detail. Instead, I have chosen six novels which, if not the 'greatest' of Dickens' works, illustrate most fully his development as a novelist. I have analysed these works in relation to their development of the form of the novel. In order to do so I have employed the terms 'fiction' and 'narrative' in a way which will perhaps seem unfamiliar, for I have attempted in the use of these terms to locate the 'form' of the novel as a product both of an internal, individual and structuring imagination, and at the same time of an externally 're-ceived', social, cultural and historical imagination, which has the generic, rather than the structural, as its priority. While I would wish this book to stand upon its practical analysis of the novels, and its active generation of a terminology which I have found necessary in approaching the novels, I will attempt

1

to provide in this Introduction some initial indication of the ways in which these terms have been used.

In a famous essay D.H.Lawrence saw the novel as divided against itself, writing in frustration that

> Greater novels, to my mind, are the books of the Old Testament, Genesis, Exodus, Samuel, Kings, by authors whose purpose was so big, it didn't quarrel with their passionate inspiration. The purpose and the inspiration were almost one. Why, in the name of everything bad, the two should ever have got separated, is a mystery! But in the modern novel they are hopelessly divorced. (2)

Lawrence here recognises two opposing concerns in the novel as those of 'inspiration' and 'purpose'. We can see how these might relate to an 'outer' concern with genre and an 'inner' concern with structure if we consider a division in the philosophy of interpretation, between 'intuitionism' and 'positivism'. E.D.Hirsch expounds these words in his excellent book, *The Aims of Interpretation.* Intuitionism, first of all,

> is probably the oldest principle of hermeneutics, being associated from the start with sacred interpretation. The letter killeth, but the spirit giveth life. (3)

Positivism, on the other hand, represents the opposite position:

> Under positivism, the mystical distinction between the letter and the spirit is repudiated. The interpreter should ignore the ghost in the machine and simply explain how the machine actually functions. ... Positivism shows itself to be the natural ally of stylistics and linguistics. The spirit killeth, but the letter giveth life. (4)

These two approaches correspond to our literary terms of 'genre' and 'structure'. Intuitionism places faith in the spirit of the work, and initially in the spirit of the Bible, the received word of God. This becomes the source, as Lawrence recognises, of generic authority, the speech that is not individual. Positivism, meanwhile, depends upon analysis of language and structure. Lawrence's position is clearly intended to be intuitionist, but he also provides us with an insight into the divided but mixed nature of the novel itself. In the novel, Lawrence tells us, intuitionism is constantly interfered with. The interference comes, of course, from the opposite position to the one he advocates, from the positivist side; the 'ghost in the machine' is disturbed by a concern with purpose, for purpose has to understand and show 'how the machine actually functions'. Lawrence champions the ghost, and does so because it *is* a ghost, constantly under the threat of analysis. At the

[handwritten margin note top: "Isn't the great thing about the novel that the structure is so pliable, it can bend to any narrative? Does it have any structure besides it ought to be between book covers?"]

same time, however, Lawrence's position is not itself as divisive
and one-sided as it at first appears, for his concern with the
division of the letter and the spirit is also informed by a
positivist concern for their structural unity, hence his impa-
tience with the disunity of the novel.   His intuitionism exists
by virtue of his knowledge that it ought to be at one with a
concern for purpose, and the knowledge of division produces
by interaction his own, apparently one-sided passion.   Because,
as he recognises, the novel is unlike the Bible, and is divided,
realisation of the threat of purpose and intention is *also*
realisation of the ghost.   The ghost survives by virtue of the
machine, and vice versa, and the interference and the frustration which comes about as the result of their inevitable
inter-association produces and affirms the vivacity and energy
of Lawrence's writing, and of the novel itself.   While one part
of the novel attends to its genre, the other part is concerned
with structure, language, and the non-literary but 'literal'
concerns received with them.   And while this second is
'positivist', regards the letter of the truth, and reproduces the
languages of reality, the first is 'intuitionist', regards the spirit
of the truth, and produces literary genres.   What has also
emerged, moreover, is that the division of these two parts of
the form of the novel is in some sense at least a 'modern' concern, attributable to the strictly secular nature of the form.
   This modernity shows us moreover a distinct capacity in
the novel for the accommodation of a very modern crisis, closely
related to the division of authorities which, as Lawrence and
Hirsch imply, is post-religious and secular, and that crisis is
represented by Darwinian theory.
   Gillian Beer's study of the assimilation of this radical adjustment of traditional beliefs into the novel in her book,
Darwin's Plots, brings us closer to a direct application of the
terms we have so far used, of 'genre' and 'structure',
intuitionism and positivism, to the form of the novel in both its
post- and pre-Darwinian capacities.
   Gillian Beer calls her final chapter on Thomas Hardy,
'Finding a Scale for the Human: Plot and Writing in Hardy's
Novels'.   She explains this title by demonstrating a division
within Hardy's work.   She tells us that on the one hand "plot
in Hardy is almost always tragic or malign": she continues,

> Darwin had sought to share Wordsworth's testamental lan-
> guage in his image of 'Natural Selection', which identified
> nature with benign planning and makes of natural selection
> a more correct form than man's merely artificial selection.
> Hardy reads such plans as plot; plot becomes malign and
> entrapping, because it is designed without the needs of
> individual life in mind.   Human variety is oppressed by
> the needs which generate plot. (5)

[handwritten margin note bottom: "Is the "structure" of the novel built on its exceptions?"]

3

On the other hand, however, Hardy's novels contain a very different kind of writing. Gillian Beer quotes Oliver Elton, one of the early critics to draw a comparison between them. He wrote of George Eliot, first, that

> While exhaustively describing life, she is apt to miss the spirit of life itself. Its unashamed passion, its careless gaiety, the intoxication of sunshine - so far as she understands these things, she leaves us feeling that she rather distrusts them. (6)

Hardy's work, Elton continues, is on the other hand

> characterised by these qualities. He does not distrust passion, gaiety, and sunshine, but records how through event and time they are threatened, thwarted, undermined. And how for each organism, and through writing, they are recuperated. (7)

The consequence of this co-existence of two different kinds of writing is that

> Hardy's writing is characterised by creative vacillation, by a shiftiness which survives the determination of plot. Life is devious and resourceful, constantly reassembling about new possibilities which lie just off the path of the obliterative energies of event. Happiness and hap form the two poles of his work. (8)

Once again, this language of 'happiness and hap' accords with what are becoming two significant groups of terms. 'Happiness', the 'ghost in the machine', faith in category, 'intuition', oppose 'hap' or 'event', the working of the machine, structure, 'positivism'. And once again these two groups of terms are seen side by side, as a matter of 'vacillation' between two forms of validity: "Happiness here does not share in the powers of narrative. Indeed it is almost at odds with narrative, because it is at odds with succession" (9).

We seem, now, to be approaching a language for this dualism which relates specifically to the novel. Clearly 'plot', or as Gillian Beer suggests 'narrative', would seem to provide one clear term, and does so with specific reference to the novel, since we recognise that in plot or narrative we identify the construction of the novel; and narrative is perhaps a more helpful term than plot, since it also offers the figure of 'narrator', the maker of the plot, the positivist writer who seeks to express himself through structure. This constructed writing and the narrator behind it is of course the writing Lawrence distrusts when in his famous maxim he tells us to 'trust the tale' and not the 'teller'.

how will he make that distinction?

'Narrative' is that part of the novel which is ordered, structured, and arranged by the individual writer. I will use the term to refer to that part of the novel which is formed within the writer's consciousness, and is constructed between beginning and ending. In constructing experience within this space, narrative is concerned with its 'literal' reflection of reality, which is its translation of experience into its own, internal terms of words, sentences, and so on. It disregards the 'spirit', the concern of genre, and seeks unity with it only through the primary medium of its own literal vision. Its approach is the positivist one, for the belief of narrative and narrator is in the order which its own writing, the writing it has itself constructed, can generate to make coherent, first itself, and, through itself, the world beyond it. To a narrative sense of the world, 'the spirit killeth, but the letter giveth life'; and that life is invested in its own structure and language.

What, then, of the other part of the novel, the part that operates in Hardy through 'happiness'? What language can we use for the 'intuitionist' part of the novel?

"Happiness", we have been told, "is almost at odds with narrative" and depends upon "the full sense of *life* elated in us by the range of sense perceptions which throng Hardy's writing" (10). These are 'recuperated' through writing; and this writing, we must assume, is different from plot or narrative, and constitutes the other part of the novel. Unlike the first kind of writing, it constitutes happiness because it believes, intuitionistically, in the spirit of things, and in *things themselves* through 'sense perceptions', in spite of the way they become constructed by plot. "The letter killeth"; so here, *'life'* belongs to the writing which does not plot, but which simply observes. Such writing is characterised by faith in immediate objects, and by its own immediate potency, not to construct but to observe the world, implying, but never of course in Hardy realising, a greater, outer genre.

Where we can call the first kind of writing 'narrative', then, we might call this second, intuitionist prose 'fiction', for it would seem to invoke, not the literal truth of reality, but a fictive spirit to the truth of reality. Whereas narrative places its faith in its own integrity and structure, and in a literal truth, the faith by which fiction occurs in the novel is the faith that is placed in what is not exclusively itself, in what is 'received' as genre. The belief of fiction is that what is written in the spirit of fiction will observe the world in the spirit of the truth. In the novel, this fictive perception places its faith in the outer world as if it provided genres, and instead of producing the story of beginnings and endings, of narrative, gives us as its substance a story composed, as Gillian Beer suggests, of immediate observations of reality.

Simultaneity of these two parts of the novel expands the scope of each, moreover. Plot, in a dualistic relation with the faith of fiction, can become the novel's means of dealing with the scepticism of the constructed novel, so that narrative might embrace both the possibility and the impossibility of literal truth in the positivist manner. Faith, meanwhile, in its simultaneous relation with plot, offers in the fictive nature of the novel to embrace both the possibility and the impossibility of spiritual truth in the intuitionist manner. The simultaneity of these two aspects becomes the novel's means of dealing with the uncertainty which surrounds our sense of their interrelation, for between them we find precisely the wavering and confirmation of our faith in reality, the certainty and uncertainty which is our perception both of the machine and of the ghost in it.

Between these terms and within them, then, we perceive an 'unstable liberty' which is the dualistic condition of the world we enter when we read, or write, the novel, the point of meeting which is necessarily the vacillation between two kinds of validity; and we perceive this vacillation by means of a language best founded, I want to suggest, upon the terms of 'fiction' and 'plot', or 'narrative'. These words offer us terms for truth in the novel which do not impose a dogmatic unity, and which require only an affirmation of our normative critical sense of the words, supplying us with the beginning of a language for the structure and nature of category of the novel's content. The difference between fiction and narrative is that where a narrative can be either literally or figuratively true as long as it has structure, a fiction is never the literal truth, and can be either structured or unstructured as long as it is written in the spirit of the reality it represents.

These two parts of the novel can be further distinguished by comparing the voices they produce in the novel. Narrative produces literal speech in the novel, whether authorial or otherwise, whereas fiction produces literary, but non-literal, speech. The natural voice of narrative is the single voice of the writer, for narrative has its truth invested in itself and in the way it internally constructs the world. The natural voice of fiction, meanwhile, is the common, literary voice of genre, for the fictive has its truth invested in the generic understanding of its words, and attempts to speak for everybody, as a received and culturally understood form. The novel is then the interaction of these two voices.

In summary, the structure of the novel tells as narrative tells, in sentences and plot; the nature of the novel is to be written as fiction is written, in the spirit of the truth; the simultaneous but discordant occurrence of the letter and the spirit of reality constitutes the novel.

Turning now to Dickens, I want to show that in being deeply, and increasingly self-consciously divided, between fiction and narrative, his novels are of formative imortance in the expression of what is essentially a 'modern', post-Biblical, and potentially post-Darwinian position. The novel anticipates and contains the Darwinian predicament, and expresses this position by means of the very discordance and indeterminacy of the fictive and narrative within it, for this uncertainty is endemic within the novel's form.

What I want to suggest is that in Dickens these opposing forces are brought together and explored by a self-conscious imagination capable of using all the various resources available to the novel, resources which include the ability to register both the literal and the literary, containing within the former both the full seriousness of the autobiographical story and the comically diverse detail of reality; and within the latter both the seriousness of moral, mythical genres and the many popular genres of early nineteenth century literature. Dickens admits every aspect of the novel into his work, and does so, as we will see, not in a haphazard and arbitrary way, but within a developing and even methodical intelligence. It was Dickens' achievement, I will argue, to locate the novel quite consciously, as a serious endeavour, in the midst of this tension, and to establish the form as primarily expressive of the conflict which we have defined as the one between fiction and narrative.

It will be my purpose here to trace the development of Dickens' novels and of the form of the novel in first attempting to resolve, and then to contain this opposition. In doing so, I will argue, he provides us with the beginnings of the modern novel.

Footnotes

(1) A comprehensive list of works on these respective aspects of the novels would be impossible; but among the works on Dickens' historical development which I have found valuable are the biographies by John Forster, *The Life of Charles Dickens* (London 1872), and Edgar Johnson, *Charles Dickens: his Tragedy and Triumph* (London 1953), and criticism by Barbara Hardy, in *The Moral Art of Dickens* (London 1970), H.M.Daleski, *Dickens and the Art of Analogy* (London 1970) and F.S.Schwarzbach, *Dickens and the City* (London 1979). Among the works on Dickens' language I have found the following most helpful; *The Violent Effigy* (London 1973), by John Carey; Steven Marcus, *Dickens: from Pickwick to Dombey* (New York 1965); S.J.Newman, *Dickens at Play* (London 1981); J.Hillis Miller, *Dickens: the World of his Novels* (Cambridge, Mass., 1958); and the brief section on Dickens in M.Bakhtin, *The Dialogic Imagination* (Austin 1981),p.302-8. In addition, I have found the following shorter essays most helpful, both in their analysis of the texts and in their hints at ways in which the novels develop and are related; Gabriel Pearson on *Dombey and Son* (in *The Modern English Novel* Ed. Josipovici (London 1976)) and on *The Old Curiosity Shop* (in *Dickens in the Twentieth Century* Ed. Josipovici (London 1962)); John Bayley on *Oliver Twist* (in *Dickens in the Twentieth Century*); and Robert Newsom, on *Bleak House* in *Dickens: on the Romantic Side of Familiar Things* (New York 1977).
(2) D.H.Lawrence, 'The Novel', reprinted in *A Selection from Phoenix*, 164.
(3) E.D.Hirsch, *The Aims of Interpretation*, 20.
(4) E.D.Hirsch, *The Aims of Interpretation*, 22.
(5) Gillian Beer, *Darwins' Plots*, 239.
(6) *Darwins' Plots*, 242.
(7) *Darwins' Plots*, 243.
(8) *Darwins' Plots*, 246.
(9) *Darwins' Plots*, 247.
(10) *Darwins' Plots*, 248.

CHAPTER ONE

The Division of the Novel

Dickens began his career as a writer when he submitted his first brief sketch to *Monthly Magazine*. This was followed by others, and later published as the collection, *Sketches by Boz*. These sketches are a remarkable collection of short pieces of prose; and they are remarkable in the variety and range of the stories they offer, for they almost immediately begin to develop a sense of what I have called the fictive and narrative parts of writing. They do so by proposing a fictive faith in the benevolence of the outer world, and then a capacity to understand reality in both of the ways I have described, by finding that faith more difficult than it at first instinctively appears.

The initially dominant part of the writing turns instinctively towards the fictive; for clearly, in the brief, episodic form of these stories, Dickens is not at first interested in questions of inner structure and formal unity. He very evidently begins his career as the participant in a common reality manifested in writing, in the conviction that writing exists as an outer, protective medium; as genre. (It is interesting, and indicative of the difficulties latent in the genre of the novel, that in doing so Dickens finds himself writing brief, episodic stories.)

The fictive, generic sense is very strong in Dickens at this early stage of his career. As a child, he tells us in 'Household Words', reality itself seemed to him to be almost a literary affair, and the world to be like one of the books of which he was an avid reader (1). When Dickens gives us his account of being lost as a child in London, it is as if he wanders among the contents of a popular literature, finding a place of 'monsters' and 'giants' (2), a world peopled by childhood stories of Jack and the beanstalk and Dick Whittington (3). So Dickens tells us,

> I wandered about the city, like a child in a dream, staring at the British merchants, and inspired by a mighty faith in the marvellousness of everything.(4)

He continues

> In such stories as I made, to account for the different places, I believed as devoutly as the City itself.(5)

This faith is precisely a fictive faith, and what it believes in is the world as a work of fiction, although even here we find in it an underlying fear which betrays the child's sense of the protective nature of this literary world. We find such faith in the *Sketches* as a celebration of the streets, crowds and popular entertainments of the city, and we also find it as a series of jokes against what we might recognise as the 'literal' understanding of the world, the understanding of narrative. We repeatedly find Dickens, in this fictive mood, making a series of jokes about coherence and continuity, which, of course, is the literal, structured medium of narrative, the province of sentence and plot.

These jokes occur in a variety of forms. Some are parenthetical asides - "We pause for reply; and, having no chance of getting one, begin a fresh paragraph" (6); "..looking forward as anxiously to the termination of our journey, as we fear our readers will have done, long since, to the conclusion of our paper" (7); "A troublesome form and arbitrary custom ... prescribe that a story should have a conclusion, in addition to a commencement" (8) - and others occur in the course of story telling. We are told of Mr William Barker, for example, that he "was born - But why need we relate where Mr William Barker was born, or when?" and Dickens continues,

> Mr William Barker *was* born, or he had never been. There is a son - there was a father. There is an effect - there was a cause. Surely this is sufficient information for the most Fatima-like curiosity; and, if it be not, we regret our inability to supply any further evidence on the point. Can there be a more satisfactory or strictly parliamentary course? Impossible. (9)

- shrugging off the consequential responsibilities of the literal writing of narrative, which would want to know precisely where and why William Barker was born. Barker belongs immediately to the generic sense of popular literature; cabs, hackney-coaches and omnibuses, and their drivers, become the metaphors for Dickens' roving instincts in these stories, but they also become metaphors for an apparently irrepressible popular will, so that their exploits are erected effortlessly to legendary status: we are told of Mr Barker, for instance, that

> Mr Barker it *ought* to have been who, honestly indignant at being ignominiously ejected from a house of public entertainment, kicked his landlord in the knee and thereby caused his death. We say that it *ought* to have been Mr

Barker, for the act was not a common one, and could have emanated from no ordinary mind. (10)

The figures that dominate this anarchic world seem above the law, providing the magistracy with "half their amusement" as well as "half their occupation" (11); when in jail, the driver of one particularly ubiquitous red cab "lies on his back on the floor, and sings comic songs all day" (12).
This ability to defeat the restriction of the world by amusement is at the heart of the world of fiction, which refuses to conform to the narrative's insistence upon the forces of literal truth; those of law and order, and justice. Consequence is ridiculed by immediacy: it does not matter where William Barker came from, and he replaces the consequential morality of narrative with an 'ought' that defeats responsibility.
These figures are almost the deities of a street culture, untouchable even by the laws they consistently flout. They are the authors of a world that opposes cognitive expression and exists, untouched by the concerns of organised existence, in a story which they dominate by the vitality of their power to amuse. Their life is properly expressed by the episodic, for their values are immediate and non-consequential. Courtroom and prison are not bad endings so much as occupational hazards. They signify the potency of literature by showing that the common, generic will is above law and consequence, acting (as the magistracy acts in these sketches) in the spirit rather than to the letter of communal existence.
Where the early *Sketches* are not dominated by the outright lawlessness of this humour, moreover, many are still governed by a continuity, a 'stream of men and moving things' (13), which both defeats comprehension and engages the imagination. Fairgrounds, pawn-brokers, shops, theatre, gardens, the river - any place where people gather and entertain themselves, or conduct their business is fastened upon by Boz's vagrant vision. The continual movement of the city (14) becomes the popular context of the fictive imagination, inviting the childlike faith in the literary organisation of reality which Dickens shows us in 'Household Words', and is the theme of all the *Sketches* classified under 'Scenes', most of which were published before 1836.
In some of the *Sketches*, however, we begin to see a sense of the qualities of narrative developing within them. Boz has always shown the awareness that his is not merely a passive participation in the life of the city. As a lost child, we hear of his 'mighty faith' in it; but we also, and inseparably hear of his fear (15), and this fear is a partial detachment and reservation from the marvellousness of everything, registering a possible lack of and need for control. The *Sketches* half accept that the voices of the city are fictive, generic voices, and Boz half assents to them; but he also reserves his own distinctive authority, and with it his own narrative, literal

11

control. "Romance can make no head against the Riot Act"(16), 'the First of May' uncompromisingly declares, "and pastoral simplicity is not understood by the police." The cabbies' irresponsibilities are suddenly confronted by a justice that threatens real restriction, and jokes themselves begin to show a social conscience: "We were disturbed from our slumber by some dark insinuations thrown out by a friend of ours to the effect that children in the lower ranks of life were beginning to *choose* chimney sweeping", we are told in the course of this Sketch. The former "mighty faith in the marvellousness of everything" gives way to the beginnings of a scepticism and suddenly actions begin to have consequences after all. This scepticism, of course, is still not a serious one; but it does begin to piece the fictive world together into a narrative - and disappointed - sense which overturns childhood faith.

> We have shut out conviction as long as we could, but it has forced itself upon us and we now proclaim to a deluded public, that the May-day dancers are *not* sweeps. The size of them, alone, is enough to repudiate the idea. (17)

The consequence (as narrative now dictates) of this discovery is a vision of 'things as they are' which for the first time is governed not by attraction and fascination but by disillusion and contempt. The conclusion, "How has May-day decayed!"(18) threatens the willing suspension of disbelief which Dickens professes in the *Preface* to the *Memoirs of Joseph Grimaldi* ("we.. still believe ... as devoutly as we did before twenty years' experience had shown us that they were always wrong" (19)).

The difference between this disillusionment and those earlier stories - in 'Private Theatres', or 'Vauxhall Gardens by Day' - where the fun and laughter of illusions have fallen flat is that here the failure of enjoyment, finding disillusionment a process of growing up, and needing to revert for the full and original illusion to childhood, finds that a benevolent reality is not capable of containing a general disillusion. Where enjoyment is a confirmation of a fundamentally benevolent environment, and the success at the same time of the protagonist and of the participation of the writer in the life of the world, failed enjoyment finds that reality falls short, and is a failure, in the same way, for the writing.

The failure of amusement here means the beginning of a questioning of the generic control of reality, and the conditions provided by the real world for human existence. While amusements have failed in the *Sketches* before, they have been theatrical failures, only rash self-exposures, in which the sufferer by the joke was after all its perpetrator. Such failures are deserved, and function as a kind of judgement. The sufferers in this joke - the sweeps - have suffering imposed upon them, and, in spite of the story's pretence otherwise, that suffering is in turn imposed upon the story; our attention is firmly fixed to the writing's social conscience by the telling of the story as if it *were* a failed joke, and the failure the fault of the sweeps. We know that their choice is no choice, and that knowledge focuses our attention, like the story's, not upon individual vitality, but upon something which excludes coincidence - as it excludes the possibility that most sweeps are princes; the inevitable process of degradation and decline.

Suddenly, we are on the side of narrative, understanding the hardship of the sweeps in its literal rather than literary implications, as a real suffering, and looking for an individual responsibility in the writing rather than for a common faith in a reality which here seems irresponsible. The social environment no longer appears to be a source of benevolence. Responsibilities begin to be taken more seriously, so that, from now on, the courts have no humour, and the former freedom of anarchic behaviour is hedged around by restrictions: the boy of thirteen tried for pickpocketing in 'Criminal Courts' produces no general laughter in court:

> Finding it impossible to excite compassion, he gives vent to his feelings in an imprecation bearing reference to the eyes of "old big vig!" and as he declines to take the trouble of walking from the dock, is carried out, congratulating himself on having succeeded in giving everybody as much trouble as possible. (20)

'Everybody' is here no longer on the side of irresponsibility: we no longer see the joke. The writing begins to be more interested in the external business of control than in the inspiration of the character it portrays, and finds itself excluded from its former intimacy with everyday life. The participant writer who was as much a part of his London as the cabbies now wears the hat of investigator and begins to feel uncomfortably and even guiltily out of place in his own scenes. Reality becomes the subject of self-conscious inquiry. "Often have we strayed here... to catch a glimpse of the whipping-place," Boz writes at the beginning of 'Criminal Courts' - 'straying' in default of the right to be there; 'We could not help observing them'; and 'curiosity has occasionally led us' (21). Those 'thoughts' have usurped spontaneity as writing becomes conscious, losing the 'faith in everything', at first naively taken for granted, controlling reality within a distancing prose. This kind of thinking, which is frequently encountered in the 'Characters' sequence, sets the writer unwillingly apart. In 'the Hospital Patient', Boz is 'impressed with those thoughts' (22) and finds himself only self-consciously a part of 'everybody', of the crowd: "somehow, we never can resist joining a crowd, so we turned back with the mob" (23). We have heard nothing of the 'mob' in the earlier pieces, for Boz has been at home in it. The 'mighty faith' in things is replaced by an outside vision which is most noticeable in 'A Visit to Newgate' where we are told of a girl seen in prison that she

> Belonged to a class - unhappily but too extensive - the very existence of which should make men's hearts bleed. Barely past her childhood, it required but a glance to discover that she was one of those children, born and bred in vice, who had never known what childhood is. (24)

Dickens' treatment of the prostitute is the opposite of his treatment of William Barker, whom good humour and anarchic imagination made apparently indestructable in a chaotic world which nevertheless invited common assent and seemed to express a generic will. The vision of this woman divides the fictive world created by the cabby, for in her fate and suffering lies the cruelty of a real world which 'should' have done better for her. The world outside, for the writing its generic sense of audience and readership, has failed, so that the writer becomes dissociated from it. The new, narrating voice of the writer is now isolated from its audience which is no longer trusted. Whereas in the case of William Barker narrative, and its concerns of coherence and continuity, could be abandoned in a 'mighty faith', here the writer finds that he must insist upon the validity of consequence in order to find judgement and, inseparably, dissociation. Her story 'requires but a glance' in its identification as a missing 'childhood'.

This narrative, however, is problematic, since its narrative voice also represents an absence of the common organisation of reality; its coherence depends upon the literal but solitary observation of the writer's voice, which suddenly seems to stand alone, abandoned by the former cheerful presence of 'everybody' in the crowd. This loneliness leaves the narrator vulnerable, and while it is born of responsibility, it becomes clear that, in the absence of a benevolent outer reality, that responsibility is to the writer and the writing, but not to the world outside. Narrative, unlike fiction, has as its primary concern itself, and upholds its own sense of consequence in looking immediately to the prostitute's missing origin, to the fact that she herself has no narrative.

It is for this reason that Dickens does not abandon the fictive, which was after all the instinctive expression of Dickens' imagination, to confine himself within the literal, linguistic imagination of narrative. Instead, the remaining sketches maintain a fascination with those things which are most problematic to narrative, with prisons, criminals, crowds, and degradation; and neither would it be true to say that a moralising, narrative voice comes to dominate his writing. Just as the fictive, episodic form of the *Sketches* seemed to belong to the 'marvellousness of everything', and was half-natural to the way that Dickens saw and experienced reality, so the dissociative voice of the narrator, and its moralistic distance, seems half-alien to him. One of the last of the *Sketches*, 'Horatio Sparkins', demonstrates clearly the fictive energy which is always latent, re-employing the Bill Barker jokes about narratives:

> "What!" said Horatio, who became more metaphysical and more argumentative, as he saw the female part of the family listening in wondering delight -
> "What! Is effect the consequence of cause? Is cause the consequence of effect?"
> "That's the point," said Flamwell.
> "To be sure," said Mr Malderton.
> "Because, if effect is the consequence of cause, and if cause does precede effect, I apprehend you are wrong," added Horatio.
> "Decidedly," said the toad-eating Flamwell. (25)

Here, as earlier, narrative makes itself the subject of a joke about its own dogma of consequence although it now does so within the framework of a story. The protection and continuation of such fictive, literary enjoyment, moreover, is the purpose of the *Pickwick Papers*. Mr Pickwick himself represents a subtle protective action against the conflicts and divisions of these questions of narrative and fiction, and is a means of continuing to combine the comedy of fiction with the responsibility of narrative. He replaces external values, as a surrogate for the benevolence of a reality now viewed with discomfort and distrust. He personifies benevolence, in order to release the kinds of individualistic irresponsibility constrained since the early *Sketches* by the need felt by Dickens for his writing to be a watchful and protecting, and not simply participating, activity.

Like Bill Barker, Pickwick defies cause and effect; his life is continually in mid-story, for we know neither his past history nor, ultimately, his future. His peculiarity is that he exists in the course of a narrative. When the cab drivers and omnibus cads begin and end in the middle of things in the *Sketches*, they do so because what matters is not where they come from, or go to, but what they unselfconsciously do. Pickwick really does nothing; what matters about him, since he exists in the context of a long narrative and not a single episode, is paradoxically the fact that he seems to come from and go nowhere at all. He is simply *there*, static in terms of progressive action. The secret of the novel's 'plot' - which revolves around sexual suspicion of Pickwick - is no real secret, for there is always that undercutting knowledge that his flirtation with illicit activity must be utterly harmless, given our immovable and unmoving assurance of Pickwick's inactive innocence. (26)

While the jokes of *Pickwick*, then, do not stand up on their own - since there is always Pickwick to come before and after them, robbing them of their independence - his stasis at the same time defuses the sense of story. He turns the idea rather than the reality of irresponsibility into a joke (27); and makes a story of the idea, rather than the reality, of action. While it might be claimed that he thereby gives us both fictive irresponsibility and the moral sense of narrative - the Victorians evidently thought he did - there is an equally good case for saying that he really gives us neither.

The *Papers*, and the figure of Pickwick himself, are a monument to the profundity of Dickens' faith in the 'marvellousness of everything', as well as to the depth of his real knowledge of the nature of the novel even at this early stage of his development as a novelist. The energy of the book, however, - what Gabriel Pearson called Dickens' "immense high spirits" (28) - is the energy of avoidance and dissociation from that real knowledge, and the darker shadows of the late *Sketches*. The book, under Pickwick's protection, is set apart from the real forces of the world, which have to be compromised in order to ensure his survival. Jingle, Mrs Bardell, Dodson and Fogg, Sam Weller, and even the financial and business world to which we know Pickwick must have once belonged, all have their edges blunted upon Pickwick's ineffectuality, and the book depends upon their recognition of him. He conquers them all, friend, enemy and lawyer, by implicating them within the Pickwickian 'you may do with me as you please' (29), his ultimate compliance with any condition the world might set him. This works two ways; for his compliance is traded for conditions which are only superficially malevolent, so that even the law seems subject to his magnanimity.

The *Pickwick Papers*, then, are very much an aside to seriousness; in dissociating writing, through Pickwick, from the real world, from the real problems of the novel, and from both fiction and narrative, the book succeeds in avoiding the questions of association and dissociation, of irresponsibility and responsibility, and of anarchy and control, which had threatened to become problematic in the course of the *Sketches*.

While the form of the *Pickwick Papers* is in some ways a resolution of the problems which Boz had already begun to face, it also presents a problem for the novelist in itself, for it avoids identification as any single kind of writing. It is not a series of sketches; yet neither is it a continuous narrative. In trying to be both, it succeeds in becoming neither. While Pickwick seems at first to be a large enough figure to protect the position of the writer, and to allow the kind of freedom Boz enjoyed in the *Sketches*, we are left by the end of the book to wonder what secrets produced Pickwick; for nowhere else in the English novel do we encounter such a purely protective figure.

What Pickwick excludes, and what we begin to wonder about, is the relationship of what is left out of *Pickwick Papers*, of Pickwick's respectable past to the full irresponsible force of Sam Weller's sense of humour, for both the literal, consequential

detail of the narrative and the common will of the fictive are left
out of the novel.

This compromise can be treated as an evasion; but it is
also a remarkable success, and one means of producing a unity
of the narrative and fiction that seemed so mutually hostile by
the later *Sketches*. For its energies of compromise are new
energies, taking up the mixed themes of the *Sketches* and developing them into a single work. The book was, of course, a
phenomenal success; as Robert Patten tells us,

> Though *Sketches* inaugurated Dickens' career, *Pickwick*
> made it. Dickens' first continuous fiction - many would
> deny that it is a novel - ushered in the age of the novel
> ... The success of the flimsy shilling parts, issued in
> green wrappers once each month from April 1836 to No-
> vember 1837, was unprecedented in the history of
> literature. (30)

He continues

> ...parts publication became for thirty years a chief means
> of democratizing and enormously expanding the Victorian
> book-reading and book-buying public. (31)

While Patten suggests that this means to success was discovered "virtually by accident", I would argue that it was
evolved as a way of understanding contemporary reality in
writing, and that this publication of a long novel in short parts
expresses in itself the mixed nature of the work, providing the
characteristic Dickensian compromise between the plot of the
narrative and the immediate faith in the literariness of the
endeavour, its generic appeal to its public. This way of writing
and publishing was, or rapidly became, integral to Dickens'
imagination, and at the same time, as Patten indicates, newly
established the novel in its modern character, as a mediation
of fiction and narrative. The *Pickwick Papers* does not achieve
a unity of the world so much as a new way of expressing it,
'in-between'; a voice which comes about as if by accident,
falling between irresponsibility and respectability.

The novel, however, remains fundamentally unsatisfactory
as we have seen. Its haphazard universality depends upon the
naivety of its own modernity, its willingness to forget both real,
consequential narrative and real, anarchic fiction, and be content to bring them together at their least demanding. For both
Dickens and his public, however, *Pickwick Papers* is a 'modus
vivendi'; but for both, the problem it exists in the middle of
continues unsolved.

By the end of the *Pickwick Papers*, however, we see that
Dickens has the invaluable and necessary capacity to exist and
work between the divided parts of the novel, the dual impulses

of writing towards narrative and fiction, and to find an expression for a new reality.

What this new world seems to lack is a common, popular story which can at the same time have the fully responsible structure of narrative; and this story is the biblical, mythical one that Lawrence laments, the sense that genre offers plot. It is this that we saw was lacking in the prostitute at Newgate; she "had never known what childhood is". *Oliver Twist* turns towards this lack of a common story in an attempt to supply one in the novel.

It does so without losing sight of the division that Pickwick exists between. The story of Oliver exists from the beginning upon both sides of that division. On the one hand, he is to provide the narrative that was missing from the prostitute, showing us the beginning of a story which can exist in spite of her. He is to be an innately 'good', moral child, born into an irresponsible and chaotic world, and his story is to be the story of his restoration to his proper place. In the course of this fable, the respectable world is to be definitively separated from the lower and criminal world, so that Oliver is not only to end the 'in-between' vision of the middle classes which became compromise in Pickwick, but, by naturally belonging to them and providing them with his narrative of identity, to establish their security and to place the power of narrative and writing in their hands. Narrative, the authority of coherence, is to be established as belonging to this novel's Pickwick, Mr Brownlow, and to be removed from the fragmentation and chaos which threatens, in Sikes and the underworld, to destroy narrative in the 'endless stream of things'.

Oliver's story, meanwhile, is to authorise this middle-class vision by existing at the same time upon the other side of the Pickwickian world which narrative would normally, in its role as the medium of social respectability and morality, exclude. His innocence is proposed as a way of seeing everything - both narrative and fiction, coherence and the fragmentariness it fears - and of making the 'middle' vision inclusive in spite of the division of higher and lower worlds that narrative must inevitably sustain. Oliver takes us back in this way to that mythical time before cruelty began, to the fairyland of amusement, the point before the disillusion of childhood that we saw in the *Sketches*.

In Oliver, we seem to be offered the narrative we seek, the narrative that can also take on the observing role of fiction, and see everything. The narrative, moreover, is to have the mythical force missing from the *Sketches*, and present only in a limited way in Mr Pickwick, and to combine and unify fiction and narrative in an authoritative way; Oliver is to confirm and enforce the outer justice of the world, the presence after all of that all-inclusive genre and structure which Lawrence identified in the Bible, whose source was nothing less than God.

Oliver Twist does not however set out to believe in but to investigate this unity. In order to do so, Oliver is set to grow up into a world directed by this faith, a world which at the beginning of the novel we doubt. We have never, as yet, heard the voice of external authority; it seemed to be missing from the *Sketches* and from the compromise Pickwick makes. This means that the question of the location of the narrator in the novel, the question that Boz found so problematic in 'A Visit to Newgate' (32), is an immediately interesting one, for as I have suggested the voice of narrative and the voice of fiction differ radically, producing isolation and community respectively. *Oliver Twist* asks this question from its beginning; where is that (godly) authority that can both narrate and afford to register everything, and be both narrative and fictive?

Our first expectation must be that this voice will be located, with Oliver, in the middle class world, for it is in the latter that we see the values of responsibility, justice and protection, inherited from Pickwick, to be most active, and they provide the projected end of Oliver's story. Oliver is to see everything; Brownlow is to provide the story.

Oliver's relationship to the latter and to the Maylies, and their relationship to him, is my first concern here, for it is strangely uncomfortable. Mr Brownlow, the Maylies and Mr Losberne consistently represent the novel's middle-class narrative concerns; and it is their very narrative sense which fails to welcome Oliver, for in their strict concern with his true origin he is always to some extent under suspicion. Mr Brownlow, who is very much the leading figure of the group, is burdened (as Dickens' narrating consciousness is) by the cruelties of inconsistency discovered by his own past; he has been 'deceived before', and sees and fears the precariousness of middle-class respectability at the expense of understanding Oliver: "you need not be afraid of my deserting you" he tells him "unless you give me cause"(33). Instead of relieving Oliver of the responsibility for himself and for his thoughts and feelings which makes his world so private, confused, insecure, and frightened - which should be the proper function of an organised, narrative respectability - Mr Brownlow makes that responsibility even greater. Oliver's obligation is to him not simply emotional and moral, but social and economic. "Speak the truth, and you shall not be friendless while I live" (34), Brownlow tells Oliver: 'speaking the truth' requires him to know and adhere to an identity which Brownlow himself feels the insecurity of. Oliver's 'natural' knowledge will provide Brownlow with his own true nature and knowledge of the world.

The authority here, then, rests with Oliver rather than with Brownlow. Oliver is not adopted by a middle-class narrative; he is its author. Brownlow's generosity is a disguised demand for something that he needs from Oliver, and needs desperately:

> I only say this, because you have a young heart; and knowing that I have suffered great pain and sorrow, you will be the more careful, perhaps, not to wound me again. (35)

'Pain and sorrow' is the pain and sorrow of a faltering narrative which needs Oliver to be its good ending, and to turn out well. In so doing the cause of the pain, the lack of identity and the difficulty of recognising one's own nature in others, will be at least relieved. Mr Brownlow is like Dickens and a middle class public, in that he needs Oliver to turn out to be the narrative he wants to believe in, and so to confirm his own place and perception in the world.

Rose and Mrs Maylie treat Oliver the same way, the only difference being that they are the more willing to accept him, never, presumably, having been 'deceived before': Mrs Maylie tells Oliver

> You shall give nothing at all ... for, as I told you before, we shall employ you in a hundred ways, and if you only take half the trouble to please us, that you promise now, you will make me very happy indeed. (36)

As with Mr Brownlow, Oliver is given responsibility for making and fulfilling promises and turning out well; and the Maylies' happiness, and not his, is what is at stake. The abstraction from Oliver's real and immediate presence is once again a determination to wait and see what he becomes. The Maylies are not interested in the present, but in the future, and in the inauspicious past. They provide Oliver with a novel which abandons fiction for narrative, so that the whole of Oliver's relationship to them becomes abstracted from the present, and purely a matter of his past, and future, life. Action in this narrative world is invested in Oliver's story.

This makes things that happen when Oliver is with them oddly unreal. The unreality begins with the way they treat Oliver, for what they say to him relates, not to the present but to their expectation of the future. In the case of both Mr Brownlow and Mrs Maylie, what Oliver is told is a formalisation of his position which has no immediate relevance for or effect upon him. "You shall give us nothing at all," Mrs Maylie tells him; there is nothing Oliver can do to establish any immediacy in his relationship to these 'good' people.

Moreover, they never seem to do anything themselves; their mannerisms and eccentricities seem gratuitous and pointless. Mr Losberne demonstrates the inability to act spontaneously from which they all suffer; impetuosity, the price of such action, is avoided by a curious kind of middle class committee, so that action, where action involves individual responsibility, becomes unnecessary. Eccentricity becomes in this context meaningless, and what does happen spontaneously seems unreal and irrelevant to what has become the concerted narrative. When Mr Losberne attempts to raid the thieves' house single-handed his action seem absurdly desperate, and is made even more confusing by Oliver's own nightmare encounter with the cripple who

> looked into the carriage, and eyed Oliver for an instant with a glance so sharp and fierce and at the same time so furious and vindictive, that, waking or sleeping, he could not forget it for months afterwards.(37)

This is an extraordinary and disorientating observation, for in it Dickens betrays how little the middle class world controls the novel. We are thrown upon Oliver once again as the writer's medium, bewildered by these middle-class expectations and doubts of his true nature. We are dependant upon his narrative as a confirmation of the reality of this oddly inactive and expectant world; and at the same time, existing in Oliver's present, find the middle-class concern with past and future to create an existence which is oddly dreamlike, abstracted from real events. "It was almost too much happiness to bear" (38), we are told at one point, when Rose recovers from illness; "Oliver felt stunned and stupefied by the unexpected intelligence." We share Oliver's bewilderment here, for we find it impossible to place Rose's recovery as an event. It seems to occur at random, and to depend upon Oliver, as much as anyone, to bring it about by gathering flowers. Like all the other events of the middle-class world, it seems to be curiously dislocated, so that Oliver finds his existence in it to be like a dream, in a world that awaits the organisation of wakefulness. This inactivity seems to be particular to the world of the middle classes, for in it everything seems to depend upon Oliver. When Oliver sleeps in Fagin's den, and watches the Jew through "half-closed eyes" (39), sleep is only his disguise, for we know that what he sees happens; when he sleeps in the Maylie world, sleep becomes a way of seeing, not a secret wakefulness but a participation in itself. What Oliver sees becomes part of a general ambivalence. When in Chapter 34 Oliver, half-asleep, sees the Jew and Monks through the window of his room (40), there is afterwards no trace of either to be seen by anyone else; but we are not told that Oliver was making it up, or even, derogatively, daydreaming. Narrative, with its preoccupation with beginning and ending, is incapable of - or not interested in - distinguishing between real and imaginary things which do not relate to its inner plot, so that the dream has in the Maylie world a status equal to reality. It is as active as any other form of perception in it, and the truth of Oliver's seeing is later confirmed as valid:

...It was the same man he had met at the market-town,
and seen looking in with Fagin at the window of his little
room (41)

we are told when Monks' identity is revealed.

As with Brownlow's warnings, Mrs Maylie's assurances, and
Mr Losberne's action, the details are not what matter here; what
matters is the end - the narrative. So that even when Oliver
is not asleep his own vision, which registers details rather than
outcomes, often seems to have the quality of a dream. The
following passage occurs just after Rose's recovery, when Oliver
goes out to gather flowers:

> The night was fast closing in, when he returned homeward:
> laden with flowers which he had culled, with peculiar care,
> for the adornment of the sick chamber. As he walked
> briskly along the road, he heard behind him, the noise of
> some vehicle, approaching at a furious pace. Looking
> round, he saw that it was a post-chaise, driven at great
> speed; and as the horses were galloping, and the road
> was narrow, he stood leaning against a gate until it should
> have passed him.
>
> As it dashed on, Oliver caught a glimpse of a man in
> a white night-cap, whose face seemed familiar to him, al-
> though his view was so brief that he could not identify the
> person. In another second or two, the night-cap was
> thrust out of the chaise-window, and a stentorian voice
> bellowed to the driver to stop: which he did, as soon as
> he could pull up his horses. Then, the night-cap once
> again appeared; and the same voice called Oliver by his
> name. (42)

The truth, here, has become stranger than fiction, for in
the Maylie's narrative world, detail, the material of the fictive
and fragmentary, has the secondary status of dreaming and is
displaced from reality, taking its place instead in the confusion
of Oliver's imagination. Reality becomes a 'kind of sleep', a
dream-world where objects seem to have the extraordinary
quality of not belonging to anything. This strange passage
heralds, in terms of the plot, nothing more portentous than the
arrival of Harry Maylie. Everything here seems to be contingent
and dislocated, undermining the security that the flowers are
meant to celebrate. Things that ought to be familiar are made
anonymous and mysterious: first, Oliver hears "the noise of
some vehicle"; then the white nightcap has a face which "seemed
familiar" although Oliver "could not identify the person". The
voice is dislocated from its body, and, while it knows Oliver's
name, belongs to nothing more identifiable than a nightcap.
This dream-world half claims us, as it half claims Oliver,
using his name, but not allowing any mutual recognition. Any
such recognition is alien to the Maylies' world.

It does have a security of a kind, however, a specific ideal, represented, not by affections or friendships, but by its paragon of beauty in Rose. It is not the fact that she is alive and survives her illness, moreover, - a mere detail which Oliver finds too much for him - that matters to this respectable world, but what Rose stands for. We are told that she was

> ...cast in so slight and exquisite a mould; so mild and gentle; so pure and beautiful; that earth seemed not her element, nor its rough creatures her fit companions. (43)

The Maylies dream not, as Oliver does, as the function of a waking consciousness in a bewildering world, but to stop that consciousness, and to separate their own world from it; and Rose is a symbol of the end of the dream. Physically, she hardly exists; she is "slight and exquisite" so that "earth seemed not her element". Living or dead, Rose is something that the middle classes can dream of, a consciousness apart from the physical reality of the world. Rose is not there to be recognised, or felt for, as another human being, but to be aspired to. She is not so much a character as the condition of abstraction from details and the gross immediacy of the fictive, the possible subject of an ethereal sexual relationship that Mr Brownlow and the committee, the plot of the novel and a part of Dickens' self all want. In her, goodness is defined as apart from the world and its rough creatures. Rose is the end of the story Brownlow wants Oliver to tell, and with her as his ideal we are shown glimpses of Oliver in heaven: when he is first recovered by Rose and Mrs Maylie, his

> ...pillow was smoothed by gentle hands that night; and loveliness and virtue watched him as he slept. He felt calm and happy, and could have died without a murmur. (44)

This happiness is the happiness of a virtuous death. And a holiday with the Maylies in the country similarly has the power of restoring men to heaven:

> Crawling forth, from day to day, to some green sunny spot, they have had such memories wakened up within them by the sight of the sky, and hill and plain, and glistening water, that a foretaste of heaven itself has soothed their quick decline, and they have sunk into their tombs, as peacefully as the sun... The memories which peaceful country scenes call up, are not of this world, nor of its thoughts and hopes. ... There lingers, in the least reflective mind, a vague and half-formed consciousness of having held such feelings long before, in some remote and distant time, which calls up solemn thoughts of distant times to come, and bends down pride and worldliness beneath it. (45)

The narrative Oliver is to give this perfect vision will place it as the true end of the human world, and locate this ideal middle class narrative with its retirement to the countryside and to peace, as the substance of reality. The confirmation of it all as 'natural' in Oliver's past is the endorsement that the middle class world awaits, the proof of its ability to recognise and to be recognised, and so to identify itself.

The narrative we are given, however, is probably the least convincing part of the novel. The convoluted tale that Brownlow pieces together in Chapter 49 with Monks' help does not make a unity of the novel's world in any sense, for it installs Monks as the chief villain. As a middle-class criminal he can not only be dealt with upon Brownlow's own terms, but also does away with the need to confront the criminal world as Oliver has experienced it. We find Oliver's story taken over at this last moment by what Mr Brownlow knows - as he tells Monks, "denial to me is vain" - so that, instead of confirming Brownlow's status by his story, Oliver seems excluded from it, and Brownlow's narrative fulfils the condition of the narrative voice by being sufficient to itself alone. Its authority is at least doubtful, moreover. Its power seems to depend very much upon Monks' weakness; when Brownlow asks him "do you still brave me?",

> "No, no, no!" returned the coward, overwhelmed by these accumulated charges.(46)

As a denouement this is unsatisfactory; narrative is endowed by Monks and not Oliver, and instead of discovering a natural middle-class origin it discovers an unnatural one. Oliver was to have discovered the truth and strength of respectability; instead Monks discovers respectability for us in a weakness we could scarcely imagine in Sikes, or even Fagin, producing Brownlow's story for him by effectively protecting him from their world.

Oliver, however, has not relinquished his original function, to see the whole of reality. The world that he enters in doing so conflicts directly with narrative and respectability both in the way that it treats him, and in the way that he perceives it.

The middle-class world seems unreal to Oliver, because it is presented as a set of narrative limitations which he was to overcome through his wider narrative; - not as an organised world, but a restricted one, which Oliver was to give a full authority. When Oliver enters the novel's other world, we see why he could never bear that responsibility. His imaginative, fictive vision sees too much to provide the Maylies and Brownlow with the narrative they require; his innocent vision exceeds the limitation of their world.

But where reality is unlimited by respectability, innocence in turn becomes a limitation. Whereas Oliver is the active agent among the Maylies' values, seeing everything as a matter of detail, and showing us the fictive in their narrative sense as an unreality of their consequential and sequential, carefully plotted world, in Fagin's den he finds himself overwhelmed by a world of detail. The odd, visionary authority he had in the world of narrative disappears in the underworld, where he sees things too late, or not at all.

This restriction, which is the restriction of innocence, is amenable to the middle class, in-between vision, in the spirit of which Oliver was conceived; but it means that he cannot fulfil that intended function and become our vision of this lower, fragmented, fictive world. Here, he simply becomes a child again - and this return to his childish status has frequently been noted as something of a restoration. John Bayley notes that Fagin was in real life the boy who showed Dickens kindness at the Blacking warehouse (47); and it seems that the reversal can be taken further than this. Kellow Chesney tells us that "the open-minded reader of *Oliver Twist* may find himself thinking that there is something to be said for Fagin and his establishment" (48), observing that "for the first time in his life, the workhouse boy finds himself with enough food, cheerful companions and a fair chance of not being wantonly flogged" and that "these managers of child thieves did in fact train them in the way described". The moral, narrative world treats Oliver as the human being (and not specifically child) it wants him to be; while the fictive and chaotic place that Fagin represents offers to educate (however wrongly) and to recognise childhood. In this simple recognition are contained the feelings Oliver needs so badly, and has never yet found, of human association; for what is most important about Fagin's world is not the abstract construction of narrative, but the physical immediacy of details. Fagin is not concerned with what Oliver adds up to, but with what he is - just as the real Fagin was with Dickens.

Mr Brownlow, Mr Losberne and Mrs Maylie had no physical appearance; Fagin by contrast "was a very old shrivelled Jew, whose villainous-looking and repulsive face was obscured by a quantity of matted red hair" (49), while Sikes "was a stoutly built fellow of about five-and-thirty" who had "a broad heavy countenance with a beard of about three days' growth, and two scowling eyes" (50). Where Rose was so ethereal as to almost have appearance without presence, Nancy, described with her friend Bet,

> wore a good deal of hair, not very neatly turned up be-
> hind, and were rather untidy about the shoes and
> stockings. They were not exactly pretty perhaps; but
> they had a great deal of colour in their faces, and looked
> quite stout and hearty. Being remarkably free and

agreeable in their manners, Oliver thought them very nice girls indeed. (51)

Sexuality, and in Fagin repulsion, immediately comes to the fore in these descriptions; and in the case of this description of Nancy and Bet it is immediately problematic to a middle-class narrative voice. "As no doubt they were" (52), it adds testily to Oliver's impression of them as 'nice girls'.

Already, here, Oliver's innocent vision of this fictive world is at odds with a narrative that wants to establish its respectable voice as the unifying voice of the novel. Oliver, moreover, has not seen everything here; it is clear that much of the action in this novel will take place beyond the comprehension of the innocence that might protect narrative from fiction, and from the realities we begin to glimpse in Nancy and Bet.

The exchanges we hear in this underworld certainly pass beyond Oliver's understanding; and through his innocent eyes we discover a different world, and one which is far from innocent. The most important of these exchanges, of course, form the relationship between Sikes and Nancy, and these are remarkable, both in that they appear in the novel at all, and in the function they perform.

"Whining, are you?" said Sikes. "Come! Don't stand snivelling there. If you can't do better than that, cut off altogether. D'ye hear me?"

"I hear you," replied the girl, turning her face aside, and forcing a laugh. "What fancy have you got in your head now?"

"Oh! You've thought better of it, have you?" growled Sikes, marking the tear which trembled in her eye. "All the better for you, you have."

"Why, you don't mean to say you'd be hard on me tonight, Bill," said the girl, laying her hand upon his shoulder.

"No!" cried Mr Sikes. "Why not?"

"Such a number of nights," said the girl, with a touch of woman's tenderness, which communicated something like sweetness of tone, even to her voice: "such a number of nights as I've been patient with you, nursing and caring for you, as if you had been a child: and this the first that I've seen you like yourself; you wouldn't have served me as you did just now, if you'd have thought of that, would you? Come, come; say you wouldn't."

"Well, then," rejoined Mr Sikes, "I wouldn't. Why, damme, now, the girl's whining again!"

"Its nothing," said the girl, throwing herself into a chair. "Don't you seem to mind me. It'll soon be over."

"What'll be over?" demanded Mr Sikes in a savage voice. "What foolery are you up to now, again? Get up and bustle about, and don't come over me with your woman's nonsense." (53)

These voices, suddenly, have little to do with the narrative of the novel, and the language of relationship sounds real and immediate.

I want, first of all, to point out the way in which the novel signifies that this exchange does not occur in the narrative world. The only interjection the novel itself makes comes in the middle of this passage, and tells us that Nancy speaks "with a touch of woman's tenderness, which communicated something like sweetness of tone" to her voice. These narrated words register the distance of Nancy from the narrative world, where "woman's tenderness" and "sweetness of tone" belong to the perfection of Rose as a part of the language narrative has in her for femininity. They are abstractions for a world which deals in the abstractions of past and future, beginning and ending. These qualities are made to belong to Nancy by becoming "a touch of" and "something like" themselves; and in the process of meeting Nancy in a real and coherent place these terms become real details. By meeting fiction in Nancy narrative becomes a real language, and a part of her fictive world. The ideals of femininity become small and even incongruous fragments of Nancy's life and in this fragmentation the fictive brings them alive and makes them real.

The approximation that these impressions are made into does not give Nancy a narrative, but instead gives her a fictive presence, and brings, what the Brownlow narrative missed, real feelings to her life. What is permanent and stable but abstract is replaced by what is momentary but felt: and these feelings are by their very nature not solitary but associative, reaching out to include Sikes. "Such a number of nights," she tells him, "as I've been patient with you, nursing and caring for you as if you had been a child; and this the first that I've seen you like yourself." Nancy reaches for the moment between illness - where Bill has been 'as if ... a child' - and health, where he will be "like himself", and inevitably mistreat her, for the fictive instants where similitude governs reality. There, Bill is both like a child and like himself, and the approximation creates momentarily a humanity which narrative would deny in making Bill either a child like Oliver - innocent while ill of the evils around him - or the force like himself that the moral world must control and destroy. Nancy recognises - and indeed inhabits - and momentarily asserts the other world of fiction, which evades the values of narrative; and Sikes, momentarily, accepts its immediacy, "Well, then, I wouldn't."

This fictive peace momentarily overturns the narrative. For an instant, we rest with Nancy's fictive intelligence as the authoritative vision of a form of knowledge that the Maylies can have no part in, and from which even Oliver, in his innocence, is excluded. Nancy's fiction seems for this second to be adequate to reality as a vision for the novel and narrative to be unnecessary, and defeated.

If fiction seems to have excluded narrative, however, what now happens makes it clear that narrative will reciprocally attempt to exclude and destroy fiction. Nancy inhabits the fragmentary and chaotic world, and does so quite passively, and without the control that Sikes asserts upon the underworld. If Nancy is the most purely fictive figure of this world, Sikes is the least fictive; when he is 'himself' he is not so much a counternarrative figure as a part of the narrative world that narrative seeks to reject, a part of the story of good and evil that Brownlow seeks to tell.

As we have seen, Nancy absorbs the narrative world in her fictions, bringing it to life by making it 'like itself'. Her feelings do not distinguish between the tenderness of Rose and the violence of Sikes; she feels for both, and she feels for the part of the middle-class world that has intruded into her own, for Oliver (54). This, she knows, is her undoing, for narrative works, as fiction does not, by separation and exclusion. Narrative, she knows already, will end her fictive imagination: as she tells Sikes, "It'll soon be over",- acknowledging at the same time her own distraction from what is real to her, "It's nothing."

We begin to see that Sikes has his own narrative; he rejects Nancy's words as 'nonsense' - which, to his own sense of continuity, they are - and takes over the story himself, imposing his own control upon Nancy, telling her, "come and sit aside of me, and put on your own face; or I'll alter it so, that you won't know it when you *do* want it" (55).

Sikes does not understand fictive approximations; for him, to be like yourself is to *be* yourself, and his demand is the assertion of his own kind of narrative power which, like Brownlow's, denies that people can exist as small parts of other realities, or as anything other than the entity that constitutes themselves. He is interested, not in some momentary harmony, a fragmented security in a fragmented world, but in the security of a knowledge which is like Brownlow's, but which replaces moral control with physical coercion.

We begin to see that the fictive is trapped by these rival narratives, and condemned by them both to a life of suffering; and that the life of attraction, amusement and feeling will be opposed by and even sacrificed to the ends of narratives which value control above sympathy. Nancy exists as a fictive vision in a world occupied by the narrative of Brownlow opposing Sikes, the novel's two 'good' and 'evil' ways of making a sequence of things.

There follows a passage in which we see this good and evil directly opposed:

> The girl obeyed. Sikes, locking her hand in his, fell back upon the pillow; turning his eyes upon her face. They closed: opened again; closed once more; again opened.

He shifted his position restlessly; and after dozing again, and again, for two or three minutes, and as often springing up with a look of terror, and gazing vacantly about him, was suddenly stricken, as it were, in the very attitude of rising, into a deep and heavy sleep. The grasp of his hand relaxed; the upraised arm fell languidly by his side; and he lay like one in a profound trance. (56)

Here, through Nancy, the two parts of the narrative meet. The moral, Brownlow narrative sees in this description of Sikes only the effect of laudanum, the drug Nancy has given him, and waits for Nancy to further the interests of the narrative by escaping from him, and by going to Rose.

But Sikes subverts this narrative by making the description belong to his own story, and his own potency. The terms by which he does so are disguised; but "they closed" seems to refer as much to an embrace as to Sikes' eyes: "The upraised arm fell languidly" clearly has a phallic double meaning; and its fall, and Sikes' 'profound trance', follows his orgasmic restlessness, with its climax "as it were, in the very attitude of rising". Sikes, having gained Nancy's obedience, imposes *his* version of things, upon her and upon the novel.

But the most important thing about this passage is that there is no real place in it for Nancy. She half-performs the function of the Brownlow-narrative - certainly in terms of what she afterwards does - but there is no place for her in the Brownlow world. This she knows herself; and we are forcefully reminded of the fact when, arriving at the 'family hotel' at which the Maylies are staying, we are told that an

allusion to Nancy's doubtful character raised a vast quantity of chaste wrath in the bosoms of four housemaids, who remarked, with great fervour, that the creature was a disgrace to her sex; and strongly advocated her being thrown into the kennel. (57)

No matter how much Nancy refuses to 'wear her own face' for Sikes, she is unable to put on the face that belongs to these family hotels and housemaids of bourgeois existence; and their hostility to her needs no further prompting. She may be half in the Maylies' world here, but she is still half in Sikes' as well.

We have seen, meanwhile, in the passage I quoted above, that the division of one narrative, represented by plot, from the other kind, represented in Sikes' potency and sexual presence, is absolute. There is no way that these two strands of the narrative action of the novel can be unified, for they exist by opposition; and they work against each other to such an extent that the writing here becomes endowed with two entirely separate meanings. Neither of these meanings are conclusive, however, and capable of seeing everything as well as constructing a story; so that in addition to this contradiction of narrative, moreover, there lies the third perspective, of fiction, which belongs to Nancy.

It is Nancy who now becomes the most important figure for the novel, for, without a universally authoritative narrative, we have begun to see through her eyes. Oliver's vision has been left far behind; for he is all too clearly at the mercy of whichever world happens to possess him. Nancy has become his protector, and, for his sake, the mediating figure between the two worlds. The novel's vision of opposing narratives becomes her own; and so it is she who experiences both the use of the laudanum, which is a part of Brownlow's story of Oliver, and Sikes' own version of things, which is clearly imposed upon her.

This imposition leaves no room for Nancy's own world, for it excludes her momentary vision. Nancy is left *without* that fictive world which was her own. Her status as a maker of fictions rather than of narratives, of 'as if's rather than of narrative identifications, makes her the victim of both the chaotic and harsh narrative she suffers through Sikes and of the dissociative will of the moral narrative.

It is Nancy then who provides the 'middle ground', the way for the novel to see both parts of the narrative; without her, we would remain in Brownlow's plotted world, or occupy the underworld with Sikes. Nancy takes over Oliver's initial role of seeing everything - but in doing so of course she loses the innocence which made Oliver oddly immune from both good and evil narratives, and the bewilderment which was his protection from the comprehension becomes suffering.

This represents a crisis for the primary purpose of this novel, which was Dickens' own purpose, to seek a unifying authority in the novel; Nancy survives and exposes the impotence of narrative, and in doing so becomes the point at which both parts of the narrative see its opposite. What now happens is the final test of narrative, the direct opposition of good and evil which *must* produce justice.

The Brownlow plot, which began as the representative of justice, however inadequate it has meanwhile seemed, tries to claim her as a part of itself. At the very last moment, before her murder, she says to Sikes,

> the gentleman and that dear lady, told me tonight of a home in some foreign country

and continues

> let us both leave this dreadful place, and far apart lead better lives, and forget how we have lived, except in prayers, and never see each other more. (58)

Here, Nancy appeals to the justice of the novel, and even though we know that her fictive imagination expects nothing - she has already told Rose of Sikes that

> I am drawn back to him through every suffering and ill-usage; and I should be, I believe, if I knew that I was to die by his hand at last (59)

- and that she belongs to neither narrative, we nevertheless recognise this appeal, as Dickens does, as a final and unequivocal appeal to a higher authority.

Sikes kills Nancy; and what he kills in her is the goodness of the Brownlow plot which in her death is presented with an opportunity to recover its tarnished potency. Her fictive detachment from the interests of the narrative - our knowledge that she does not belong to the respectable world - here restores our sense that it may yet be capable of sustaining our faith in its action, if it can provide justice in the face of this final and absolute challenge.

Nancy's murder is an extraordinary event; for in killing Nancy narrative attempts to eliminate and to take over the novel. What actually happens, however, at this point of confrontation and crisis, is very different:

> Of all bad deeds that, under cover of the darkness, had been committed within wide London's bounds since night hung over it, that was the worst. Of all the horrors that rose with an ill scent upon the morning air, that was the foulest and most cruel.
>
> The sun - the bright sun, that brings back, not light alone, but new life, and hope, and freshness to man - burst upon the crowded city in clear and radiant glory. Through costly-coloured glass and paper-mended window, through cathedral dome and rotten crevice, it shed its equal ray. It lighted up the room where the murdered woman lay. It did. He tried to shut it out, but it would stream in. If the sight had been a ghastly one in the dull morning, what was it, now, in all that brilliant light!
>
> He had not moved; he had been afraid to stir. There had been a moan and motion of the hand; and, with terror added to rage, he had struck and struck again. Once he threw a rug over it; but it was worse to fancy the eyes, and imagine them moving towards him, than to see them glaring upward, as if watching the reflection of the pool of gore that quivered and danced in the sunlight on the ceiling. He had plucked it off again. And there was the body - mere flesh and blood, no more - but such flesh, and so much blood!
>
> He struck a light, kindled a fire, and thrust the club into it. There was a hair upon the end, which blazed and shrunk into a light cinder, and, caught by the air, whirled

up the chimney. Even that frightened him, sturdy as he was; but he held the weapon till it broke, and then piled it on the coals to burn away, and smoulder into ashes. He washed himself, and rubbed his clothes; there were spots that would not be removed, but he cut pieces out and burnt them. How those stains were dispersed about the room! The very feet of the dog were bloody. (60)

This passage is the turning point of the novel; for at its beginning Dickens' voice is still indistinguishable from Brownlow's, and believes at least in the possibility of a generic structure in the narrative, in spite of the peculiarity of Oliver's treatment by it. Murder necessitates and tests the unity of fiction and narrative, as an ultimate wrong which must be judged, if nothing else is, as if by God: "Of all bad deeds that, under the cover of darkness, had been committed ... that was the worst". The story that morality tells wants the murder to bring a language of faith to narrative, and to see the generic, fictive nature of at least this literal deed.

This appeal to the unity of the novel does not last for long, however, and no God appears in judgement upon it, for the sun does not provide the omniscient, divine vision we lack; and, instead of providing a way of seeing everything which is greater than and exists outside of the novel, merely shows us everything within it more clearly, and without order, as, with the sunrise, the murder literally bursts out. The sun "burst upon the crowded city in clear and radiant glory" so that "Through costly-coloured glass and paper-mended window, through cathedral dome and rotten crevice, it shed its equal ray. It lighted up the room where the murdered woman lay. It did." Here, there is no control over what is happening. What the sun lights up in defiance of morality exceeds the grasp of the moral language of evil by making the crime horribly brilliant. The "clear and radiant glory" of the sunlight is not the glory of Mr Brownlow's narrative, and instead of uniting fiction and narrative by providing a great and outer, generic framework for the story, does so by reducing both faith and plot to the chaotic meaninglessness of mere animal detail. Sikes finds that the physical, brute reality of his action overtakes and is worse than its conception and performance, and when the sunlight reveals it to him "He tried to shut it out". Sikes' narrative reacts in the same way as the narrative of morality, for that, too, tried to shut the sun out "under the cover of darkness". Morality and criminality are united in their opposition to the exposure of action.

What the sunlight reveals is a terrible world, a world worse than the imagination of narrative, making the murder, what murder cannot possibly be, worse than before: "If the sight was a ghastly one in the dull morning, what was it now, in all that brilliant light!" Narrative cannot comprehend this worsening of the deed, or its brilliance, and finds itself faced by a world that becomes mysteriously alive. The 'stream' of light seems to have a bright activity, and nowhere else in the novel do we see the sun with such clarity; Nancy's corpse itself seems to have eyes that move, and a supernatural existence beyond 'mere flesh and blood'. Things seem to happen arbitrarily, and to have their own vitality; when Sikes burns his club a cinder, 'caught by the air, whirled up the chimney'; and blood seems to be everywhere, defying rational precaution.

At the very point where narrative reaches its crisis it loses control; and this is true both of the story Sikes tells, and of the moral narrative of Brownlow. We are plunged back into a world of details and incoherence, and reality suddenly seems to become fragmentary and to have no narrative. Nothing really seems to be itself any more. The sunlight transforms everything, and the reasons for the murder - which Sikes did have - are dissolved in the immediacy of brilliance. We find ourselves back in the world of fiction, the world where human action is not authoritative but passive.

And suddenly, we find that Sikes, of all people, is the passive figure in the scene. "He had not moved; he had been afraid to stir"; the reality of things outside his own crude rationale takes over his consciousness in this fear. It is fear that does have the effect, as John Bayley suggests (61), of humanizing Sikes. The sun, we are told, "brings back, not light alone, but new life, and hope, and freshness to man". To Sikes, it brings back imagination; when he hides the body away

> it was worse to fancy the eyes, and imagine them moving towards him, than to see them...

This new humanity is the gift of the fictive; Sikes suddenly becomes a man, doing what anybody would do in trying to shut out the light and hide murder away. In this, moreover, the novel sees through his eyes, and he takes over Nancy's role, becoming the way the writing can see everything.

Narrative, then, finds itself in the fictive world; and we find that it has no ultimate authority. Incapable of bringing the world to a unity in its own judgement, it finds itself faced instead with chaos, and a world in which neither generic nor narrative meanings have survived, a world of brute detail from which the novel must now escape.

Sikes reacts as narrative must, by fleeing from the sunlight and seeking darkness. This is the rationale of a fear which now cares nothing for any narrative but the narrative of hiding away, and in this hiding narrative finds its true nature, as a selection of the real truths of the outside world, unable to include this extremity of fragmentation.

Sikes then finds the place he seeks, and in doing so almost accepts the ending which the Brownlow narrative would now impose; he returns to London, and to London's darkest place, in conformity with the rhetoric of 'all bad deeds',

> Near to that part of the Thames ... where the buildings on the banks are the dirtiest and the vessels on the river blackest with the dust of colliers and the smoke of close-built low-roofed houses (62)

to

> the filthiest, the strangest, the most extraordinary of the many localities that are hidden in London (63)

to Jacobs Island. Here Sikes dies, hanging himself while "endeavouring to creep away in the darkness and confusion" (64).

In returning to the darkness Sikes returns and submits to the narrative which, even in killing him, is at least some form of rationale, and in his death there narrative hides his murder away at last.

With Sikes receding to this moral and coherent darkness the rest of the underworld can also be consigned to the darkness of the justice that narrative, Brownlow, and even by now Sikes have all consented to uphold against the chaos of the fictive. The criminal gang is dispersed, Charley Bates re-formed, and Fagin subjected to a dark and cautionary death.

With Sikes and Nancy gone, the narrative is, it seems, given its authority to govern the end of the novel. Mr Brownlow is left with Oliver, and we begin to expect that the novel will fulfil its initial conception, forgetting Nancy and the in-between world, and assert the unity and harmony of its final justice. Brownlow tells Oliver his story, and takes him to Fagin in prison, as if to show how the justice of narrative has dealt with the criminal world, by concealing it in a darkness where middle-class narrative can forget and disown it.

But this is an authority in which we can now hardly believe, and even here we see it discredited. At the very end of what now begins to be Oliver's story once again, Oliver "was in a flutter of agitation and uncertainty which deprived him of the power of collecting his thoughts, and almost of speech" (65). This confused vision gives us the real ending of the book, usurping the coherence that narrative seeks: when he is shown the dark justice of Fagin's fate Oliver asserts his own control over the text. "Strike them all dead," we hear Fagin cry. "What right have they to butcher me?" (66). The child's consciousness is still, in innocence, a fictive, fragmented vision which registers the fact that reality offers details, incoherent words and phrases, which are still the real vehicle of feeling, and which the narrative vision cannot include, and here it shows us that Fagin is stil a human being, and not a moral lesson.

The fictive, then, refuses to the very end of the novel to be integrated within the narrative and coherent; and authority seems to be invested only in the limited world of darkness. Where narrative attempts to assert a control over the whole of reality - over all the world that the bright sun illuminates - it is overcome by the horror, not of the violence and brutality of coercion itself (which belongs, as we saw, as much to Brownlow as to Sikes) but of its arbitrariness and its meaninglessness. This suffering sends even Sikes back to the darkness by which morality and narrative control the fictive.

The novel however retains the sunlight as its vision; in Oliver, then Nancy, then Sikes, and then again Oliver, it adopts the vision which is most inclusive, and which runs counter to narrative, the vision of fiction. *Oliver Twist* finds narrative to be inadequate to a reality which, even in its fullest horror, it finds irresistible. Ultimately, it is with Oliver and innocence that the novel leaves us, a conclusion which leaves us where we began, not quite belonging to narrative, morality and respectability, but not, in innocence, suffering the fate of the suffering to which fiction, in a world without control, finds itself subject.

In the meantime, however, we have now seen what Pickwick protected us from, the real meaning of a narrative which seeks to control - and its limitation - and of a fictive world that both enjoys and suffers - and the strength and inclusiveness of its feeling. *Oliver Twist* gives us for the fist time in the English novel a full experience of both fiction and narrative; and as Bayley again notes (67) it is not a 'liberating' experience, for it leaves us withdrawing from a crisis of the novel into the child's vision it set out to mature and develop, and into the innocence which we saw Boz lose. This ending will remain important for Dickens' writing, which by the end of this novel begins to understand the extremities of its two integral aspects of fiction and narrative, and the problems which the form of the novel faces in its radical division between them.

THE DIVISION OF THE NOVEL

Footnotes

(1) See John Forster, *Life of Charles Dickens* , I, 9; also Edgar Johnson, *Charles Dickens: his Tragedy and Triumph*, 20-2, and 'Books that Dickens read', in *The Dickensian* XLV, 81-90, 201-207 (1949).
(2) *Miscellaneous Papers*, 397.
(3) *Miscellaneous Papers*, 398-9.
(4) *Miscellaneous Papers*, 400.
(5) *Miscellaneous Papers*, 400.
(6) 'Hackney Coach Stands', *Sketches by Boz*, 94.
(7) 'Early Coaches', *Sketches by Boz*, 158.
(8) 'The Tuggses at Ramsgate', *Sketches by Boz*, 411.
(9) 'The Last Cab Driver, and the First Omnibus Cad', *Sketches by Boz*, 169.
(10) 'The Last Cab Driver', *Sketches by Boz*, 173.
(11) 'The Last Cab Driver', *Sketches by Boz*, 174.
(12) 'The Last Cab Driver', *Sketches by Boz*, 169.
(13) The phrase is Wordsworth's, and expresses a similar (and for Wordsworth hostile) comprehension of reality. See *The Prelude* (1805), VII, 158.
(14) For a specific discussion of the *Sketches* in relation to the city see F.S.Schwarzbach, *Dickens and the City*, 35-42.
(15) *Miscellaneous Papers*, 401.
(16) 'The First of May', *Sketches by Boz*, 196.
(17) 'The First of May', *Sketches by Boz*, 201.
(18) 'The First of May', *Sketches by Boz*, 203.
(19) *Miscellaneous Papers*, 3.
(20) 'Criminal Courts', *Sketches by Boz*, 230.
(21) 'Criminal Courts', *Sketches by Boz*, 228.
(22) 'The Hospital Patient', *Sketches by Boz*, 277.
(23) 'The Hospital Patient', *Sketches by Boz*, 778.
(24) 'A Visit to Newgate', *Sketches by Boz*, 236.
(25) 'Horatio Sparkins', *Sketches by Boz*, 426.
(26) Pickwick continually creates the plot passively, through his good feelings and benevolence, allowing himself to be led through the novel. See, for instance, 278, 298-9, and 358.
(27) We are reminded of the force of this irresponsibility at Chapter 13 (238) when we hear of the suspected death of one old gentleman from the stage-coach driving of Tony Weller; but we only hear about this at second hand, through his son Sam.
(28) Gross and Pearson (Eds.), *Dickens in the Twentieth Century*, xxiii.
(29) *Pickwick Papers*, 760.
(30) R.L.Patten, *Charles Dickens and his Publishers*, (Oxford 1978), 45.
(31) R.L.Patten, *Charles Dickens and his Publishers*, 45.
(32) See page 14 above.

(33) *Oliver Twist*, 146.
(34) *Oliver Twist*, 146.
(35) *Oliver Twist*, 147.
(36) *Oliver Twist*, 285.
(37) *Oliver Twist*, 287.
(38) *Oliver Twist*, 301.
(39) *Oliver Twist*, 106.
(40) *Oliver Twist*, 309.
(41) *Oliver Twist*, 456.
(42) *Oliver Twist*, 301.
(43) *Oliver Twist*, 264.
(44) *Oliver Twist*, 271.
(45) *Oliver Twist*, 290.
(46) *Oliver Twist*, 439.
(47) Reprinted in Gross and Pearson (Eds.), *Dickens in the Twentieth Century*, 53.
(48) *The Victorian Underworld*, (Pelican 1972), 167.
(49) *Oliver Twist*, 105.
(50) *Oliver Twist*, 105.
(51) *Oliver Twist*, 111.
(52) *Oliver Twist*, 111.
(53) *Oliver Twist*, 346.
(54) See *Oliver Twist*, pp.197-8: "I have tried hard for you," she tells Oliver on the evening before the house-breaking.
(55) *Oliver Twist*, 347.
(56) *Oliver Twist*, 357.
(57) *Oliver Twist*, 359.
(58) *Oliver Twist*, 442.
(59) *Oliver Twist*, 365.
(60) *Oliver Twist*, 423-4.
(61) Gross and Pearson (Eds.), *Dickens in the Twentieth Century*, 60.
(62) *Oliver Twist*, 442.
(63) *Oliver Twist*, 442.
(64) *Oliver Twist*, 451.
(65) *Oliver Twist*, 454.
(66) *Oliver Twist*, 472.
(67) Gross and Pearson (Eds.), *Dickens in the Twentieth Century*, 51.

CHAPTER TWO

The Novel as Fiction, I: The Old Curiosity Shop

The ending of *Oliver Twist* leaves us with the human world, a secular world in which there is clearly no god and no divine justice.   The 'radiant glory' of the sun has become a harsh, neutral, amoral light, and it leaves us with two opposed and clearly limited ways of living.   Nancy perceives without control, and while she sees everything she suffers; Brownlow orders, and ultimately controls the novel, but does so in a limited way which sees only what it can afford to see.   The outer, generic voice of fiction and the inner voice of the narrative   seem   as   far   apart   as   ever,   and   each   suffers   from   the separation.   The inner voice is constricted by its division from commonality to the darkness and limitation of its own story; the outer voice suffers for its division from narrative by failure to find any authority and structure for itself.   Meanwhile, we have seen that the world that exists outside these two limited ways of understanding reality, the sunlit world from which the compromise of innocence retreats, is a terrible chaos in which the fictive and the narrative, brought together, only produce the worst of all worlds, an outside world with neither faith nor structure.   We   are   again   left   where   we   were   in   both   the *Sketches* and *Pickwick,* with a compromise between fiction and narrative, as the mixed nature of the novel.   The naivety of the earlier works has, however, been significantly objectified by the end of *Oliver Twist,* for we are shown its innocence in Oliver's childhood.   The failure of compromise to grow up into the daylight reality which withheld justice signifies the beginning of a new self-consciousness about the difficulty of writing the novel in what is now the sure knowledge that authority in the   novel   will   have   to   be   generated   by   human,   and   not mythically authoritative, figures.   What I want to suggest is that this   self-consciousness   now   prompts   Dickens   to   explore   the novel in two distinct directions, which correspond directly to the division we have seen to be dominant in the novel, between fiction and narrative, and to find what Gillian Beer might call a scale for the human (1) in Dickens.   Fiction and narrative seem capable of providing distinctively different human figures in the novel just as they were capable of providing distinctive voices; for these voices have been located in very different kinds of figures. The voice of narrative has produced figures such as Brownlow and Sikes; authoritative and individualistic, they are the would-be narrators of the action. The fictive voice, meanwhile, has produced Nancy and in the *Sketches* Bill Barker; passive figures who are concerned to live 'as if' the world were the just and protective place they clearly lack, and who relate the action to us in the spirit of that missing, propitious world, through the medium of their own imaginative elasticity. In doing so they lead us towards, not the literal reality they occupy, but a literary, ideal and commonly sought after world, the world 'we all' want; and this world of course is a perfect world. And, briefly and incoherently, they create such a world.

These latter figures do not narrate; they see everything without ordering, placing a faith in outer, generic reality, and at the same time expressing such a faith. These figures are not then narrators but fictive voices, speaking in the spirit of a common world which expresses itself as a sense of genre, of common kind, in the spirit of a commonly believed in, ideal world, and disregarding the letter of reality, and its narratives. Nancy and Bill Barker do not construct, as Brownlow does, but adopt, belonging to the outer reality of things rather than to the internal reality of narrative. They are inclusive figures, absorbing any part of the world they encounter, and are in turn adopted by Dickens - just as Brownlow is constructed by him - as authentic, common, non-literal voices. We do not so much hear their story as see through their eyes, for we remain un-committed to but in sympathy with what they say and do; they are not so much narrators as the fictive equivalent, personae.

Narrator and persona seem to offer sharply contrasting ways of developing human experience in the novel. The novel must evidently understand both if it is to include the whole of a human experience unmediated by a divine justice, but the question now must be one of how it is to do so, and retain some kind of unity; for we have seen in *Oliver Twist* that the fictive and narrative, left to the sunlight which now stands in the place of god, will oppose, misunderstand, and eventually destroy each other.

There would then seem to be two distinct ways of com-prehending the fictive and the narrative; and while one would produce a fictive novel, the other would produce a novel con-trolled by narrative.

The first is suggested by Nancy. She was never the narrator of the story, for she never told the details of her life as narrative, but instead presented them to us 'as if' the world had been a better place. Her failure was to attempt to include narrative within that world; while to be ignorant of narrative would be to find oneself with Oliver, in innocence, it would seem that a fictive novel might be written by making the figure of Nancy into a more intelligent figure still, into a persona of the

writer, self-consciously abstaining from narrative (as she did
not) in order to perceive the world whole through the medium
of the writing, and to show us its personae under the neutral
perspective of observation. Such a novel would include narrative
by investing nothing in the authority of narrative.

The second way of writing the novel is suggested by
Brownlow. He was the narrator in *Oliver Twist*, but his authority failed because what he hoped was the common story -
and protective of Oliver - turned out to be Brownlow's own,
to a great extent protected *by* Oliver. A narrative novel, it
would now seem, might be written by a more intelligent figure
than Brownlow, an authorial narrator undertaking the task
converse to that of the fictive writer, and self-consciously abstaining from fictive universality in order to tell his *own*, individual story. Such a novel would include fiction by investing
nothing in the universality and omniscience of fiction.

The novel thus suggests division within itself into these
complex and opposite strands which each, separately, show us
the capacity of human self-consciousness to bring fiction and
narrative together in the modern novel. What I want to suggest
is that Dickens' works undertake to explore and, for the English
novel at least, establish the possibilities and limitations of each
of these approaches to the novel.

The least obviously limited of these approaches, perhaps,
is the fictive; for Brownlow remains at the end of *Oliver Twist*
as a figure of limitation. Dickens' first instincts were towards
the common feelings and popular, generic sense of the fictive,
expressed in the episodic form of the *Sketches,* and so it is
not surprising that upon completing *Oliver Twist* it is to the
fictive that he first turns, beginning work on a new miscellany
in "the hope, that, by invention of a new mode, he might be
able for a time to discontinue the writing of a long story" (2).
This work was entitled *Master Humphrey's Clock:* the evasion
of the necessity of writing 'long stories', the evasion of the
difficulties of the responsibility of narrative in it, did not last
long, for the periodical began to fail. In order to recover it,
Dickens began work to turn one of the stories he had written
for it into a new novel, *The Old Curiosity Shop,* expanding the
hints contained within 'the little child story' set up for publication 25 April (3).

This story is introduced by the figure of Master
Humphrey; and this odd and apparently insignificant figure is
of formative importance to the development of the form of the
novel, for he is the first figure in it to attempt to recognise
the divisions of the form, and to bring about a 'fictive' novel
by both possessing and withholding control. He develops the
Pickwickian authority into a more evidently mature voice which
narrates, not as it is acted upon, but as it observes. He is
an attempt, not to blunt authority as Pickwick does, but to take
order into the disorganised, fictive world where things happen,
as we have seen, without such order. He refuses to make the

Pickwickian compromise, and attempts to lead us self-consciously
into a world of fiction unqualified by any part he might play
himself.

While Master Humphrey narrates, he does so in order to
offer protection to an unqualified world of the fictive, and this
produces a novel which appears to be extremely odd, and one
which has been the most problematic of Dickens' works to modern criticism. *The Old Curiosity Shop,* and particularly Little
Nell - and certainly it is impossible to have the novel without
Little Nell, as recent criticism has tried to do - has often seemed
the most dated of Dickens' novels.

"Nell is a poorly realised character" is Malcolm Andrews'
observation in the most widely read current edition of the novel
(4), while on its back we read that "Nell attracted from her
creator an admiration we can no longer share" (5). Other
critics have been less generous, in extending their criticism
beyond the figure of Nell.

> There is not much doubt that *The Old Curiosity Shop* is
> Dickens' least successful novel, a work in which he seems
> to have lost much of his intellectual control (6)

is Steven Marcus' extraordinary verdict in *Dickens from
Pickwick to Dombey,* and more recently F.S.Schwarzbach spoke
of its "cloying necrophiliac sentimentality" (7).

It is clear that Dickens' intellectual control is fully engaged
at the beginning of the novel, for in the figure who was to have
been Master Humphrey we are given a full recognition of the
lessons learnt by *Oliver Twist.* Master Humphrey is not an
ordinary narrator, since he initially exists, not to control a
'long story', but to make something longer and more coherent
of the episodic conception of the 'little child story'. To him,
darkness does not offer limitation, for his function is not to
provide the Brownlow protection of the narrative. Instead, he
offers a protective kindness to a different sort of imagination.
As he tells us, "Night is generally my time for walking", and
he continues

> I have fallen insensibly into this habit, both because it
> favours my infirmity and because it affords me greater
> opportunity of speculating on the characters of those who
> fill the streets. The glare and hurry of broad noon are
> not adapted to idle pursuits like mine; a glimpse of passing
> faces caught by the light of a street lamp or shop window
> is often better for my purpose than their full revelation
> in the daylight, and, if I must add the truth, night is
> often kinder in this respect than day, which too often
> destroys an air-built castle at the moment of its completion,
> without the smallest ceremony or remorse. (8)

Master Humphrey is interested in the protection of the fragmentary and momentary imagination which prefers to catch snatches of reality and not to see it whole, in daylight. This imagination no longer believes in the outside world as a complete and coherent, structured place, and has its faith in a night-dreaming world of 'air-built castles' which the disorder of reality destroys. Under this narrator, narrative itself is an illness in the remorseless and chaotic light of day:

> Think of a sick man in such a place as Saint Martin's Court, listening to the footsteps, and in the midst of pain and weariness obliged, despite himself (as though it were a task he must perform) to detect the child's step from the man's, the slipshod beggar from the booted exquisite, the lounging from the busy, the dull heel of the sauntering outcast from the quick tread of an expectant pleasure-seeker - think of the hum and noise being always present to his senses, and of the stream of life that will not stop, pouring on, on, on, through all his restless dreams, as if he were condemned to lie dead but conscious, in a noisy churchyard, and had no hope of rest for centuries to come. (9)

Master Humphrey's authorial consciousness dissociates the action of novel from the action of reality in which, as we saw in *Oliver Twist*, there is no judgement, and no inherent order. He rejects the narrative in which Brownlow expected us to believe, for the "stream of life", the sequence of things upon which narrative most depends, has become the oppressive insistence of 'men and moving things', "pouring on, on, on". Narrative is not so much the life of things as a disrupter intruding into the literary imagination, the imagination that attempts to perceive and record it. It produces by its intrusion the worst of all worlds, the chaos of a defeated coherence which even Sikes fled from. The sickness which this book attempts to evade is what was revealed in *Oliver Twist* to be the remorselessness of a daylight without a god or justice, which becomes the remorselessness of action and plot; and what the darkness is there to hide is the unconnectedness of things, the sheer incoherence of the 'stream of life' and the torture which its endless shifting and changing becomes to the purposive will.

To Master Humphrey, sickness becomes a sign of health. His own physical presence enforces this. We are told in *Master Humphrey's Clock* that Master Humphrey is a "misshapen, deformed old man" (10) so that his own vitality and character are withdrawn from our attention. Through his eyes, the novel becomes the fruit of a "lonely, solitary life" (11). Moreover, he shows an imaginative sympathy for a life of death represented for the first time here as drowning. We are told that

drowning was not a hard death, but of all means of suicide
the easiest and best. (12)

Drowning disrupts and fragments the "stream" of things,
and stops the sequence. It reasserts the private world of fiction against the relentless course of narrative; the drowning
man sees his life pass before him as he drowns, and dead, or
even half dead, as Rogue Riderhood is much later in *Our Mutual
Friend* - and as Sikes was when ill in *Oliver Twist* - passes into
a kind of sleep which sanctifies an individuality made chaotic
by the incoherence of the narratives of the world. So that
Riderhood, unconscious, seems a 'better' man, as Sikes did to
Nancy, the latter humanised as he is in murder by the momentary suspension of narrative consciousness (13). Drowning,
Master Humphrey knows, is a form of the kindness that darkness offers, *creating* the fictive in a world whose worst cruelty
is to murder sleep.

In this affinity with weakness, and with death, Master
Humphrey is an extraordinary narrator, for he rejects narrative. In doing so, he is not so much the teller of the tale as
an image of Dickens, an expression of his will to dissociate self
from the oppressive responsibility which *Oliver Twist* places
upon narrative, to order and control a chaotic world. Master
Humphrey exists between persona and narrator, and combines
the function of both. He does so, not as Nancy did, by participating in and attempting to belong to both worlds, but by
standing in the place of the teller and by personifying the
narrator himself. He does not relate events, so much as observe
the world; but, again, this observed world is not governed by
narrative. What kind of novel, then, does Master Humphrey
lead us to discover?

Our first answer to this question must lie in the figure
whom he first encounters, and who sets off what we would call
in a narrative the action of the novel, the figure of little Nell,
and, inseparably from her, the old curiosity shop itself in which
he finds her. It is indicative of the strangeness of this book
that Nell is the strangest of all Dickens' often oddly conceived
females; and darkness, the old curiosity shop and Little Nell
are all integral parts of Master Humphrey's imagination. The
curiosity shop is a symbol of the kind of sleep he seeks, a place
of complete withdrawal where daylight cannot penetrate. It

was one of those receptacles for old and curious things
which seem to crouch in the corners of this town and to
hide their musty treasures from the public eye in jealousy
and distrust. There were suits of mail standing like ghosts
in armour here and there, fantastic carvings brought from
monkish cloisters, rusty weapons of various kinds, dis-
torted figures in china and wood and iron and ivory:
tapestry and strange furniture that might have been designed in dreams. (14)

Nell herself then appears to him, not so much as a character as a part of the furniture of the dream, so that in reflection upon his first encounter with her Master Humphrey finds it impossible to separate her from the place to which she belongs (15):

> We are so much in the habit of allowing impressions to be made upon us by external objects, which should be produced by reflection alone, but which, without such visible aids, often escape us; that I am not sure I should have been so thoroughly possessed by this one subject, but for the heaps of fantastic things I had seen huddled together in the curiosity dealer's warehouse. (16)

Already, Master Humphrey's reverence for the darkness has taken its effect; in allowing - as his 'habit' - the outside world to take over reflection, a licence which expresses the faith of fiction in external reality, those external objects take on the force of reflection, so that through the strange reciprocation of Master Humphrey's consciousness reality becomes a dream world. Nell, of course, is a part of the dream, to the extent that she is unimaginable without the 'fantastic things' which now occupy the external world about her:

> If these helps to my fancy had all been wanting, and I had been forced to imagine her in a common chamber, with nothing unusual or uncouth in its appearance, it is very probable that I should have been less impressed with her strange and solitary state. (17)

Again, it is the kindness of the darkness which the old curiosity shop concentrates which does *not* force Master Humphrey to imagine Nell in a "common chamber", helping and preserving the approximation of real to ideal. "As it was," he continues, "she seemed to exist in a kind of allegory." The power of the fiction the darkness has made of reality has been to replace narrative with something different from a story. We may not see the direction in which Master Humphrey's allegory will lead us - unlike traditional allegory moral or religious associations are obscured by the identification of Nell by darkness or fantasy, and by dreaming, rather than by anything recognisably evil or wrong - but what we do see is that the image of Nell is different from a character in a narrative, as the novel's 'fictive' approximation to an allegorical symbol in a fragmentary and incoherent reality. The fictive imagination offers us in Nell and her surroundings a kind of secular myth.

Nell's unconventionality is sufficient to seem to arrest and drown narrative. When Master Humphrey, dutifully taking up his role as narrator, begins "to imagine her in her future life, holding her solitary way among a crowd of wild and grotesque companions" he finds that

> the theme was carrying me along with it at a great pace, and I already saw before me a region on which I was little disposed to enter. (18)

That region is the pain and trouble of the progression of narrative itself; and it is significant, and indicative of Nell's peculiar power, that Master Humphrey can withdraw from it, and return from the beginnings of a story to the stable image of his fiction:

> But all that night, waking or in my sleep, the same thoughts recurred and the same images retained possession of my brain. I had ever before me the old dark murky rooms - the gaunt suits of mail with their ghostly silent air - the faces all awry, grinning from wood and stone - the dust and rust, and worm that lives in wood - and alone in the midst of all this lumber and decay, and ugly old age, the beautiful child in her gentle slumbers smiling through her light and sunny dreams. (19)

What Nell stands for does not unfold like a narrative, but recurs, as the 'same thoughts' and the 'same image'. Nell has made the river of things stand still, and has made a world of the fictional chaos of dark and decaying things. She is at the centre of this chaotic fictive world, as its brightest and purest aspect, so that in her, and in the darkness that surrounds her - in the dust and rust, and lumber and decay - daylight is transferred from the world of narrative to the fictive world which finds its ideal in her dreams. Nell, it appears, has effected through her narrator a complete transformation of Oliver's world, so that where Oliver had to live in a waking, conscious world, Master Humphrey allows Nell to create a world for herself, a world where the objects which governed Oliver - the material differences and responsibilities of a harsh reality - are absorbed by darkness and decay, and in which her dreams shine out as light and sunny, untroubled by the light of day, or the narrative that made that light destructive.

Nell seems to be the most prominent of the 'personages' introduced by Master Humphrey. The other figure who promises to be significant at the novel's beginning is of course Quilp.

Quilp is very much a part of the fiction to which Nell belongs, generated, not so much by narrative, as by Nell's presence in the book and by the darkness and decay which brings that presence about, in order to supply the novel with what she lacks: he is the very opposite of Nell. Where she has no speech and no self-generated activity, Quilp seems to be all speech and activity; and his energy is born out of what Nell precisely is not. Master Humphrey's vision divided her from "the dust and rust, and worm that lives in wood" and from "this lumber and decay, and ugly age"; things which seem entirely appropriate to Quilp, who is

> an elderly man of remarkably hard features and forbidding aspect, and so low in stature as to be quite a dwarf, though his head and face were large enough for the body of a giant. His black eyes were restless, sly, and cunning; his mouth and chin, bristly with the stubble of a coarse hard beard; and his complexion was one of that kind which never looks clean or wholesome. But what added most to the grotesque expression of his face was a ghastly smile, which, appearing to be the mere result of habit and to have no connection with any mirthful or complacent feeling, constantly revealed the few discoloured fangs that were yet scattered in his mouth, and gave him the aspect of a panting dog. (20)

Quilp is conceived as a part of the dream-world Nell inhabits; he resembles a creature from a fairy-tale, a cross between a dwarf and a giant, both sub-human - resembling a 'large panting dog' with his 'fangs' and his 'dog's grin' (21) more than he does a human being - and superhuman in his near-magical powers of mobility and his mastery of circumstance. With these two figures, Master Humphrey creates what promises to be a work of fiction in its purest sense, and not a work of narrative, for neither Quilp nor Nell are ordinary characters, and, it apppears, will be the active figures of what will be a fictional, allegorical novel, rather than a narrative. Quilp promises to be a disruptive figure, but offers in his disruption to be a part of the darkness which protects Nell, as a part of her fictional identity in Master Humphrey's dream. He becomes another aspect of "the strange furniture that might have been designed in dreams", of the wild and grotesque things which impress Master Humphrey with Nell's "strange and solitary state".

By the end of the first chapter of the novel, then, it appears that we have a book which offers to have no real hero or heroine in any conventional sense. While Nell and, secondarily, Quilp are offered as central figures, neither promise in the first chapters to become the book's protagonist. Instead, they together appear as the central image of an allegory which, with its refuge in the darkness of the old curiosity shop, seems, even without Master Humphrey's presence, to promise to control the action; and the narrative, the movement of things, and the pain attached to the consciousness which sees the daylight reality of the real world - as Oliver did - appears to be soothed into inclusion within Nell's light and sunny sleep.

While this is one resolution of the ending of *Oliver Twist,* it also represents a new dilemma: for while Dickens may not have a narrative heroine in Little Nell, or a hero in Quilp, he still has a projected novel in which to put them both. Unlike Master Humphrey, he cannot simply retire from anything that promises to be narrative - that, after all, is why the persona exists in the first place. If Nell, and the figures surrounding her, are to be fictive and allegorical, what are they to do when they are called upon to act in a narrative, a demand which the novel must necessarily place upon its characters? Without the self-conscious presence of Master Humphrey, we begin to see a formal opposition developing in the novel. A world asleep may work as an image or an idea, but the very stasis which Master Humphrey discovered as a comfort must be highly problematic to a novel which, as Dickens has already discovered, must as a matter of necessity be committed to the telling of a long story. The image and idea of Nell and her surroundings - of the old curiosity shop and Quilp - satisfy the night-time, fictive world Master Humphrey brings about; but they hardly satisfy the requirements of a narrator who, unlike Master Humphrey, must remain active in his novel. Master Humphrey begins the novel by providing the eyes through which its strange world is seen. With his disappearance, the question of how to see the fictive world in the novel begins to arise as a matter of urgency, for we have in Nell a character who, unlike Nancy, does not even half-exist in the world of narrative, and is incapable therefore of undertaking even Nancy's harsh mediation of suffering; Master Humphrey has protected her from that, but has done so, it begins to appear, at the expense of the narrative, and the novel's story. Nell, and Quilp, emerge as surprisingly powerful figures.

Nell continues, not surprisingly, perhaps, to be a central figure in the novel; Master Humphrey's image of her, once established, remains in Dickens' mind as a central intention. He wrote, much later, in his preface of 1848, that

> in writing the book, I had it always in my fancy to sur-round the lonely figure of the child with grotesque and wild, but not impossible companions, and to gather about her innocent face and pure intentions, associates as strange and uncongenial as the grim objects that are about her bed when her history is first foreshadowed. (22)

A few pages before Master Humphrey makes his exit from the novel, we are once more shown her as we have seen her before:

> Nell joined us before long, and bringing some needle-work to the table, sat by the old man's side. It was pleasant to observe the fresh flowers in the room, the pet bird with a green bough shading his cage, the breath of freshness and youth which seemed to rustle through the dull old house and hover round the child. (23)

But the novel continues rather uncomfortably,

> It was curious, but not so pleasant, to turn from the
> beauty and grace of the girl, to the stooping figure,
> care-worn face, and jaded aspect of the old man. (24)

While this is essentially the image which Master Humphrey
promised as allegory, the dark things among which Nell was
conceived seem to be less a part of the 'kindness' of darkness,
than a source of discomfort and anxiety, a contrast which is
"not so pleasant". The pressure which produces this uneasiness
is made more apparent in the next paragraph when the narrator
- still, at this point, Master Humphrey - asks of Nell and her
place with her grandfather,

> As he grew weaker and more feeble, what would become
> of this lonely little creature; poor protector as he was,
> say that he died - what would her fate be then? (25)

Clearly, this is the region upon which Master Humphrey
was previously "little disposed to enter"; the region of the pain
and troubles of narrative. But this time, with his own withdrawal from the novel imminent, Nell's sunny dreams, which
brighten the darkness around her, seem to be less important
than their vulnerability. Master Humphrey worries about her
future protection; for previously, as a figure who existed in
order to perceive fiction, he was himself her chief protector.
His withdrawal will mean that Nell must in some way perceive
life for herself, and cease to be simply an object of perception,
and this necessity is not a requirement of Nell's fictional existence, as a figure who can be a small but ideal, 'sunny' part
of an incoherent world, and exist as a child, but a requirement
of narrative, which demands that Nell must see her story as a
responsibility to reader, writer, and novel, and see it whole.
With Master Humphrey's departure Nell, if she is to remain at
the centre of the novel, will have to move through it, and, in
some way at least, become a part of its narrative. Master
Humphrey's retirement means that the novel, as a long story,
which cannot itself participate entirely in Nell's stasis, must
make some effort to include Nell within its narrative.
Nell, however, is absolutely resistant to any such attempt.
We find her treating the progression of the novel as something
which is almost profane, so that her encounter with it is in some
ways like a kind of Pilgrim's Progress. As death will mean
heaven to Christian, if only he can renounce life with sufficient
determination, so Nell must encounter each new experience
which narrative forces upon her as a sleep walker, in order to
return to the sunny dream she was able to live out under the
protection of Master Humphrey at the novel's beginning. Everything that happens to her happens as a test of her power
to preserve the kindness of darkness and her own fictive ex-

istence.   So that while the narrative exists in order to wake
Nell up - as it exists in the *Pilgrim's Progress* to make a sinner
of Christian - we find that Nell constantly resists and opposes
its pressures.

Her position in the novel can, perhaps, be more fully understood however if we compare her to another, very much more
Dickensian precedent, whom I have already mentioned in reference to Master Humphrey.   This precedent is Mr Pickwick.

Pickwick, of course, seems a strange figure to cite as a
precedent for Nell.   But the testing to which she is subjected
is very much like that which earlier proved Mr Pickwick's vitality in spite of his apparent responsibility and well-meaning
morality.   The difference between them is like the difference
between Pickwick and Master Humphrey; for Nell is surprisingly
a more realistic figure, and as such a more intelligent figure.
Where Pickwick imposes the values of fiction upon narrative,
Nell, like her ally Master Humphrey, preserves them by withdrawal.   Where Pickwick's transcendent enthusiasm was a celebration of his will to participate in the world, but at the same
time a compromise with the harsh values of reality, Nell's resistance to much the same environment is a celebration of her
power of self-preservation; and of the power of the fictional to
survive in a world where things are seen whole, as narratives,
without compromising with those narratives.

Like Pickwick, then, Nell sets out to travel through the
world as a matter of choice.   This choice is her first real threat,
and her first test.   Should she fail it, her future would appear
to be a Pickwickian freedom, and Nell to be committed to dominate the forward movement of the plot.   Encounter with worldly
values of life and survival would supplant the dream which
governs her purity.

She passes this first trial by presenting what is actually
her future to us as a restoration.   She sees in her journey

> a return of the simple pleasures they had once enjoyed, a
> relief from the gloomy solitude in which she had lived, an
> escape from the heartless people by whom she had been
> surrounded in her late time of trial, the restoration of the
> old man's health and peace, and a life of tranquil happi-
> ness. (26)

Nell sets out upon her story; but she does so regarding
her future not as a plotted progression to a better world, but
as a simple return to the childlike world she has once known.
Nell defeats the necessity the novel has discovered in Master
Humphrey's retirement to *be* narrative at this first stage by
making the pressure to grow up, and see things whole, into a
commitment to remain what she has always been, and to preserve
both her own fictional childhood existence and its fragile protection in her grandfather's health and peace.   She makes of
her future, not a narrative plan, but the same sunny dream that

Master Humphrey saw her sleeping out as her own small part of the chaotic reality she occupied;

> Sun, and stream, and meadow, and summer days, shone brightly in her view, and there was no dark tint in all the sparkling picture. (27)

Nancy could only live 'as if' she occupied this ideal world, and in *Oliver Twist* it was removed even from the reach of Oliver's innocence in the unattainable goodness which was the end, and not the reality, of narrative, in Rose. Here, heaven itself seems to become the real substance of Nell's life. This non-literal, half-mythical (heavenly) reality becomes both the novel's discovery of a generic world capable of fulfilling dreams, and a world which denies the claims of narrative to present and order its perception of the world literally.

This world is the world of the curiosity shop. Nell remains at home in it; and she remains, as she was at the beginning of the novel, strangely both dependent upon the dark curiosity shop world around her, and at the same time in a light and sunny world of her own. The only difference in her real presence as the novel progresses comes about as the 'grotesque and wild' things which surround her change; but these only show us different aspects of the curiosity shop, and do not alter the brightness of her image. The landscape through which we are taken with Nell is not so much the first sign of a social realism which never really interested Dickens, and for which he would have been much the lesser writer, but the manifestation of the darkness of the world Nell occupies, and which is, again very oddly, her protector, on a truly grandiose scale. Through Nell and the industrial landscape, the dream-life of things is extended from the boundaries of childhood and child-consciousness, the territory it occupied with Oliver, to a full vision of the bewilderment which the outside world offers.

> On every side, and as far as the eye could see into the heavy distance, tall chimneys, crowding on each other, and presenting that endless repetition of the same dull, ugly form, which is the horror of oppressive dreams, poured out their plague of smoke, obscured the light, and made foul the melancholy air. (28)

Nell discovers the whole world as a curiosity shop, and finds herself quite at home in it. So that "she lay down, with nothing between herself and the sky; and, with no fear for herself, for she was past it now, put up a prayer for the old man" (29). Mr Newman, in *Dickens at Play*, calls Nell a 'monster' (30) for the sympathy she finds in this environment; and to the book's narrative interest, she is precisely that, for "that endless repetition" of the landscape constitutes the defeat of the progressive structure and expectation of narrative, and is the landscape which in the curiosity shop, with its senseless and non-progressive jumble of dark objects, was the natural environment of the image Nell began as. Her affinity with the sheer turmoil of this monstrous and irrational scene then is equally natural; so that what the narrative treats as anarchic and abhorrent Nell can contemplate with "no fear or anxiety" (31).

The monstrosity of Nell to the interests of narrative is shown to the full when she attempts association with others. She is only once tempted into a relationship which could be seen as anything like a friendship, with the single exception of her long-term association with Kit (which, because of her withdrawal from the novel's action, could more legitimately be called a dissociation), and this temptation is another test of her dream-nature, and of her resistance to narrative.

In Chapter 32, she witnesses the reunion of two sisters, and afterwards "could not help following at a little distance" (32). This is the first and only time that Nell has any response to the outside world other than one of avoidance or self-preservation. She comes closer here than she does anywhere else to fulfilling the function of a character in a narrative, and to family ties and associations with the figures around her - hitherto, her only relation with them has been insofar as they exist as a part of the chaos and jumble of the grotesque which constitutes the curiosity shop of Nell's existence.

But what she does with the relationship the novel offers her here hardly supports the normal substance of character and plot:

> Their evening walk was by a river's side. Here, every night, the child was too, unseen by them, unthought of, unregarded; but feeling as if they were her friends, as if they had confidences and trust together, as if her load were lightened and less hard to bear; as if they had mingled their sorrows, and found mutual consolation. It was a weak fancy perhaps, the childish fancy of a young and lonely creature; but night after night, and still the sisters loitered in the same place, and still the child followed with a mild and softened heart. (33)

Far from offering the normal, active relationship we would expect of Nell in any ordinary narrative, she is again here very much like Master Humphrey. Where Pickwick would have dominated the two sisters with his vitality, disarming their story by including it within his own energy, Nell stands back, as Master Humphrey would, knowing that to join in would not be an assertion of her right to dream and to construct 'air-built castles', but a sacrifice both of that right and of her own identity to the story of the two sisters. Sympathy is an integral part of the dream-world, and Nell - like Master Humphrey - can truly sympathise only if she does not act.

Nell's inaction preserves Master Humphrey's night-time world, and the episode of the two sisters is precisely as he would wish it; a "glimpse of passing faces", affording "greater opportunity of speculating on the characters" (34) of figures seen only briefly. In the fragmented world such vision produces sympathy as the unifying emotion; what the fictional worlds of Nell and Humphrey, and Pickwick too, have in common is the good feeling that forms the basis of each.

But this very inaction also produces a problem for the narrative and plot of the novel. The emotions and affections of the passage above remain utterly unshared, so that to the associative demands of narrative they seem almost impossible. Nell's experience here is very much like the later experience of David Copperfield when, running away from London to his aunt, he sleeps in the company of the sentry at Greenwich; like Nell, he is unseen, unthought of, unregarded. But in *David Copperfield* the novel gains at least a partial triumph over childhood; his experiences, ultimately, exist in order to be communicated as part of the story of his life; his 'friendship' had to be silent at the time, but the narrative makes its own sense of his feelings by asserting that they were felt only in order to be expressed later, and not really for their own sake. In doing so, the narrative betrays the dream-world of the child.

But for Nell, there is no later. We find that we must watch her, as a part of the curiosity shop of life, where the narrative wants to watch *with* her, and to see through her eyes, for Nell's experience here has nothing to do with telling a story: it is purely momentary, purely fictive. She does not in any sense tell us what happens; there is no retrospective or indirect speech. Instead, Dickens writes for her, finding it necessary to adopt her own principle of sympathy. Nell remains silent, refusing to do anything more than feel, and to be anything other than felt for.

The 'as ifs' in the passage above are not like Nancy's in *Oliver Twist*, for Nancy mediated, however unwillingly, between fiction and narrative; her 'as if' was a concession to the literal reality which prevented her dream from realisation as anything other than a momentary truth. Nell's make no such concession. When Dickens writes "as if they mingled their sorrows, and found mutual consolation", the 'as if' is not accessible to narrative as Nancy's was. These words do not publicly establish the emotion they contain, but instead privatise and hide it: was it there 'in reality', as the potential substance of narrative? In Nell's mind? In Dickens'? In Master Humphrey's? Or even, as we ask, in the reader's own?

This uncertainty suggests that Nell's feelings exist outside the normal characterisation of narrative, for they belong specifically neither to Nell nor to a narrating voice. Instead, they are generalised feelings, and belong, as Nell does, to all of us. They are the feelings of fiction which do not exist literally but in the spirit, here, of emotion itself. They gesture towards, not real feelings, but a generic, mythical speech we all know and understand, and belong to a world of the literary which asks for common assent. Nell's privatisation of association paradoxically makes her a personification of associative feelings, and Dickens' private persona for a goodness which he found missing from the public world. This fictive privacy belongs to Nell, to Dickens, to Master Humphrey and to ourselves, and above all to a world in which, as we saw in *Oliver Twist*, loneliness itself is a generic condition, left without the justice which brings fiction and narrative together without conflict.

Dickens begins to work secretly, in writing feelings for Nell, participating in Nell's withdrawal by making her feelings up for her. He does so in order to put them into a narrative which in *Oliver Twist* admitted such feeling only as a childish dream, and he finds it necessary to make an apology for the story he has thereby violated; "It was a weak fancy, perhaps" - but, given the harshness of the narrative's terms, it was the best he could do.

Nell shows us the importance and function of the persona in the novel, to present feelings unreservedly 'as if' they belonged to us all; but in doing so she becomes a threat to the very motive forces of the narrative - to its speech and its action. The only way that narrative can deal with her is ultimately to write her out of the book, and to drown her in its own course. Nell is too extreme a figure, too special in her nature, to afford any ground for compromise with her. We find as the book progresses that much of its everyday life begins to betray the dream that Nell lives, and to portray her as the static idea that narrative would like to see in her. So that her encounter with Mrs Jarley, for instance, gives the story the opportunity to make her 'the wax-work child' (35), an image which comes both from the exasperation of the narrative and from the irresponsibility of the everyday life which we have previously seen working against narrative. Nell the waxwork child becomes another aspect of her curiosity shop personality, viewed from the perspective of narrative.

But, for the novel's narrative interests, this small revenge upon Nell's fictive nature only suspends the problem of what to do with her; it does not solve it. The narrative continually finds itself forced to treat Nell as a curiosity - an exhibit in the curiosity shop. Each image it produces for her has close affinities with death, for narrative sees the fictive world, in its stasis, as a world of death. The waxworks, the child in the graveyard with the Punch and Judy men, Nell's sympathy with the sadness of the two sisters, and with the favourite pupil who dies - all these identify Nell's presence as a series of associations with a melodrama whose very life is born of its relation to death. It is natural, then, that the story should turn to death in order to solve the problem that Nell has become.

Nell's death offers itself to the narrative as a kind of final exhibit, the last great curiosity of her life, and appears to be an end of the odd problems that Nell raises, an ending to the resistance she has produced to the forward movement, and to the speech and action of the narrative.

At the end of her story, she fulfills her nature as a curiosity to the extent that people actually come to view her. As Mr Newman points out in *Dickens at Play,*

> By Chapter 55 parties of visitors come to the village as much to inspect the child as the mouldering church. (36)

But Nell's death itself presents the problem she is to the narrative interests of the writing at a much deeper level than these half-joking images of her nature. At her death-bed we are told,

> She was dead. No sleep so beautiful and calm, so free from trace of pain, so fair to look upon, She seemed a creature fresh from the hand of God, and waiting for the breath of life; not one who had lived and suffered death.

And the writing continues

> Where were the traces of her early cares, her sufferings, and fatigues? All gone. Sorrow was dead indeed in her, but peace and perfect happiness were born; imaged in her tranquil beauty and profound repose.
> And still her former self lay there, unaltered in this change. Yes. The old fireside had smiled upon that same sweet face; it had passed like a dream through haunts of misery and care; at the door of the poor schoolmaster on the summer evening, before the furnace fire upon the cold wet night, at the still bedside of the dying boy, there had been the same mild lovely look. So shall we know the angels in their majesty after death. (37)

What the narrative wants to do, here, as it does in its former images of Nell, is to relinquish her to her own changelessness, and to leave her in death as a kind of 'via negativa'; so that her whole life and the whole life of the novel insofar as it has focused upon her has been like the landscape she once walked through, "like a dream". Release from Nell, the narrative hopes, will be release from her changelessness, and from the dream-world she inhabits, and an end of the resistance she has offered to real action, and to real speech.

But we have only to read of Nell's death to realise, paradoxically, the value and power of the world she occupies, even in dying. For death as Nell experiences it is not an ending, but a form of protection, and mythical presence has in this real potency, in spite of its apparently private and secular nature. Death is the culmination and continuation of the fiction she offers, for it is the very nature of her changelessness not to end

- or rather, perhaps, to be a continual ending: "Still her former self lay there, unaltered in this change." Nell herself remains the same, with the "same sweet face" and "the same mild lovely look". In dying, Nell is born to the future life she once foretold for herself, to her own dream, experiencing the

> return of simple pleasures they had once enjoyed, a relief from the gloomy solitude in which she had lived, and escape from the heartless people by whom she had been surrounded ... and a life of tranquil happiness. (38)

In death, these dreams come to fruition:

> Sorrow was dead indeed in her, but peace and perfect happiness were born. (39)

Nell has in a sense always been dead; she has "lived and suffered death", we are told, and not life, so that even death changes nothing in her. We see in the darkness which falls and surrounds her as she dies that death is only another form of the kindness that Master Humphrey seeks, and, in Nell, provides. Moreover, it is the ultimate form of that kindness, threatening no sudden revelation of the 'stream of life' in daylight, and no destruction of any 'air-built castle' by some terrible clarity of action or plot, as Sikes destroyed Nancy's by murder. The dream of this final image of Nell is finally a secure one, for in death, and only in death, can we recognise that Nell always was the same - and, for the purpose of the novel, always will be.

Once again, here, Nell is shown to be what should in narrative be an impossibility - a creature without a narrative voice. Living in death as she was dying in life, she seems to be "a creature fresh from the hand of God, and waiting for the breath of life". As such, she again creates what Dickens wants for his novel, the space for the feelings which the realism of the narrative in *Oliver Twist* devalued and excluded. Once again, Nell's nature makes a commonality of the private nature of her death, and defeats its literal occurrence. We cannot be sure whether she achieves her happiness in reality, in her own mind, in Master Humphrey's, or in Dickens'. Once again, we are made aware that the feeling here exists beyond the scope of the associative values of the narrative, and of the novel insofar as novels consist of narrative, for the emotion she embodies is not an emotion which can exist within a narrative context, but instead one which is hidden away from the 'stream of life' Master Humphrey so feared.

Death, then, does not undo Nell, but secures the value of her dream-world for the novel. Her absence is at least as potent in this as her presence. The difficulty of Nell for the narrative, however, remains.

The nature of her death does not allow the story to reassert its own values, and the problem Nell sets narrator (as distinct from novelist) remains unsolved. Her death does not change the substance of the novel, for its action continues in her absence just as much of it in any case occurred in her absence before her death, still dominated by her, as I suggested near the beginning of this chapter, through the curiosity shop world created around her, and more actively by the figure of Quilp. Quilp, I have argued, is a part of the fiction to which Nell belongs, a part of the curiosity shop which represents consciousness in its fragmented, inconsequential form. While Dickens' conventional villains always have some origin for their criminality - whether it be of race, as with Fagin, or of class, as with Carker or Uriah Heep (and bound up with these conventional origins are their more complicated roots in Dickens' own obsessively class-orientated past) - Quilp's kind of villainy has no such source, for he belongs to Nell's world, the world of dreams. As one of the 'wild and grotesque' figures surrounding Nell, his energies compliment and indicate hers, as hers do his.

Quilp is in important ways a very similar figure to Nell herself, and is similarly resistant to the demands of narrative and plot. Near the beginning of the novel, Quilp is described as follows:

> The creature appeared quite horrible with his monstrous head·and little body, as he rubbed his hands slowly round, and round, and round again - with something fantastic even in his manner of performing this slight action - and, dropping his shaggy brows and cocking his chin in the air, glanced upward with a stealthy look of exultation that an imp might have copied and appropriated to himself. (40)

Quilp appears here to be more object than man. Just as Nell seemed more curiosity than character to the 'stream of life' of the novel, so Quilp seems to be more spectacle than human being. Dickens uses the same word, 'creature', to describe them both - the difference being of course that where Nell seems "fresh from the hand of God" (41) Quilp appears to be fresh from a very different source. In each case, the novel's narrative sense indicates that, if it is a human function to narrate, to plot, and to see life whole, as a story, these two figures are something different. And while we might be tempted to identify something less than human, and animal-like in the word - particularly in the case of Quilp, who is described later as "a large panting dog" - it is necessary to remember that Nell's life in death, and Quilp's near-magical mastery of physical objects and circumstances also suggest that these 'creatures' are something more than merely human.

It is Quilp's peculiar kind of potency which is the key to his nature and to his close relationship to Nell, and, like Nell's, his character has been repeatedly misread. A.O.J.Cockshut, for example, makes the dark observation that "Quilp's sadism" "is not content with ordinary violence and terrorism" and that "his cruelty is .. linked in true sadistic fashion with sexual morbidity" (42).

For Quilp's violence is always directed at objects, rather than directly at other figures in the book. Most obviously, he never actually strikes his boy, but always misses and hits something else; while instead of beating and torturing Kit - as he would like to - he beats and tortures a wooden effigy. In each case, his violence is curiously self-contained. Moreover, it governs not simply occasional outbursts, but the whole of his action. John Carey's remarks in *The Violent Effigy* are helpful here in demonstrating the extent of Quilp's energies:

> Much of his time is spent in driving to ludicrous excess the components of Dickensian cheerfulness. Conviviality trails a hair-raising image of itself around with it. Food consumption, for instance, is an indispensable accompaniment of Dickensian bliss. Quilp approaches meals with horrible ferocity. (43)

- and he goes on to cite the eating of eggshells, the smoking of 'hideous pipes', the biting of forks and spoons and the drinking of boiling spirits.

Quilp does 'drive the components of the Dickensian world to excess', and he does so by physically assaulting them; and Carey is entirely right in indicating food as a prime target for assault.

Food in Dickens' novels is frequently a kind of social contract; it provides a medium in which associations can appear to be real and tangible, and is always important in the portrayal of its eaters. We see it at its most threatening in Sikes, who simply absorbs it without any enjoyment or appreciation (44), indicating to us at the same time his use and absorption of Nancy for his sole purpose of survival. Quilp is less merely brutal, however, and does not offer this kind of threat. He does threaten the contracts which narrative values, but he does so, not by threatening to dominate them, but by refusing to take them seriously. Quilp turns eating into sport, and the 'horrible ferocity' with which he approaches food constitutes his determination not to be beaten. As for Nell - and for Pickwick - the world is not a coherent story to Quilp but a series of tests, or episodes; and his energy is directed at the mastery of every new event. And, like these other figures, he competes, not against other characters, as a hostility of relationship, but against the world at large, and in isolation. He does not eat eggs with shells on in order to intimidate his guests, but simply because eggs *have* shells. The intimidation may be quite real, but it is secondary to the affrontery of the world of objects.

While Quilp is threatening, his threat is not directly to other characters, as Sikes once threatened Nancy, but to a world which is materially inconvenient to him, and to material inconvenience itself. Where Sikes saw contracts - as he saw food - as a means to an end, Quilp sees them as an end in themselves. To Quilp, a contract - a relationship - is an object which has got the better of him if he fails in some way to consume it. Quilp's contracts with other people turn them, at least as far as he is concerned, into things. So that Kit can really become for him a wooden figurehead, into which he can drive screwdrivers and red hot pokers (45). By doing so he fulfills his relationship to Kit in exercising his violence 'as if' he were present. The 'as if' has the same function as Nell's, even if it is here put to the opposite use. Instead of establishing Quilp's violence as a public fact, it hides it away. We can ask the same questions about it as we earlier could of Nell's emotions; does it exist in reality, as the substance of the narrative? In Quilp's mind? In Dickens'? In Master Humphrey's? Or, again, even in the reader's, for we recognise it as evil in much the same way as we recognise Nell's goodness, as a human impulse, rather than as the direct action of narrative.

Again, we are made aware that Quilp's violence exists outside of the ordinary bounds of narrative, just as the dreams of Nell did. Like Nell, Quilp's nature is the stuff dreams are made of; fiction, but not a story.

This fiction governs Quilp's nature - just as it governed Nell's - in all of his dealings with the world. It even governs his marriage, and his relationship with his wife - something Nell's dream-world never has to include.

The scene when he returns to his house in Chapter 4 to find his wife and mother-in-law entertaining friends, for instance, demonstrates what Quilp's odd nature does to the ordinary course of relationship and association.

Before his entrance, first of all, we are told that

it is no wonder that the ladies felt an inclination to talk.
and linger, especially when there are taken into account
the additional inducements of fresh butter, new bread,
shrimps, and water-cress. (46)

Food here represents quite normally the comfortable Dickensian contract of social discourse. Quilp siezes upon this immediately on interrupting the party:

"Go on, ladies, go on," said Daniel. "Mrs Quilp, pray ask
the ladies to stop to supper, and have a couple of lobsters
and something light and palatable." (47)

And, having driven the ladies away with this challenge to their indigestions, goes further when left alone with Mrs Quilp herself:

"Oh you nice creature!" were the words with which he broke silence; smacking his lips as if this were no figure of speech, and she were actually a sweetmeat. (48)

What Quilp did to Kit he here more subtly does to his wife, substituting an 'as if' for the reality, and making her into a 'creature' like himself and Nell, a part of the dream-world of the curiosity shop. Quilp has the effect upon his wife that he has upon everyone else, making her an object of his own grotesquery. Unlike Sikes, whose actions were specifically menacing, Quilp makes us all look ridiculous. Like Nell, the pretence involved in his attitude to other figures, the 'as if' which comes between his attitude to his wife and any real intention of eating her, makes of his action a fantasy rather than a crime.

In this context, it is only of partial use to point out, as many critics have done, that Quilp and Nell both have a source in Dickens' own circumstances. John Carey tell us,

> Thomas Wright notes that Quilp's mother-in-law, Mrs Jiniwin, was modelled on Dickens' mother-in-law Mrs Hogarth. Quilp was, in a sense, Dickens himself, as seen through his mother-in-law's disapproving eyes. (49)

In the same way, it has frequently been suggested that where Quilp, his wife and his mother-in-law are one caricature of Dickens' early married life, Nell is its complement, in being closely related to his wife's sister, Mary Hogarth, with whom Dickens had a very close and odd friendship; whom he probably loved better than his own wife; whose innocence and purity obsessed him; and who died suddenly at the age of seventeen, only three years before *The Old Curiosity Shop* was begun. While these correspondences are undoubtedly to some extent accurate, we misunderstand both Quilp and Nell if we assume that they characterise Dickens directly. Dickens recognises in his mother-in-law, in himself, and in Mary his own fantasies; and he brings these fantasies into the novel, not as his story but as his fiction. They are figures which, as fantasy, are an end in themselves. It is extraordinary, and a mark of Dickens' extraordinary genius, that they appear as characters in a novel at all; the life they live and die is the dream life of the normal consciousness of narrative, and only Dickens' intelligence as a writer can bring that dream life actively into the novel as part of a realisation made in *Oliver Twist* that that essential part of human life and feeling is threatened by the realism of narrative and novel.

As I pointed out above, the occupation of the realm of the fantastic, which Quilp shares with Nell, makes his feelings, like Nell's, not directly attributable to his nature as a character, but instead a common property. If Quilp, like Nell, is a fan-

tasy, we cannot then say that he is simply his own and Dickens'
fantasy - although that is evidently partly true. He is also
Master Humphrey's fantasy; and he is the novel's fantasy, it
then follows, of what it normatively does to its characters; and
if he is all these, he is also the reader's fantasy, both of what
happens in novels, and, insofar as the novel represents a set
of expectations about what happens in reality as narrative, he
is the reader's fantasy of what happens in the real world. His
actions parody life, and so include us all;

> Mr Quilp planted his two hands on his knees, and
> straddling his legs out very wide apart, stooped slowly
> down, and down, and down, until, by screwing his head
> very much on one side, he came between his wife's eyes
> and the floor. (50)

Like his hands, which were rubbed "slowly round, and
round, and round again", Quilp's actions, in their endless
deliberacy, are a parody of narrative since they occur for their
own sake and not to any end. Quilp 'acts'; and the deliberacy
of his action is his enjoyment in its execution, and not in its
consequence.
Much the same goes for his speech; as fantasy, it is enjoyed for its own sake, rather than for the sake of what follows
upon it:

> Am I nice to look at? Should I be the handsomest creature
> in the world if I had but whiskers? Am I quite a lady's
> man as it is? - am I, Mrs Quilp? (51)

It is the very concept of Quilp as a 'lady's man' which
pleases him - and which pleases us.
We cannot always accept what Quilp stands for quite as
comfortably as this, of course, for what he most consistently
represents is a fantasy of sexual exploitation. In the passage
above, where Mrs Quilp is like a 'sweetmeat', Quilp tells her

> If you ever listen to those beldames again, I'll bite you
> (52)

and in the following passage, where he forces his wife to sit
with him,

> The sun went down and the stars peeped out, the Tower
> turned from its own proper colours to grey and from grey
> to black, the room became perfectly dark and the end of
> the cigar a deep fiery red, but still Mr Quilp went on
> smoking and drinking in the same position, and staring
> listlessly out of the window with the dog-like smile always
> on his face, save when Mrs Quilp made some involuntary

movement of restlessness or fatigue; and then it expanded into a grin of delight. (53).

The innuendo here, with the end of Quilp's cigar 'a deep fiery red' and Mrs Quilp consumed (as she is in the illustration by Phiz) in his smoke, is obvious. The 'as if' is taken as far as it ever is into reality; but what Quilp does to his wife remains a fantasy, with the same deliberacy and pantomime of his former actions and words and with the same parodic universality, in which we all recognise his intent, and at the same time are unable to give its direct attribution - to Quilp, to the novel, to Dickens, to Master Humphrey, or to ourselves.

As the novel and narrative progress and draw to a close, the dream life recedes into its prevailing and protecting image of darkness. And just as darkness has been a protection for the fictive from the glare and hurry of the story, so it fends off the approach of narrative from both Nell and Quilp.

Nell dies, in the gloom of her church cottage, in the peculiar, dream-darkness of the snow through which Kit and the Garlands, the Brownlow-like agents of the story in this novel, have to travel to reach her. As they do so we see in her death a source of brightness - Kit finds himself "shading his eyes from the falling snow" (54) in the middle of the night - of which narrative can make no sense. Kit, in the snow-light, "could descry objects enough .. but none correctly" (55) and objects encountered on the road "as they were passed, turned into dim illusions" (56). Narrative simply cannot comprehend the dream which it approaches in Nell.

Quilp disappears similarly at the approach of the story, lost in a darkness it cannot penetrate. It is no coincidence, of course, that he dies by drowning, "of all means of suicide the easiest and best" (57). Both Quilp and Nell in a sense drown in their dream, defeating narrative in a death in which Master Humphrey recognised the fragmentation of the cruelty of the relentless course of daylight.

Death, then, is an intrinsic part of the fantasy world which both Quilp and Nell occupy, and both are protected and absorbed quite naturally by the darkness in which they have lived. The dream which they together make of life drowns Nell in sleep, and Quilp, quite literally, in the Thames. But death, for them, becomes a protection from narrative. It paradoxically secures the life and integrity of dreams and fantasy in the novel, and secures the dream world as a separate but necessary part of a novel whose narrative can only preserve it in death, and cannot approach or understand its darkness. Death really fulfils both Quilp and Nell, and confirms their special nature as figures outside narrative. Their death preserves and establishes their fictive natures, but it is also problematic for the novel that remains. Nell and Quilp provide the novel with its world of fiction, and with its feelings, but they do not offer a way of seeing and experiencing that world. Master Humphrey offers one way, at the beginning of the book; but his retirement from the novel provides a space which Nell and Quilp can use but do not entirely fill. The withdrawal and subsequent absence of the narrator leaves room for the fictive world to dominate the novel; but it also creates the need for a mediator between fantasy and the requirement of the novel and novelist for some form of narrative, if only as a means of perceiving the fantastic. Since narrative cannot see through the eyes of Nell and Quilp, it finds it has to develop a way of viewing them.

It does so, as I hinted above in relation to Nell, by making a kind of exhibition of them, in order to find some middle ground for fiction and narrative. Nell often apppeared to be an exhibit; while Quilp was in some ways an articulate version of Punch. The novel develops its own knowledge of these figures, and does so by placing them in the context of fairgrounds and entertainments, of races and waxworks and puppets. So that, outside of Nell and Quilp and, as it were, released by them, lie those figures which exist in every novel by Dickens, but which are never elsewhere given the powers of observation which they here possess quite freely of the usually dominating world of authoritative respectability; the incidental figures who enter the novel accidentally, and who have no preconceived allegiance to any part of it. In this novel, and very much more in this novel than in any other until perhaps the writing of *Our Mutual Friend,* these figures become the book's ears and eyes.

From Codlin and Mrs Jarley to Dick Swiveller, we are given a broad response to the world of fantasy, ranging from the overtly cynical to the innocent - but a response which exists between narrative (which has been unable to approach fantasy) and its morality, and the world of fantasy and dreams, in the everyday world.

Codlin, the Punch and Judy man, shows us with Thackerayan worldliness the utilitarian attitude to that world:

> If you stood in front of the curtain and see the public faces as I do, you'd know human nature better. (58)

Codlin's 'branch', as he calls it, of the Punch and Judy 'business' is of course to collect the money; and he does so

> protracting or expediting the time for the hero's final triumph over mankind, according as he judged that the aftercrop of halfpence would be plentiful or scant. (59)

As his partner Short says of him,

> When you played the ghost in the regular drama in the fair, you believed in everything - except ghosts. But now you're a universal mistruster. I never see a man so changed. (60)

Not surprisingly, perhaps, it is the character in the novel who is least a 'mistruster' in this sense who turns out, quite accidentally in terms of Dickens' first intentions, to be one of its most important figures, filling the gap Master Humphrey leaves between Nell and Quilp and novelist, and providing the pair of eyes we need in order to view the world the novel has become.

Dick Swiveller is the one character in the book who engages with and believes fully in both fantasy and narrative. While he has a strictly non-bourgeoise naivety and lack of sophistication and is fully immersed in his consumption of entertainment, quite at home in the dreams and ideals of music-hall fantasy, he is at the same time an intelligent figure, capable of attempting to construct the incoherence and irresponsibility of his own life and the world around him into some kind of articulate whole.

Where Nell and Quilp, then, have no voice as characters in a narrative, and speak the language of fiction, Dick restores the fictive to narrative, mediating between fantasy and reality by recognising the ideal as quotation - respecting at the same time both its fictive nature and its real importance to his own existence. By doing so, Dick Swiveller gives fiction a voice in narrative.

Through him, then, as a kind of everyman, the fantasies of the novel are brought into the daylight of consciousness; and it is through fantasies that his life is made into something other than a continual hardship and sadness. And it is not simply dressed up, but really transformed, as he demonstrates upon his first appearance in the book, when he visits the old curiosity shop with Fred in Chapter 2:

> "Before I leave the gay and festive scene, and halls of dazzling light, sir" said Mr Swiveller, "I will, with your permission, attempt a slight remark. I came here, sir, this day, under the impression that the old man was friendly." (61)

In calling the Old Curiosity Shop a 'gay and festive scene' and 'halls of dazzling light' Dick recognises it for what, to the fictive consciousness, it is, a source of comfort, protection, and inspiration. The music-hall quotations, the mock-speechifying, and the formality of address - all these are in a sense pretence, and conscious pretence; but what they do is to recognise and to quote the dream world and the chaotic order of Nell, and the grotesque things which surround her, to the literal reality of a world in which Fred has come to extort money from his uncle. By quoting fantasy to reality, they also supply reality with what is patently missing from it, the good feelings, the 'friendliness' which Swiveller knows instinctively must be the basis of any transaction. These feelings are lost, as they were in *Oliver*

Twist. Dick Swiveller, as a go-between for two separated worlds, becomes the novel's restorative (62).

For Dick Swiveller's consciousness exists in both worlds of the novel; so that he can see what is missing from reality, and articulates that loss by voicing the chaos of fantasy for narrative. Because he half-exists in narrative, as Quilp and Nell do not, he survives in a world which ultimately demands progression and some form of success where Nell and Quilp, who are purely fantasies, must die. He survives by quoting dreams back at reality, even in the most desperate of real circumstances:

> "Quilp offers me this place, which he says he can ensure me," resumed Dick after a thoughtful silence, and telling off the circumstances of his position, one by one, upon his fingers: "Fred, who, I could have taken my affidavit, would not have heard of such a thing, backs Quilp to my astonishment, and urges me to take it also - staggerer, number one. My aunt in the country stops the supplies, and writes an affectionate note to say that she has made a new will, and left me out of it - staggerer, number two. No money, no credit; no support from Fred, who seems to turn steady all at once; notice to quit the old lodgings - staggerers three, four, five, six. Under an accumulation of staggerers, no man can be considered a free agent. No man knocks himself down; if his destiny knock him down, then it must pick him up again. Then I am very glad that mine has brought all this upon itself, and I shall be as careless as I can, and make myself at home to spite it." (63)

The comfort Dick offers himself here is the comfort of the fictive world, outside narrative. His resolution to "be as careless as I can" and "make myself at home" is a resolution to ignore the ends and 'destiny' of his story, a resolution very much in the spirit of the earlier cab-drivers of the *Sketches*. But Dick differs from figures such as Bill Barker in acknowledging the existence of the practical world of narrative, and of circumstance. He enumerates and orders the necessities of his life - in their absence - before undertaking to 'spite' them. While concluding with a universal truth about bad luck - that no man intentionally brings it upon himself - the price of the status he thereby achieves as a kind of everyman is the practical difficulty of this fictional kind of comfort and reassurance as a means to the end of survival. While Dick shows himself to be an attractive figure in every sense, preserving good feeling in a world of harsh realities and so bridging the gap between Nell and the demands of the story, he is able to do so only at great cost. For of all the figures in the book it is Dick who really suffers the most hardship, lacking as he does the resources of withdrawal that preserve Quilp and Nell as fantasies.

He does succeed in making a home of the novel. He talks to himself when there is no one else for him to speak to, and makes other people belong to his names for them. He answers back to his position and circumstances, taking swipes at Sally Brass with his ruler, and christening her 'the dragon' and doing business on his own initiative with the mysterious lodger. Unlike Nell and Quilp, he is capable of participating in either side of the fantasy world, and his feeling can be both bad and good. His good feeling, of course, is concentrated about the Marchioness; and his ability to participate in the world of fantasy is again at the root of his relationship with her. Only Dick Swiveller could make a Marchioness of the little servant girl at the Brasses.

But his suffering is also real; if the novel is his home, it is hardly a comfortable one. It is almost inevitable that he, too, should fall ill, and do so as a direct result of physical hardship, and it is a part of the narrative's cruelty to Dick that he should not be allowed the comfort of withdrawal. His illness is never allowed, as Nell's is, to become the kind of rest which would allow Dick to slip into the dream world he is temporarily allowed to occupy. The novel must end: and it falls upon Dick, who alone of all its figures has seen all parts of the world it offers, and seen its life as we see it, neither as a dream nor a reality, but as a strange and chaotic mixture of each, to end the book for us.

His response upon being re awakened to this task is typically brave:

> "I'm dreaming," thought Richard, "that's clear. When I went to bed, my hands were not made of eggshells; and now I can almost see through 'em. If this is not a dream, I have woken up by mistake in an Arabian Night instead of a London one. But I have no doubt I'm asleep. Not the least." (64)

Dick Swiveller's peculiar and pervasive energy is active in even this extremity of physical weakness, making himself at home by placing his own imagination between the unkindness of reality that Master Humphrey feared and the protection of dreams and of sleep.

It is this energy which makes Dick so central to this novel, and to Dickens' role in writing it; for only he can carry us through the experiences the novel offers without the continual threat of termination which Nell and Quilp represent, without the aloofness and detachment of Kit, and the Garlands, who are too safe in their cottage for their principles to have any effect on the course of the book, and without the cynicism of Codlin which tells us that art is a mere exhibition, and fantasy a delusion. Dick Swiveller keeps fiction alive by adapting his imagination to reality, and reality to his imagination. He succeeds in making the literal literary and the literary literal, much as Dickens did in the *Sketches,* by quoting his ideal world, his 'as ifs', back at reality. In doing so the story of the novel becomes in a strange way his story; for his sensitivity to what happens to him and around him becomes the medium in this novel for our own identification of the action.

The correspondence between Dick Swiveller and Dickens, as existing between the worlds of fantasy and reality - and between the fictional and the real - now seems quite obvious; and it is obvious, too, I think, that in this novel Dick Swiveller is Dickens' ally both in recognising the value of Nell's fictive world, and in resisting the pressure of narrative against that world, to drown the ideal, and the fantasies which the fictive world can contain, in action.

But Swiveller is also in some ways a highly problematic figure for Dickens. The book began as an attempt to insert the ideal feelings of a dream-world into the action of the novel; and yet what emerges from it is the figure of Dick Swiveller, who is compromising in every sense, for it is no coincidence that of all the characters in the book it is Dick who experiences life, as Nancy did, as a constant hardship - even if it is at the same time often amusing and even half-enjoyable. The Swiveller compromise is only brought about by a belief in the world and by a trustfulness of reality, in spite of everything, which makes him consistently and repeatedly the victim - albeit the apparently willing victim - of the chaotic world of the novel, of both its fantasy and its narrative. And it is as the victim of the novel that Dick is so useful to it.

This presents us with a very odd situation, for, insofar as Dick represents Dickens, and he does to the extent that the action of this novel simply could not be seen as a narrative without him, Dickens becomes the victim and sufferer in his own novel, as its writer. And that insofar as fantasy and fiction constitute the imagination and feeling of this novel, which, in the novel's avoidance of Sikes' violation of the imagination of narrative, they do, Dickens finds that his own persona and his own feelings have become the surviving but quite passive victims of his narrative. So that he finds himself reduced by the course of the narrative, and by the rejection by narrative of his dream-world, to the amoral, suffering, lower-class and subjected status of Dick Swiveller; to the status of everyman. While there is a real heroism in this, both for Dick Swiveller and for Dickens, there is also the threat of the world Dickens wanted the novel to write him out of; the real world of his own unprotected childhood. Narrative, *The Old Curiosity Shop* finds, will not have real feeling without the past, and the trouble of the past. *The Old Curiosity Shop* is at the very root of Dickens' greatness as a writer; for it not only achieves a position which is in every way a common position for reader and writer in reconciling the dividedness of dreams and reality, and of fiction and narrative, but it does so as the resolution of a difficulty *in* difficulty. *The Old Curiosity Shop* solves nothing. But it faces difficulties at a price - the admission of the writer's own immersion in them - which is great, and which, like all true resolutions, creates both its own real problems, and its own real triumphs.

Dickens *cannot* be Dick Swiveller; but in *The Old Curiosity Shop* he is. He compromises himself in him for his reader, and no novelist can make a greater sacrifice, or in any real sense achieve more, than that.

Footnotes

(1) See page 3 above.
(2) R.L.Patten, *Charles Dickens and his Publishers*, 105.
(3) R.L.Patten, *Charles Dickens and his Publishers*, 110. See also R.L.Patten, 'The Story Weaver at his Loom'; Dickens and the Beginning of *The Old Curiosity Shop*, in R.B.Partlow (Ed.), *Dickens the Craftsman: Strategies of Presentation*, (Illinois, 1970) 44-64, and particularly 50-3 for a detailed account of the novel's conception.
(4) Malcolm Andrews (Ed.), *The Old Curiosity Shop* (Penguin 1972), 29-30.
(5) This summary judgement from the back of the current Penguin edition illustrates the popularly accepted modern opinion of the novel.
(6) Steven Marcus, *Dickens from Pickwick to Dombey*, 129.
(7) F.S.Schwarzbach, *Dickens and the City*, 75.
(8) *The Old Curiosity Shop*, 43.
(9) *The Old Curiosity Shop*, 43.
(10) *The Old Curiosity Shop*, 675.
(11) *The Old Curiosity Shop*, 673.
(12) *The Old Curiosity Shop*, 44.
(13) See *Oliver Twist*, 346: *Our Mutual Friend*, 503.
(14) *The Old Curiosity Shop*, 47.
(15) J.R.Kincaid observes this, remarking that "the dominant critical error is to separate Nell from her surroundings". See *Dickens and the Rhetoric of Laughter*, 81.
(16) *The Old Curiosity Shop*, 55-6.
(17) *The Old Curiosity Shop*, 56.
(18) *The Old Curiosity Shop*, 56.
(19) *The Old Curiosity Shop*, 55.
(20) *The Old Curiosity Shop*, 65.
(21) *The Old Curiosity Shop*, 83.
(22) *The Old Curiosity Shop*, 42.
(23) *The Old Curiosity Shop*, 70.
(24) *The Old Curiosity Shop*, 70.
(25) *The Old Curiosity Shop*, 70.
(26) *The Old Curiosity Shop*, 148.
(27) *The Old Curiosity Shop*, 148
(28) *The Old Curiosity Shop*, 423
(29) *The Old Curiosity Shop*, 426.
(30) S.J.Newman, *Dickens at Play*, 72.
(31) *The Old Curiosity Shop*, 426.
(32) *The Old Curiosity Shop*, 315.
(33) *The Old Curiosity Shop*, 316.
(34) See page 41 above.
(35) *The Old Curiosity Shop*, 308.
(36) *Dickens at Play*, 76.

(37) *The Old Curiosity Shop*, 654.
(38) *The Old Curiosity Shop*, 148.
(39) *The Old Curiosity Shop*, 654.
(40) *The Old Curiosity Shop*, 69.
(41) See page 54 above.
(42) A.O.J.Cockshut, *The Imagination of Charles Dickens*, (1970), 93.
(43) John Carey, *The Violent Effigy*, 25.
(44) See *Oliver Twist*, 356.
(45) *The Old Curiosity Shop*, 566.
(46) *The Old Curiosity Shop*, 74
(47) *The Old Curiosity Shop*, 78.
(48) *The Old Curiosity Shop*, 81.
(49) *The Violent Effigy*, 27.
(50) *The Old Curiosity Shop*, 81.
(51) *The Old Curiosity Shop*, 81.
(52) *The Old Curiosity Shop*, 83.
(53) *The Old Curiosity Shop*, 83.
(54) *The Old Curiosity Shop*, 640.
(55) *The Old Curiosity Shop*, 640.
(56) *The Old Curiosity Shop*, 640.
(57) *The Old Curiosity Shop*, 44, and see page 42 above.
(58) *The Old Curiosity Shop*, 183.
(59) *The Old Curiosity Shop*, 191.
(60) *The Old Curiosity Shop*, 183.
(61) *The Old Curiosity Shop*, 67.
(62) Dick Swiveller has often been recognised as an 'in-between' figure - see, for instance, Gabriel Pearson, 'The Old Curiosity Shop', in Gross and Pearson (Eds.), *Dickens in the Twentieth Century*, 87-8: J.R.Kincaid, *Dickens and the Rhetoric of Laughter*, 99; but the usual view is to regard him as a mediary between Quilp and Nell.
(63) *The Old Curiosity Shop*, 330.
(64) *The Old Curiosity Shop*, 580.

CHAPTER THREE

The Novel as Fiction, II: Bleak House

Nell, Quilp, and the curiosity shop world are of formative importance, both to Dickens and to his public. Johnson writes that "no story he had thus far written so strengthened the bond between him and his readers into one of personal attachment" (1) and Dickens himself wrote that "*The Old Curiosity Shop* made, without doubt, a greater impression than any other of my writings" (2). The public response to the story, and particularly to the part containing Little Nell, was by all accounts staggering, and circulation of the final numbers reached the phenomenal figure of 100,000 (3). Nell and the curiosity shop effectively established Dickens as the writer of the age - it is ironical that she should now be the most vehemently rejected figure of his novels. The fictive nature of the novel creates in Nell and the dark things which surround her a vision which, while not directly religious, is nevertheless half-mythical; and the novel comes as close as the English novel ever does to providing us with the intuitionist authority of the biblical. Nell is 'popular' in a unique, highly emotive way which is never again achieved by a single figure in a novel, as indeed it had never been achieved before. She shows us both what the fictive world is in the novel, and what it will always be; so that, by the end of *The Old Curiosity Shop,* it becomes apparent that, while the fictive imagination is adapted to and adopts the shifting conditions of narrative by means of the mediative figure of Swiveller, fiction does not itself change or develop. It has a constant ideal, and exists as a constant idealism, which we have seen allegorised in the curiosity shop world, peopled by Nell and Quilp. Between this idealism and reality must exist an 'as if'; and in Nancy and Dick Swiveller that 'as if' constitutes the same risk of becoming, in the constancy of the ideal, the victim of the changes wrought by narrative in a world where narrative has, as we saw in *Oliver Twist,* no revealed unity of its own.

The fictive remains constant; what changes is our distance from it, the 'as if' we are offered as our relation to it. In Nancy, the mediative seemed impossibly vulnerable; in Master Humphrey, and then Dick Swiveller, we are brought close

enough to the fictive to be able to view its idealism as a separate
and distinctive world. But even Dick Swiveller is only able to
make that world real through his own, and implicitly through
Dickens', individuality. This is Dickens' own private 'as if',
forced upon him by the retirement of Master Humphrey, who
was 'not disposed to enter' (4) upon the region of suffering
involved in taking his night-time world beyond its protective
darkness, and into the place where its literary, ideal nature
met the literal and changing truths of narrative. Master
Humphrey was himself too clearly committed to the ideal, too
inflexible in his own relation to change in his effort - Dickens'
effort too, of course - to find security in the compromise he
proposes.

Security, in some form of unity in the novel, is clearly the
condition which *The Old Curiosity Shop* fails to satisfy; as
unity, it is sought by Dickens in the middle of his career - as
I will show in the second part of my discussion - in the compromise which I suggested above (5) might provide us with a
narrative novel. The ideal of the fictive, the world of the curiosity shop, remains, meanwhile, as a constant imaginative re-
source of Dickens' writing, and we find it remaining just beyond
the reach of narrative, often appearing, as Nell did, as an odd
and even grotesque sentimentality to the modern critical imagination. Its most important appearance, perhaps, is in the
death of Paul Dombey in *Dombey and Son,* which Gabriel Pearson
has convincingly interpreted as "the death of that innocent,
childish spontaneity which was the well-head of his common
humanity" (6). In Paul, the ideal imagination, the 'common
humanity' of fiction seems to be finally relinquished. But that
ideal reverberates throughout the novel as the fictive world the
narrative continually reaches towards, and often, as Pearson
himself shows, recaptures; as he concludes, the 'new self-
consciousness' is only partly a release from idealism, and the
novel remains 'radically impure' (7) as a literal work of narrative. I shall, as I have indicated, discuss this 'impurity'
elsewhere; I am concerned here with the constancy and re-
emergence of the fictive.

In *Bleak House* we find the fictive restored as the priority
of the novel, and Master Humphrey, the narrator persona,
radically changed by the movement of narrative. In this novel
the capacity of the 'as if' which he offers self-consciously is
extended to its fullest, to obviate the need for the mediation
of a Swiveller. In *Bleak House,* Master Humphrey takes the
fictive, ideal truth to meet the literal truth of narrative, and
brings it out of the night-time world into the daylight. In doing
so, he can no longer be the figure we knew at the beginning
of the earlier novel, for there his own idealism made him look
like the earlier father figures of the novel. He can no longer
be active, he can no longer be paternal, and he can no longer
even be old, for in all of these qualities he compromised with
the literal truth of his position and withdrew from the interme-

diary responsibilities of the fictive narrator by making a world of withdrawal. He refused to accept the vulnerable qualities which Swiveller found forced upon him; as a truly mediative and self-conscious figure, he must now be happy to accept those harsh and literal realities without the protection of the self-limitation of elderly, paternal activity. He must be young, and, without the refuge of paternal old age, passive and subjected to the conditions of narrative. Dickens finds no male figure to accept these conditions; for even Swiveller became at the end of his story protective of the Marchioness. Instead, he gives us Esther Summerson, and with her we find the curiosity shop brought into the world of literal truths, and given the 'real', half-literal substance of a landscape in which fiction and narrative meet in the daylight. The 'as if' of Esther's fully inverted narrative, which has shed all pretention to protect, produces a version of reality itself which is under the same condition of inversion, and is itself a world of compromise, the curiosity shop brought out into the streets and fields.

It is directly into this world, of course, that the famous opening of the novel leads us:

> Smoke lowering down from chimney-pots, making a soft black drizzle with flakes of soot in it as big as full-grown snowflakes - gone into mourning, one might imagine, for the death of the sun. Dogs, undistinguishable in mire. Horses, scarcely better; splashed to their very blinkers, foot passengers, jostling one another's umbrellas, in a general infection of ill-temper, and losing their foot-hold at street-corners, where tens of thousands of other foot passengers have been slipping and sliding since day broke (if this day ever broke), adding new deposits to the crust upon crust of mud. (8)

The landscape was one place where fiction and narrative failed to meet, and now we see that failure pictured for us. This is the daylight Master Humphrey feared, in which nothing is immediately identifiable in the mud and fog. This light is like darkness - except that it promises the stories of the waking, conscious world it disguises. Even the 'endless stream' of consciousness is broken into dreamlike apparitions; "fog everywhere", Dickens continues,

> Chance people on the bridges peeping over the parapets into a nether sky of fog, with fog all around them, as if they were up in a balloon, and hanging in the misty clouds. (9)

Where in the earlier novel the crowd threatens the fictive with the insistence of the world's stories, we now face those stories to find them - as *Oliver Twist* found them - to be themselves curiously fictive and ghostlike. The endless footsteps are silenced and stifled by the fog, which removes people from the streets and places them in the 'clouds' as 'chance' people. Even the river, we now find, loses the sense of progression it symbolised in *The Old Curiosity Shop* in the fog:

> Fog up the river, where it flows among great aits and meadows; fog down the river, where it rolls defiled among the tiers of shipping, and the waterside pollutions of a great (and dirty) city. (10)

The fog makes no distinction between meadows, docks and city, and all appear - as narrative would never have had them before - as the same chaotic, shadowy world. The clear sense of place, of country and city, and even of streets, houses, and bridges, becomes obscured in this foggy daylight, which now appears to offer neither fiction nor narrative, but a world of shadowy pretences, in-between, with neither progression nor ideals. This world has shed all pretension to do anything for us, or to appear in any way, and is 'inverted' in that it almost denies its own presence, as landscape, in the fog.

The fog breaks the city and its surroundings into fragmentary apparitions; and it does the same for the justice which we have already seen to be limited in its potency. Here, justice itself is only another aspect of the shadowy confusion of the fog:

> The raw afternoon is rawest, and the dense fog is densest and the muddy streets are muddiest, near that leaden-headed old obstruction, appropriate ornament for the threshold of a leaden-headed old corporation: Temple Bar. And hard by Temple Bar, in Lincoln's Inn Hall, at the very heart of the fog, sits the Lord Chancellor in his High Court of Chancery. (11)

Chancery, we are moreover told,

> so exhausts finances, patience, courage, hope; so overthrows the brain and breaks the heart; that there is not an honourable man among its practitioners who would not give - who does not often give - the warning, "Suffer any wrong that can be done you, rather than come here!" (12)

Justice, like the landscape, was in the earlier writing a place where we might have expected fiction and narrative to meet; the fog, here in Chancery, defeats what justice should in narrative defend, the stories of people's lives, just as it obscures the stories of the world outside, of people, streets, cities, fields and rivers. At the same time, it fails to provide the promise of fiction, of a better world, since it offers to fulfil no ideal, witholding the promise the sun held out in its 'radiant' and godlike glory in *Oliver Twist*. This justice promises neither to restore narrative nor to protect the fictive, but participates in the blank negativity of the fog. Reality, we find, offers neither literal nor literary truth, neither the beginning and endings of narrative nor the ideals of fiction. The foggy world offers the shadow of both.

If a sense of place and a sense of justice were two aspects of a world in which fiction and narrative were to cohere, the third, at the level of the human, was a social sense of place; and we find the fog in this third place, too, in the second chapter of the novel. Of the 'world of fashion', we are told,

> the evil of it is, that it is a world wrapped up in too much jeweller's cotton and fine wool, and cannot hear the rushing of the larger worlds, and is a deadened world, and its growth is sometimes unhealthy for want of air. (13)

This fashionable world is like the world of justice and the world outdoors; its daylight is a limited and restricting daylight which, like the fog, gives only a partial vision, and 'deadens' the senses. Like those other foggy worlds, this one is part-deaf, part-blind, and as such provides another negated environment, for the 'fashionable intelligence', its consciousness, is 'like the fiend'; "omniscient of past and present, but not of the future"(14). In this, it is neither narrative, for it has no ending, nor fiction, for it does have a past, and is clearly not unchanging and static. In this, we are told, it is like Chancery:

> Both the world of fashion and the Court of Chancery are things of precedent and usage; oversleeping Rip Van Winkles, who have played at strange games through a deal of thundery weather; sleeping beauties, whom the Knight will wake one day, when all the stopped spits in the kitchen shall begin to turn prodigiously. (15)

The fog does what I suggested a fictive voice must; it abstains from the search for unity, and suspends the fairy tale which any such unity, in a story which provides both ending and ideal, now appears to be. There will be no Nicholas Nickleby to perform heroic deeds in this novel, and no Martin Chuzzlewit senior to return at the novel's end to resolve the difficulties of narrative. The knight the former provided for the novel is a dream for the future, but not the present 'precedent and usage'; while the latter, who seemed even in *Martin Chuzzlewit* to be the Rip Van Winkle of the novel and to return at its end to a life passed by, has already overslept. The fog suspends these fairy-tale stories, but it does not destroy them, and in this suspension fiction and narrative meet, awaiting on the one hand the ideal world, and on the other the sense of ending which will 'one day' come about. Fiction and narrative come together in the inversion and negation of reality which the fog constitutes, and find in it a common hope, that one day the fog will lift, and we will find beneath it the missing landscape, the missing justice, and the missing human society in which they cohere and are reconciled as the fulfilment of ideal stories seen here as fairy tales. The fog provides us with a landscape, justice and humanity which can exist 'as if' such tales could be told, and becomes the Swiveller in the novel; and it is to this landscape that our reincarnation of Master Humphrey, the persona-narrator of this novel, belongs.

Esther's voice is like the fog; Robert Newsom recognises this when he tells us that

> It is in the very texture of her thoughts ... that we are presented with the same stop-and-go, circular motion that seems to be the external condition of things in the worlds of Chancery and of fashion. The mud and fog of the first two chapters, signifying confusions in the external relations between things and people, have in the the third been internalised and become the inhibited condition of a particular kind of thinking. (16)

But while Newsom is right in asserting that Esther's mind is akin to Chancery and fashion, he is wrong to see 'inhibition' in it, and in the fog it reproduces. As we have seen, the narrative and fictive meet in the fog, but in belonging to neither, it and Esther's intelligence are curiously uninhibited. The fog creates a 'fictive' novel in the sense that I have suggested, for it provides a mediative voice concerned, not with its own authority, but with seeing everything; but it is at the same time even-handed in its treatment of both parts of the novel, offering reality itself as an 'as if' in which neither are fulfilled, but in which both might be. This possibility is now a part of a whole foggy world of such possibilities, so that, where Dick Swiveller seemed to have a solitary responsibility, Esther's seems to be the voice of every part of the novel, concentrated in her.

Through Esther, it is possible to identify, not simply a common predicament, but a common world, in which we perceive fiction and narrative together through her passivity. She truly sees everything, while claiming nothing further than this perception for herself.

This of course means that her 'narrative' voice is a very odd one, perhaps the strangest to be found in all the variations the novel offers us. Michael Slater comes close to identifying its character when he observes critically and in some bewilderment that "Dickens seems, in fact, to be trying to make Esther function both as an unreliable and as a reliable narrator at the same time" (17). This is precisely the function of her fictive narrative, and it produces some strange effects. When she refers to Alan Woodcourt at their first meeting, for instance, she tells us,

> I have forgotten to mention - at least I have not mentioned - that Mr Woodcourt was the same dark young surgeon... (18)

Esther succeeds in neither mentioning nor forgetting her future husband here, for she is a secret to herself in spite of her apparent position as narrator. She remains innocent of her own ends, and has an innocent, fictive faith in her own narrative, even while telling the story of her own life. She begins her story as a voice the novel finds in the fog that reality has become, a voice of past and present; and as such her chief allegiance is to her own obscurity. Her very first words make this plain:

> I have a great deal of difficulty in beginning to write my portion of these pages, for I know that I am not clever. (19)

In spite of the fact that she is beginning an autobiography, Esther knows and can contribute only 'my portion' of the story. She begins her 'narrative' as with the reluctant coherence of a fictive vision, her voice quite different from that of Dickens' 'narrative', and curiously existing in spite of it. His voice remains quite distinct in tone from hers, and uses Esther's status as a woman, not collaboratively (as Conrad later uses Marlowe) but as an entirely different kind of vision.

It is of course true that a large part of this difference is invested in Esther's status as a woman, for it is her *accepted* obscurity that sets her apart from the world of narrative. She is a narrator without ends of her own. Narrative is active and cognitive, as even Dick Swiveller must be at the very end of his novel; the fictive is unselfconscious, passive, and inevitably suffers, as Swiveller does in the course of his story; and it is this part of Dick Swiveller that Esther takes up unequivocally and expresses. In her, the passive world narrates directly, and so turns the authority of the novel upside down.

We find that Esther's half-fictive voice is ready to do what the world's other narratives will not, and what even Dick Swiveller found to be highly problematic, and declare its own limitation. While it remains bound to its own past and present it makes a blank page of the future, much as the foggy world does, refusing to be narrative just as in admitting the past it is not quite fictive. Esther's voice, too, is a thing of 'precedent and usage', and in it her weakness becomes a strength; for language seems restored in her to what is a potency in her very lack of authority. She promises us the benevolence in others which as a faith in the outside world is the trust the novel seemed to have lost. She tells us early in the novel that

My lot has been so blest that I can relate little of myself
which is not a story of goodness and generosity in others
(20)

assuring us that her narrative will achieve the commonality
which has seemed to become the province of the fictive and
fragmentary, the province of the world that suffers rather than
of the voice that coheres and controls. Her speech claims to
be the speech and good feelings of others, and exists to express
the common feelings of fiction as we have never heard them in
narrative.

Her own story seems then as the novel progresses to be
a blank space, vacated by herself to be occupied by the outside
world. "It hardly seems to belong to anything," she tells us
when mentioning Woodcourt's name elsewhere; and when she is
established with John Jarndyce in *Bleak House* he creates her
identity for her, answering her opening words by telling her,
"you are clever enough to be the good little woman of our lives
here" (21). Esther continues,

This was the beginning of my being called Old Woman, and
Cobweb, and Mrs Shipton, and Mother Hubbard, and Dame
Durden and so many names of this sort, that my own name
soon became quite lost among them. (22)

While Dickens' characters sometimes change names - David
Copperfield does, of course (23) - Esther is the only figure in
his novels to lose one. Even her name belongs to the limited,
fictive narrative and becomes another aspect of the shadowy
world of the fog, a place for the outside world to write its own
stories, and to have its own feelings, to be fictive or narrative,
to seek endings or ideals; and as we shall see, she provides
both the novel's narrators and its personae with their opportunity. Esther refuses to choose between them, and seems to
thrive upon the very vulnerability of the existence which
undertakes to have no single identity.

We see this demonstrated most clearly when she falls ill.
Illness became in the course of the earlier novels a kind of test
of allegiance, the ultimate choice between the ideal and the literal, between fiction and narrative. Nell and Quilp, by dying,
confirmed their allegiance to the fragmentary world they occupy
and their withdrawal from anything that might threaten to become narrative; while Dick Swiveller by suffering illness signals
a compromise of fiction and narrative, but recovers to end the
novel. Illness elsewhere in Dickens' novels is frequently a
crisis of authority. We see it in Oliver, whose illness represents
the importance of narrative control over his destiny (which
answers it by the oddly-patronised illness of Rose), in Martin
Chuzzlewit at the limit of his dream in Eden, in Dombey after

Paul's death (which *is* in a sense his illness) and in David Copperfield, as we shall see later in my argument (24).

For Esther, however, illness is inverted, and becomes a *source* of authority, and of her own identity, producing and produced, not by psychological crisis, but by self-confirmation. It does not challenge her individualism so much as threaten her *with* individual action: for whereas in the other novels illness is partially welcomed as a sign of difference, a removal of the authorial consciousness from the foggy world and compromises, Esther rejects it upon precisely this ground, as removing her life from its shadowy reality. Illness directly opposes the foggy world, and divides the fictive and narrative imagination, calling upon her to enter the fictive world of death or withdrawal, or to return to life as to narrative. It is this choice that Esther, unlike those who have previously suffered illness, refuses to make.

Illness takes Esther, as it took the earlier figures of the novel into a world where fiction and narrative are clearly distinguished, and there the fictive life of the imagination seems radically separated from the literal life of narrative.

> I lay ill through several weeks, and the usual tenor of my life became like an old remembrance. But this was not the effect of time, so much as of the change in all my habits, made by the helplessness and inaction of a sickroom. Before I had been confined to it many days, everything else seemed to have retired into a remote distance, where there was little or no separation between the various stages of my life which had been really divided by many years. In falling ill, I seemed to have crossed a dark lake, and to have left all my experiences, mingled together by the great distance, on the healthy shore. (25)

In illness, Esther becomes aware of the disruption of the 'usual tenor' of her life as if of the disruption of a narrative; so that "there was little or no separation between the various stages of my life which had really been divided by years"; and her 'experiences' are "mingled together by the great distance". Her whole life no longer appears to her as the orderly procession which, in spite of her unconsciousness of the future, now becomes the 'tenor' of her life, but as the dream seen by a drowning man; and drowning, we have already seen in *The Old Curiosity Shop*, is a death which defeats progression. Esther's life begins to do what it has never before done, and deny the narrative world:

> While I was very ill, the way in which these divisions of time became confused with one another distressed my mind exceedingly. At once a child, an elder girl, and the little woman I had been so happy as, I was not only oppressed by cares and difficulties adapted to each station, but by

the great perplexity of endlessly trying to reconcile them. I suppose that few who have not been in such a condition can quite understand what I mean, or what painful unrest arose from this source. (26)

Esther finds herself forced into the identity of narrative, and dreams as narrative would dream; unwillingly, experiencing the disorder of the dream-world as "painful unrest". At the same time, the fictive becomes uncharacterisically vivid in Esther's imagination:

Dare I hint at that worse time when, strung together somewhere in great black space, there was a flaming necklace, or ring, or starry circle of some kind, of which *I* was one of the beads! And when it was such inexplicable agony and misery to be a part of the dreadful thing? (27)

Esther's own verdict upon her illness however does not have recourse to either of these extreme imaginations:

Perhaps the less I say of these sick experiences, the less tedious and the more intelligible I shall be. I do not recall them to make others unhappy, or because I am now the least unhappy in remembering them. It may be that if we knew more of such strange afflictions, we might be the better able to alleviate their intensity. (28)

Alone, both narrative and fictive inform 'sick experiences' which, we begin to see, now have no effect upon Esther's life. They are dismissed as completely as they could be, and with them is dismissed any suggestion that they might endow the imagination with any special identity. In rejecting them, Esther affirms her own foggy nature, and her denial of the individual imagination of that neutral fictive narrative which in her voice constitutes the writing. What she does establish through illness is her determination to tell no story that will be merely her own, showing us that she belongs inseparably to the landscape of the novel, and not to its individual voices. Her voice is necessarily different from Dickens', for it is the voice of the fog, a voice Dickens himself has found as the voice of the fictive novel, which comes from a common, mediative reality, and not from the purpose or intention of individual authority.

It is however capable of admitting such authority into the novel, as it is capable of admitting the other part of the world that Esther rejects, the fictive world which she experiences as the imagination of death, and which would have her withdraw from the novel entirely, as Nell did.

Outside Esther, and beneath the umbra of her shadowy imagination, we find the whole fictive and narrative life of the novel included within her passive and uncommitted imagination, for she allows both the idealism of fiction and the literal truth of narrative, much as the foggy landscape does. Typically, the lesson she does learn from her illness is applicable to both. As she tells us,

> I had never known before how short life really was, and into how small a space the mind could put it. (29)

Esther shows herself to be, like the fog, an agent of a realism which will not allow the novel to be governed by its own time. Her illness reminds her 'how short life really was', bringing us away from both the eternity of the fictive, and the progressive beginning and ending of narrative, which have previously contested to present us with the time of the novel, whether literary and ideal or literal and pragmatic. The 'real' length of life, she tells us, belongs to neither, for while it does not give us the eternal duration of fiction, neither does it give us the literal duration of narrative, for it can be adjusted in turn by the non-literal powers of the mind. This foggy realism is an inversion of the realism we might expect, again operating by negating the potency of its constituent imaginations; instead of uniting them, its accepts neither as authoritative.

In doing so, it admits both. Esther's recovery from illness is a return to the foggy world from the solitary and uncompromising divisions of illness, and with this return her impartiality has a new authority.

This authority changes Esther, and is new to the novel, since it gives the survival which seemed in *The Old Curiosity Shop* to be a kind of qualified narrative control a new and impartial grasp upon reality. Where Swiveller's recovery had to become a triumph for the novel and for the narrative over the death that threatened him - and herald a 'happy ending' - Esther's signals the potency of the life that can exist in between fiction and narrative, the potency of precisely the mediative vivacity which Dick Swiveller finds he has to sacrifice at the end of *The Old Curiosity Shop* in order to end the novel, and the term of his mediation. Esther's recovery confirms Dick Swiveller's way of seeing the world as his own recovery does not. The 'as if' of Esther's existence is strengthened, moreover, for Esther finds herself between living and death, and shows us that her narrative is now mediative between them:

> I felt for my old self as the dead may feel if they ever revisit these scenes. I was glad to be tenderly remembered, to be gently pitied, not to be quite forgotten. (30)

Whereas Dick Swiveller has to bring his former life to a conclusion after his illness, Esther's fictive narrative can die and be reborn, strengthened by death, to live a second life as if an afterlife. Esther's accepted passivity means that this indeterminacy can be absorbed within her narrative, as it cannot in the narrative that seeks authority and control, so that her resurrection contains both her knowledge of narrative, of the world whose imagination threatens her own, and of the fragmentary, fictive world to which she belongs in accepting the chaotic nature of reality.

This creates on the one hand a space for the plot of the novel, and for the control and authority which narrative still needs. This is unthreatened by the incoherence of reality and the foggy world, although its control and authority is of course limited by the special condition of Esther's narrative which allows it to occur. This part of the novel is exploited by the narrative will to become its own ideal world, a kind of heaven in which the command of action over the literal world in determining the course of the story seems to become almost godlike. Esther gives this limited narrative its fulfilment, in the space created by the inverted, fictive nature of her own narration, so that the world's stories are reawakened in her, as if they had always existed for her protection.

John Jarndyce becomes Esther's guardian angel, and takes possession of her private life, while Inspector Bucket takes possession of her public and social existence. Through these two, the agents of a Pickwickian respectability and of legal justice elsewhere in the novel become stagnant and lost in the confusion that reality seems to offer, the middle-class values of respectability and justice are re-established as parts of a narrative secured to Esther's ends. It is paradoxically because Esther's consciousness has now been proven by her illness that she can with confidence place herself in their hands, and allow her consciousness to be fully governed by theirs; for they represent narratives which need only an ending in order to be complete, and it is as a part of the knowledge of her own impartiality that Esther has gained from her illness that she knows that the narratives of the world will be complete in her own fictive story.

Esther surrenders her future to Jarndyce in promising to marry him, and in doing so surrenders herself to a narrative which has made her its end. On the night that Jarndyce writes to her to propose marriage, she tells that story over to herself:

> I began with my overshadowed childhood ... I passed to the altered days when I was so blest as to find friends in all around me, and to be beloved. I came to the time when I first saw my dear girl ... I recalled the first bright gleam of welcome which had shone out of those very windows upon our expectant faces on that cold bright night, and which had never paled. I lived my happy life there over again, I went through my illness and recovery. I thought of myself so altered and of those around me so unchanged; and all this happiness shone like a light from one central figure, represented by the letter on the table. (31)

Once again, while Jarndyce is apparently the hero of this story, the 'central figure', it would not have come about without the opportunity that Esther's narrative, the blank space that her fictive, passive and suffering self makes of the narrative *she* tells, gives. It is a small irony of the novel that Jarndyce actually gets his part in that narrative wrong, and has to give way to Woodcourt. The story he is allowed to construct, of a Pickwickian, paternal authority, however, remains unchanged, and is even endorsed by the note of sexual uncertainty:

> It was not a love letter though it expressed so much love, but was written just as he would at any time have spoken to me. I saw his face, and heard his voice, and felt the influence of his kind protecting manner, in every line. It addressed me as if our positions were reversed; as if all the good deeds had been mine, and all the feelings they had awakened his. (32)

Esther here creates Jarndyce's authorship, just as she created his speech - and indeed this letter is itself a continuation of that speech, asserting no written authority of its own - by providing the space which the narrative he wants, but elsewhere has found so difficult of achievement, can occupy. Esther reads it "as if our places were reversed", as she tells us; as if he were writing an account of *her* feelings. This 'as if' makes Jarndyce's narrative into a fictive approximation, and thereby gives it the protection it needs.

Esther's narrative has a kind of double knowledge of what it tells us, which is both fictive and narrative, locating the activity of the world around her in her own passivity. Slater's comment that she is 'both an unreliable and a reliable narrator' comes close to recognising this knowledge, for her fictive knowledge of the world, and of the suffering the foggy world imposes upon her passive, unifying narrative exists side by side with her participation in Jarndyce's narrative vision. She see things both ways, on the one hand as fragmentary and arbitrary, needing her passivity, and on the other - the way she narrates to us - as coherent and benevolent.

This doubleness reaches its extreme with Jarndyce's proposal to her. One of the most important outcomes of her illness, and the way it marks her suffering, is a change in her appearance, and much is made of the 'alteration' in her face. This, along with her illegitimacy, fully discredits the ideals that narrative has for women (for its ideal here is still Rose). After recounting Jarndyce's letter of proposal, then, in which of course he mentions neither of these things, Esther continues,

> But he did not hint to me, that when I had been better looking, he had had this same proceeding in his thoughts, and had refrained from it. That when my old face was gone from me, and I had no attractions, he could love me

just as well as in my fairer days. That the discovery of
my birth gave him no shock. That his generosity rose
above my disfigurement, and my inheritance of shame. (33)

Esther continues, "but *I* knew it" (34). Where in *The Old
Curiosity Shop* the fragmentary and immediate seems to have
no location, and to be beyond narrative, here it is contained
by what Esther knows and made into the narrative it wants to
become, and is rescued from incoherence. We cannot be sure
exactly what Jarndyce has done, and why he has done it; what
we can be sure of is that any fragmentation or uncertainty in
the story Jarndyce has to tell is answered, as it never was in
the earlier novel, by Esther's acceptance of it. We cannot be
sure whether Esther 'knows' his narrative, or his confusion,
whether she confronts him in the faith of facing an authoritative
figure or in her own passive authority which knows the end and
concedes his dislocation and his inability to control reality in
her acceptance of his kind intentions. What we do know is that
all eventualities are included in her knowledge, rather than
dissipated, as they were in *The Old Curiosity Shop,* beyond the
grasp of narrative, into a series of questions as to the location
of feelings. Esther's narrative, in leaving room for this uncertainty, is itself beyond the scope of ordinary narration.

This double nature does not only govern Esther's relationship with Jarndyce; for it is characteristic of the kind of
narrative she tells that, while she is particular to *his* narrative,
which she authorises, he is not particular to hers, and is only
one part of the world of frustrated narratives that exist in the
foggy world and which all need the ending that Esther allows.
All of Esther's relationships have a similar ambivalence about
whether she is protecting or protected; and the happiness and
reciprocal benevolence of these figures comes to depend upon
their own acceptance of Esther's benevolence.

Ada and Woodcourt come to depend upon it as completely
as Jarndyce, as we see from the end of the novel: "Don't you
know that you are prettier than you ever were?" (35) Woodcourt
asks her, and Esther replies, in her narrative voice,

I did not know that; I am not certain that I know it now.
But I know that my dearest little pets are very pretty,
and that my husband is very handsome, and that my
guardian has the brightest and most benevolent face that
was ever seen; and that they can do very well without
much beauty in me - even supposing - (36)

This, as the last word of the novel, shows us precisely how
Esther's narrative works. She is only half there herself as the
ending of the novel, making people around her the real ending
of the narrative.

In this way, she does not *need* to assert herself or her
own narrative, which is theirs, and whether she is herself

pretty or not is irrelevant to the story. She does not need the world to tell *her* story - in which case her prettiness would be the key issue, as would her birth, above - but instead fulfils the needs of the outside world to have its stories told by her. Ada, Jarndyce and Woodcourt all find that they can assert their own kind of vitality - the vitality of narrative, of coherence and of happy endings - in her; and Dickens, too, of course, is given precisely the same licence to enjoy this narrative that ends well.

This is not the only kind of narrative to which Esther gives us access, however; for as well as allowing Jarndyce's narrative its domestic happy ending, she also provides space for that wider narrative which seeks to control and cohere the whole of the world, and to bring it within the capacities of narrative to perceive and understand it.

It is in Esther that this wider narrative coherence is achieved, as a public kind of story rather than as Jarndyce's private one; and once again she is given an agent for this narrative who has a curiously double relationship with Esther herself. This agent, of course, is Bucket; where Jarndyce protects - and is protected by - Esther's private and emotional self, Bucket protects her public status, and sees to the proper discovery of her past as a public narrative should; but again there is an ambivalence in this 'protection'.

Esther's surrender to Bucket is apparently complete. She seems to be willing to return, under the authority of his narrative, to the confused, vivid and divided world of fictive imagination and plotted narrative that she left on the far shore of the dark lake she crossed in illness. Called from her bed in order to see Bucket's resolution of the plot, and to see the secret of her own identity to its end, she tells us that "I was thrown into ... a tumult" (37) so that "I did not seem, to myself, fully to recover my right mind until hours had passed" (38); her journey is "like the horror of a dream" (39); and we even see beyond her own confusion into the very substance of the disorder which this other narrative imagination seeks to control when by the river in the dead of night

> the light of the carriage-lamps reflected back, looking palely in upon me - a face, rising out of the dreaded water. (40)

This is not Esther's vision at all, of course, but the vivacity of fiction and narrative she releases. This vivacity has a double effect. It releases the full potency of the fictive; while at the same time allowing the narrative to discover in her a source of coherence with the chaotic; for while it cannot control the world of fiction, it can appear to control her, and, through her, to be omniscient. As H.M.Daleski observes of the novel as a whole,

Though Esther is made to tell the story of the Jarndyces and Chancery, *her* story is an integral part of the narrative that is concerned with Lady Dedlock; the omniscient narrative, in other words, is also *Esther's* story, and once again what appears to be separate is not. It is all one... (41)

Insofar as the novel is invested in this public narrative, this is certainly true. The discovery of Esther's relationship to Lady Dedlock seems to release a series of connections which extend throughout the world of the novel, so that Esther's past becomes a source of authority for what seemed to be chaotic and meaningless; just as her emotional life was a blank page for happiness, so her real life seems to offer a blank page for a social organisation, and Bucket, who becomes the author of that organisation, is liberated by it.

In Bucket, the plot of the novel becomes a game in which Tulkinghorn, Lady Dedlock and Hortense turn out to be the other players. In this, Bucket is simply the most expert participant;

From the expression of his face, he might be a famous whist-player for a large stake - say a hundred guineas certain - with the game in his hand, but with a high reputation involved in his playing his hand out to the last card, in a masterly way. (42)

Within this context, Mr Bucket seems omnipotent. "Mr Bucket's interpretation," we are told "is little short of miraculous" (43); and his vision too is superhuman, so that he "mounts a high tower in his mind, and looks out far and wide" (44). And he determines that the murderess Hortense

shall do nothing without my knowledge, she shall be my prisoner without suspecting it, she shall no more escape from me than from death, and her life shall be my life, and her soul my soul, till I have got her. (45)

"You are a Devil," (46) Hortense tells him; and she is right, for he becomes in a limited way a god of that 'fiendish intelligence' which is "omniscient of past and present". This godliness, however, fulfils nothing so much as itself. It discovers Esther's past for her; but in doing so the narrative that is made is oddly limited, brought about by and even at its ending unable to pass beyond Esther. Once again, we see her double narrative at work, for it is as if she fulfils the need of the world to have its stories told *in* her. Bucket's authority does not go beyond Esther - as Jarndyce's did not. Once again, this authority is secured in her rather than dissipated in that series of questions as to its real location; and once again, while we do not know whether Esther regards Bucket as authoritative or as unable to control reality - in faith or in her own passive authority - what we do know is that all eventualities are included in what we see in her knowledge.

This knowledge then allows the narratives of both Jarndyce and Bucket, as both private and public stories. But it also half-knows the world that is beyond either, and in which narratives are disappointed or fail. Esther's fictive narrative is rooted in passivity and suffering, and belongs as much to the fragmentary and incoherent - to the fictive - as to the limited narratives that she allows to exist among the incoherence she suffers. Her identity becomes a place where the world can write its stories; but it also remains a place where the chaotic is registered, for as a 'foggy' intelligence, Esther's retains a fictive sense of things alongside its knowledge of narrative, and notices everything.

We have already caught brief glimpses of this world through the vitality of Bucket's narrative. When Esther sees "a face, rising out of the dreaded water", we pass beyond the scope of Bucket's control for a moment; the river's "fearful look, so overcast and secret" (47) hides a truth which neither of the limited narratives we have seen will discover and, "creeping away so fast" (48), tells a story they can never keep up with.

Half in the foggy world of the novel's beginning, the river remains beyond the narrative world, and unconquered by it; and so do Chancery and the 'fashionable intelligence', for each claim a victim in Richard and Lady Dedlock, whom neither private nor public story can save. While these figures are excluded by narrative, they are included within Esther's vision, for while her narrative invites the coherent narratives that Jarndyce and Bucket need, it is also a readiness and a form of authority to view the world for which authority can do nothing. Just as Esther's vision allowed coherence through its knowledge of fragmentation and was prepared to accept the limitations of the authority it at the same time recognised, so it also knows and accommodates the world beyond authority, where stories go wrong, or where they do not even begin. In *Bleak House* narrative takes us in Esther to the world that is uncontrollable as it accepts the limited attempts at narrative control we have examined above.

Just as Esther suffers the control of authoritative and coherent figures such as Jarndyce and Bucket, so she suffers too the fates of those figures who reject the control of these characters, or who lie beyond their limited help. Esther accepts energy directed toward and placed in her; but she also becomes the register of the novel's misplaced energies. Richard Carstone, Lady Dedlock, Jo, the mysterious Captain Hawdon, and the more marginal figures of Mr Guppy, Miss Flite and even Krook are all curiously connected to Esther's perception in a way which goes beyond the bounds of plot and narrative.

The deaths of the first four of these figures would seem to suggest that misplaced energy is registered as melodramatic tragedy, and disposed of as such. But Esther, as we have seen, is no ordinary narrator. While Lady Dedlock provides us with the language of catastrophe we might expect when she tells Esther, "This is the earthly punishment I have brought upon myself. I bear it, and I hide it" (49), Miss Flite provides a very different vision of the same foggy world when she tells Esther of Chancery,

> there's a dreadful attraction in the place. Hush! Don't mention it to our diminutive friend when she comes in. Or it may frighten her. With good reason. There's a cruel attraction in the place. You *can't* leave it. And you *must* expect. (50)

Miss Flite's voice belongs to the fictive world which Esther's voice embraces, and shows us that the foggy world can contain the vitality of the fictive as well as of the narrative imagination. Like the landscape she occupies and expresses, Esther herself expects nothing, and so provides a place for the whole range of our responses to reality, whether they be concerned with controlling the world, as with Jarndyce and Bucket, with tragedy, or with fatalism, with coherent life or with a fragmentary existence within the confusing and unfixed terms of contemporary reality. Esther's fictive narrative gives Miss Flite a place in a narrative which would never admit her upon conventional terms: Esther asks her, in typically neutral fashion,

> "Would it not be wiser .. to expect this Judgement no more?"
> "Why, my dear," she answered promptly, "of course it would". (51)

Just as Richard does when it can be of no use to him, Miss Flite acknowledges the nature of reality; but she chooses instead to occupy her own world, and her own story, and if Esther were not our narrator there would be no real place for this eccentricity, which acts in the spirit of the way things should be rather than conforms to their literal truth, within the terms of the narrative. In *Bleak House*, however, such eccentricity has become part of the substance of the book, as another vital part of the world Esther occupies. Miss Flite is not Dickens' narrator, any more than Jarndyce or Bucket is; but, through Esther, she becomes another voice for the novel.

Miss Flite is, moreover, an essential figure for that part of the book which finds itself suffering the loss of its control over reality, for she has a kind of faith which Jarndyce and Bucket do not have. The choice she makes, of not knowing what she might know, and of living in her own story rather than in the stories of reality, is a curious, and curiously heroic, kind of faith in a world that she knows, but does not really believe, is likely to fulfil her dreams, and make an ideal world of them; producing the coherence which we have seen as the unity of narrative with fiction.

This fictive faith is as essential to the writer's imagination as the narrative will to control which we see in Jarndyce and Bucket; and once again we see that its place in this novel is Esther's gift, as a kind of energy which it had become impossible for narrative to admit. The fictive vision Esther offers shows us, not so much tragedy (which is how narrative views misplaced energy), as the faith which, being against the world's narratives, makes comedy - a fragmentary and transitory story - out of such tragedy, again showing us how passive, fictive authorship can be inclusive of both fiction and narrative, of both ideal and literal. The unity which the passivity of Esther's foggy imagination produces has effectively been written out of the novel since the fate of Dick Swiveller in *The Old Curiosity Shop,* for Miss Flite's words undermine the order of the plotted narrative of the novel, being confined to the fictive world and against the possibility of a finished, written story. At the same time, however, they are integral to the world that we discover through Esther, in which Dickens rediscovers the full fictive and narrative energies of writing, brought together within the negated landscape of the foggy world. As fiction, this energy rediscovers the faith of the writer in the right story in spite of Chancery, fog and fashion - and the pressures of narrative.

This faith is a fictive one, akin to the earlier faith and life of the figures in the early *Sketches,* which is released through the medium of Esther's neutral imagination. It runs through a large part of this novel, and speaks for characters other than Miss Flite herself. Certainly, it speaks for Richard, who even at the end of his life is able to turn one dream into another, as different forms of the same belief:

> "It was a troubled dream?" said Richard, clasping both my Guardian's hands eagerly ..
> "And you, being such a good man, can pass it as such, and forgive, and pity the dreamer, and be lenient and encouraging when he wakes?"...
> "I will begin the world!" said Richard, with a light in his eyes. (52)

Miss Flite reminded us that it is characteristic of the fictive that the end should be mistaken for the beginning. We might dissent from the sentimentality of Richard's death - and of the novel when it takes up Richard's faith to tell us that he

> began the world. Not this world, O not this! The world that sets this right. (53)

- but we can see the value of such faith, at least here, where all else seems lost.

Miss Flite speaks, too, and more importantly, for Lady Dedlock. For she too believes in the spirit of the world she lives in, in spite of her literal knowledge of it, just as she once believed in Captain Hawdon. Lady Dedlock's faith is a very much more desperate one than those we have encountered in Miss Flite or Richard, but it is of the same kind. In not choosing to know the end of things, but in believing in the ideal, in life as a dream, in spite of knowledge, their faith was not only in life but in death. Death is the end of expectation, an end which Esther's reading can perceive - though not understand - as well as it perceived other parts of reality; and it is the end of narrative, for it takes away narrative's right to end itself (as it did in Little Nell and Quilp). It is however a part of the life of that fictive vision which sees things as they happen to be, and which exists in the present as an adjustment - and often enjoyment - of the gap between the way the world is believed in and the way it is known; between what ought to be and what is. While written narratives deny the world of death, Esther's fictive narrative does not. Lady Dedlock is driven to death; but in doing so she displays the depth of the novel's faith in the spirit of things.

> A terrible impression steals upon and overshadows her that from this pursuer, living or dead ... there is no escape but in death. Hunted, she flies. The complication of her shame, her dread, remorse and misery, overwhelms her at its height; and even her strength of self-reliance is overturned and whirled away, like a leaf before a mighty wind. (54)

Here we again see through the narrative control of the novel, to a world which cannot be subject to the efforts of Jarndyce or Bucket. Lady Dedlock is driven out of the narrative and death, here, is her final remaining hope. But, far from representing a crisis for the novel, she leads us towards a central image of the fictive part of the novel's beliefs. At the end of the search for her mother, Esther, Bucket and Woodcourt find themselves at the heart of the city:

> At last we stood under a dark and miserable covered way, where one lamp was burning over an iron gate, and where the morning faintly struggled in. The gate was closed. Beyond it, was a burial ground - a dreadful spot in which the night was very slowly stirring; but where I could dimly see heaps of dishonoured graves and stones, hemmed in by filthy houses, with a few dull lights in their windows, and on whose walls a thick humidity fell like a disease. On the step at the gate, drenched in a fearful wet of such a place, which oozed and splashed down everything, I saw,

with a cry of pity and horror, a woman lying - Jenny, the mother of the dead child. (55)

Although this voice is Esther's, her narrative takes us at this point beyond ordinary narrative and into another world - "the unreal things were more substantial than the real" she tells us immediately before this - which she does not understand, as we do not fully understand ourselves, but which she perceives nevertheless. It is entirely consistent with the life of fiction that her mother has become the mother of a dead child, and fiction takes control of Esther's narrative here, making a joke of the literal qualities of her imagination and their inability to believe in the truth of an image. Esther here makes her own discoveries about the capacities of the fictive and narrative as they meet in her, and finds narrative unable to recognise death when it sees it, for a moment turning the recognition upside down and seeing a dead child where she is shown a dead mother - seeing the death that is *not* there before the death that is, and substituting imagination for the reality of the scene.   In doing so, narrative retains the order which Esther had lost from reality itself, and saves itself from the dream she witnesses, at least for a few minutes.

But the imagination which really governs the writing here is the imagination of fiction which was sought by Master Humphrey at the beginning of *The Old Curiosity Shop*. It is dominated by the darkness which in the earlier novel seemed to offer to protect: the morning only faintly struggles in, "the night was very slowly stirring", and the place is "hemmed in" by houses with "dull lights". And for all the repulsion of narrative from the place, and for all its unpleasantness - in spite of the 'thick humidity' which 'broke out like disease' - it begins to appear that protection is indeed what this place has finally offered to Lady Dedlock, who had written to her husband, "I have no home left." In death she decides to seek the home she had lost, and in this hidden place, which harbours death, she finds what she wanted. The life of the place is the life of death, with its disordered 'heaps', its 'fearful wet' and 'oozing'; but at the same time it is the life Lady Dedlock desperately needed. While the darkness which was to restore imagination to the book now offers no hope of reconciliation with narrative - it seems repellent to a sense of purpose and direction and only takes Lady Dedlock in death - it still provides a refuge for an imagination which, for whatever reason, seeks to evade the literal; and, again, it does so through Esther. Lady Dedlock's reasons are the private reasons of her past; but contained within them is the necessity she feels to find a language which can include her.

The language Lady Dedlock finds in the graveyard is the language of death; she has been there before, of course, to look at Hawdon's grave, when she shrinks into a corner - into a corner of that hideous archway, with its deadly stains contaminating her dress. (56)

Having known its 'stain', she knows that she can find inclusion here, if she can find it nowhere else. Her faith in seeking inclusion above all else is that same faith that Miss Flite had in admitting the attraction of expectation, and is itself a form of expectation, working against narrative in seeking an end, rather than knowing one. The graveyard becomes the home of an imagination which refuses to be defeated by the world's narratives, and by the failure of the real world to provide a daylight unity of ideal and narrative, and to make a universal story of the future. It becomes the common home offered by the novel; Captain Hawdon is buried there, and Jo too finds in it his refuge and his resting place - Jo, who is to the narrative sense of the novel little more than an animal:

> It must be a strange state to be like Jo! To shuffle through the streets, unfamiliar with the shapes, and in utter darkness as to the meaning, of those mysterious symbols, so abundant over the shops, and the corner of streets, and on the doors, and in the windows! To see people read, and to see people write, and to see the postman deliver letters, and not to have the least idea of all that language - to be, to every scrap of it, stone blind and dumb! ... It must be a strange state, not merely to be told that I am scarcely human (as in the case of my offering myself for a witness), but to feel it of my own knowledge all my life! To see the horse, dogs and cattle, go by me, and to know that in ignorance I belong to them, and not to the superior beings in my shape, whose delicacy I offend! (57)

These words, of course, belong to the written part of the novel - to Dickens' novelist's voice. But while they express Jo's distance and separation from the world of knowledge that the written world belongs to, they also express their own distance from and lack of understanding of Jo's world; and they recognise that the most impenetrable part of the mystery he represents to writing is the part that unconsciousness and death play in his life:

> His whole material and immaterial life is wonderfully strange; his death, the strangest thing of all. (58)

Jo occupies a world of imagination and sheer (and necessary) faith in reality which in its distance from the consciousness of narrative blurs the division of life and death; as the furthest figure from narrative, he is the figure most capable of showing in his faith a loyalty and trust not possible to the conscious world. Jo, who seems to the narrative most like an animal, is at the same time most capable of showing those associative feelings which are socially necessary; and the character in the novel who is least able to write seems most able to speak. While Jo's speech is illiterate, we hear his voice - as we hear Miss Flite's - whenever we encounter him, and once again we hear him, as we hear Miss Flite, through Esther's mediation, which not only includes him in the plot, but above all listens to him.

Jo's voice is what Dick Swiveller's voice threatened to become - a deathly one; for speech is gained at the price of innocence, and innocence paid for with the vulnerability by which he dies.

But Jo's death matters less to this novel than Swiveller's would have done to *The Old Curiosity Shop*, for nothing is invested in the fiction he tells but fiction itself, and that is registered by Esther's neutral imagination which records everything as a part of the world of the novel, and retains and preserves the character of the fictive. Esther's uncommitted voice allows the world to be believed in by Jo, Miss Flite, Lady Dedlock, Hawdon, and Richard, and at the same time written, just as she allows it to be controlled by the novel's narrators. She includes the fictive faith to the spirit of things, to the way they should be, as well as the narrative faith in their construction and purpose, and she allows both within the novel. Here, Esther allows the world of death, which would in narrative be a tragic and subversive world, to dominate the novel, and her mediation, her fictive narrative, allows fictive feelings to return to the novel here, and make the tragic appear as an act of comic faith.

The most outrageous and extraordinary of these acts of faith is the spontaneous combustion of Krook.

Krook's death clearly belongs to the graveyard world, as one of the fullest manifestations in all of Dickens' writing of its peculiar energy. In it, death is made a physical, tangible thing; it would almost be true to say that in Krook's ending death comes to life.

Mr Guppy and Tony Weevle, who we see plotting in Krook's rented room, discover his death for us. Guppy first finds that the soot which falls down the chimney is "like black fat" (59); and then, leaning out of the window, "hastily draws his hand away";

> "What in the Devil's name," he says, "is this! Look at my fingers!"
> A thick, yellow liquor defiles them, which is offensive to the touch and sight and more offensive to the smell. A stagnant, sickening oil, with some natural repulsion in it that makes them both shudder. (60)

It is as if death, or something belonging to death, has actually appeared on Mr Guppy's fingers; so that the two go downstairs to investigate "more dead than alive", to discover "a smouldering suffocating vapour in the room, and a dark greasy coating on the walls and ceiling" (61). What they find in Krook's room is too horrible to face:

> O Horror, he *is* here! and this from which we run away, striking out the light and overturning one another in the street, is all that represents him. (62)

Krook's death is more than simply repulsive; for the novel runs away with Guppy and Weevle not only in disgust, but out of the belief that it is facing death. Spontaneous combustion does not matter as a scientific fact but as a fact of the imagination, and as the imagination of what death looks like. Dickens wrote in defence against criticisms made by Lewes, among others, of the possibility of spontaneous combustion, that "I shall not abandon the facts" (63), citing several 'cases' in his support; but in reality he had already written a very much more convincing defence into the text of the novel. The doctors who attend the inquest "regard the late Mr Krook's obstinacy, in going out of the world by any such by-way, as wholly unjustified and personally offensive" (64); and their offence is not really very different from Esther's at her illness, when she complains that "if we knew more of such strange afflictions, we might be the better able to alleviate their intensity".

Esther's offence was the offence of the neutral, foggy world at the impingement of narrative and fiction upon the uncommitted commonality of her imagination; and Krook's fate is, like Esther's illness, only Dickens' demonstration of his faith and confidence in her negative control. Spontaneous combustion exemplifies that gap between the way the world is believed in and the way it is known, first shown us by Miss Flite, and Dickens shows us that the novel itself is susceptible to the very crisis we see at work in Miss Flite. In standing out for Krook's death as in one quite legitimate way true, Dickens and the novel take the opportunity Esther's double vision gives to see things momentarily as fiction would, and, in facing death, to step beyond the limitation of what narrative can itself know.

In doing so the novel restores innocence and spontaneity to the novel's narrative, even though it has become clear that they offer something quite different to the knowledge by which narrative normally controls the novel, and indeed oppose that knowledge.

Innocence and spontaneity, moreover, do not simply offer the imagination of death, although, as the imagination missing from narrative, their energies have begun to seem concentrated there. So far we have only seen the world of fiction as a world of death, and as the failure of the realisation of dreams. Even

Krook's combustion is brought about by the extraordinary nature of his obsessive expectations.

But for much of the novel failure becomes a way of life, and where it does so we see that comic sense restored to the novel which was lost when Dick Swiveller tried to realise his dream.

Miss Flite is half a comic figure; Mr Guppy is purely comic, for he blatantly opposes the vision of narrative, literally seeing what it refuses to notice in committing the sin of identifying Esther with her face.

All of Mr Guppy's plots are doomed to failure; for his imagination, like Dick Swiveller's for most of *The Old Curiosity Shop*, is the spontaneous imagination of amusement and enjoyment. So that he is convinced that every newcomer to Kenge and Carboy's, where he is a clerk, "wants to depose him" (65) and

> On the strength of these profound views, he in the most ingenious manner takes infinite pains to counterplot where there is no plot; and plays the deepest games of chess without any adversary. (66)

Mr Guppy, like Swiveller, makes amusements of boredom, and is a kind of comic writer of his life. His wisdom does not even acknowledge the wisdom of narrative, as Miss Flite's does, but exists in a comic world; "If he be ever asked how, why, when, or wherefore, he shuts up one eye and shakes his head" (67). His wisdom works against narrative, as his plots do, confusing the narrative's plot, and failing, in narrative terms, to gain its own end, for he fails to gain possession of the all-important letters, and he fails too to gain possession of Esther. Insofar as his activities are literary they end in confusion. When he makes notes of his explanation of Esther's background to Lady Dedlock on a piece of paper, it "seems to involve him in the densest obscurity whenever he looks at it"; and he tells her,

> The fact is, that I put down a head or two here of the order of the points I thought of touching upon, and they're written short, and I can't quite make out what they mean. (68)

Mr Guppy succeeds here in the direct destruction of the narrative; for what he has to tell Lady Dedlock is actually of the utmost importance to the plot, and amusement is gained at the price of clarity.

But the use of this kind of enjoyment to narrative is to provide narrative with a kind of generosity which is quite alien to it. Amusement, we see here, is actually gained from the failure and impedance of narrative; and seeing things from one end, as it were, in innocence of ending, has a power of faith in not knowing, which amounts to self-confidence and self-belief, as we are continually reminded when Guppy confronts Lady Dedlock. We gain access to this power as we gain access to Miss Flite, Krook, and Lady Dedlock, by Esther's mediation, which sees the world as both narrative and fiction.

It is as a part of Esther's consciousness that room is created in *Bleak House* for the fictive vision, just as it is a part of her consciousness that provides room for the novel's narratives. This novel does not depend upon its control of things, but upon Esther, and the foggy landscape that exists beyond her, so that when narrative or fiction fail the novel does not.

At the close of Jarndyce and Jarndyce, Esther and Woodcourt find something odd happening at the court:

> It appeared to be something that made the professional gentlemen very merry, for there were several young councillors in wigs and whiskers on the outside of the crowd, and when one of them told the others about it, they put their hands in their pockets, and quite doubled themselves up with laughter and went stamping about the pavement of the Hall. (69)

The joke, of course, is that the case of Jarndyce and Jarndyce has ended, to be absorbed in its own costs: so that the people coming out of the court "were more like people coming out from a Farce or a Juggler than from a court of Justice" (70). The narrative perception of the novel, which would in an ordinary novel be Esther's perception (for this is the end of her story), would see only failure in this amusement; but while we see that failure, it is impossible for us not also to see amusement in it, for Esther's mediation, which registers all of the world's choices, allows room for such failure in the novel; even where she is herself directly implicated in that failure, it merely becomes included as another of the reverses of her foggy intelligence.

Esther shows us no resolution of the fragmentary and coherent, but she does admit them both into the substance of the novel. The ordinary, chaotic, dangerous, fictive world returns in her narrative as it was ultimately excluded by Mr Brownlow's and even by Dick Swiveller's, while their narratives are in turn preserved in hers; she shows that she is capable of seeing the whole of the reality the novel represents, and of suffering all of its outcomes. In Esther, the uncertainty and dividedness that we saw characterised reality in its impulse towards the spirit and the letter, chaos and order, fragmentation and coherence, irrational amusement and cognitive identification, fiction and narrative, becomes the structure and organisation of the novel, and at the centre of it is her narrative, which in being passive rather than coercively authoritative is fictive in its ability to see everything. This complete vision finally becomes the unequivocal vision of the fictive novel, ending the search for a stable fictive voice that began in Oliver, and passed through Nancy, Sikes, Oliver again; Master Humphrey and Dick Swiveller; before coming to rest in her. In Esther, we are given a persona finally capable of doing what these earlier figures could not, of making the chaotic, fictive, incoherent world into a part of the novel's form and of accepting the coherent values of the world as another, different part of that same form.

Footnotes

(1) Edgar Johnson, *Charles Dickens: his Tragedy and Triumph,* I, 304. Johnson actually attributes the observation to Forster, who pays a lengthy tribute to the novel, but not in these words (see *Life,* 177-193).
(2) *The Letters of Charles Dickens,* Ed. Madeleine House and Graham Storey, Vol. II (Oxford, 1969), 365.
(3) R.L.Patten, *Charles Dickens and his Publishers,* 110. See also Robert D. Altick, *The English Common Reader,* Appendix B, 384-5, for a complete list of Dickens' bestsellers.
(4) See page 45 above.
(5) See page 40.
(6) Gabriel Pearson, 'Towards a Reading of *Dombey and Son,* in Gabriel Josipovici (Ed.), *The Modern English Novel,* 57.
(7) Gabriel Josipovici (Ed.), *The Modern English Novel,* 72.
(8) *Bleak House,* 49.
(9) *Bleak House,* 49.
(10) *Bleak House,* 401.
(11) *Bleak House,* 50.
(12) *Bleak House,* 51.
(13) *Bleak House,* 55.
(14) *Bleak House,* 57.
(15) *Bleak House,* 55.
(16) Robert Newsom, *Dickens: On the Romantic Side of Familiar Things,* 34.
(17) Michael Slater, *Dickens and Women,* p. 257.
(18) *Bleak House,* 255.
(19) *Bleak House,* 62.
(20) *Bleak House,* 647.
(21) *Bleak House,* 147.
(22) *Bleak House,* 148.
(23) Upon his arrival at his aunt's she renames him 'Trotwood'; see *David Copperfield,* 271.
(24) In this novel illness takes the form of exhaustion. See page 121 below.
(25) *Bleak House,* 543.
(26) *Bleak House,* 543.
(27) *Bleak House,* 544.
(28) *Bleak House,* 544.
(29) *Bleak House,* 543.
(30) *Bleak House,* 682.
(31) *Bleak House,* 666.
(32) *Bleak House,* 666.
(33) *Bleak House,* 667.
(34) *Bleak House,* 667.
(35) *Bleak House,* 935.
(36) *Bleak House,* 935.

(37) *Bleak House*, 825.
(38) *Bleak House*, 825.
(39) *Bleak House*, 827.
(40) *Bleak House*, 828.
(41) H.M.Daleski, *Dickens and the Art of Analogy*, 159.
(42) *Bleak House*, 780.
(43) *Bleak House*, 820.
(44) *Bleak House*, 824.
(45) *Bleak House*, 796.
(46) *Bleak House*, 793.
(47) *Bleak House*, 828.
(48) *Bleak House*, 828.
(49) *Bleak House*, 566.
(50) *Bleak House*, 553.
(51) *Bleak House*, 553.
(52) *Bleak House*, 927.
(53) *Bleak House*, 927.
(54) *Bleak House*, 816.
(55) *Bleak House*, 867.
(56) *Bleak House*, 278.
(57) *Bleak House*, 274.
(58) *Bleak House*, 274.
(59) *Bleak House*, 505.
(60) *Bleak House*, 509.
(61) *Bleak House*, 511.
(62) *Bleak House*, 511.
(63) Preface to the First Edition; reprinted in *Bleak House*, 42.
(64) *Bleak House*, 523.
(65) *Bleak House*, 327.
(66) *Bleak House*, 327.
(67) *Bleak House*, 327.
(68) *Bleak House*, 461.
(69) *Bleak House*, 920.
(70) *Bleak House*, 922.

CHAPTER FOUR

The Novel as Narrative, I: David Copperfield

We have seen that Dickens evolves in Esther Summerson a persona for fiction, a figure who is capable of making narrative half protective of the fictive; and although Esther admitted narrative equally with fiction, our interest in the novel has so far been dictated by the perspective of fiction. Esther develops the novel in one way, providing a persona who observes the world neutrally, and who is capable of seeing everything, as I suggested above a 'fictive' persona might (1). But I also suggested that a narrative novel might be written by an author self-consciously abstaining from the fictive in order to tell his own, individual story, without pretending to a unity of fiction with narrative (as Brownlow did in attempting to provide a justice for the novel) and it is now necessary to see how Dickens considers this second, very different strategy.

Narrative is not the instinctive medium of Dickens' imagination; and his early work is dominated by a peculiar distrust of individual authority in narrative. This produces a repeated detachment in the novels of Dickens' own voice from those of his narrators, which would seem to indicate self-consciousness in the writer, wherever narrative is employed as the resolution, or as part of the structure of a novel. This displacement of individual authority is evident in Nicholas Nickleby, in Martin Chuzzlewit the elder, and in Dombey; in the first in heroism - which of course provides one way for the narrator to tell his story, around a central figure; in the second in 'authorial' control in retirement; and in Dombey, in his assertion and in the failure of his authority over his world. All of these novels are qualified as narratives by what Gabriel Pearson has called a 'radical impurity'(2). This impurity mixes the ideal and literary with the literal, and produces the beginning of a self-consciousness about the aims of narrative which has played a full role in the development of the fictive voice. We saw that the personae that seemed conducive to fiction were produced by the liberation of this self-consciousness from its narrative allegiance to narrator, first rather tentatively, in Master Humphrey and Dick Swiveller, and then, with full confidence, in Esther Summerson. In this liberation, of course, narrative self-consciousness is transformed into what in the fictive world is insight and perception.

This detachment is not yet a full narrative self-consciousness, but it is a scepticism about the limitations of narrative, and the powers of the autobiographical story which is the expression of the narrative of the individual, to undertake what Esther refused to do, to assert an individual identity against the world that denies the greater unity of narrative with fiction. Dickens is sceptical about this limitation as a matter, not of his inability to reveal his secret self - as a matter of the 'Romantic' guilt which critics have been so enthusiastic to locate in Dickens (3) - but as his instinctive and intellectual refusal to accept the dangerous and isolating terms that narrative seems to offer. Dickens distrusts the insistence of narrative upon the individual and the responsibility of the life of writing, and its division from what we have seen are the terms of a whole and inclusive vision of reality, the way of seeing everything that Esther provides by sacrificing her individuality.

Throughout the earlier novels, and culminating in *Dombey and Son*, we see in the 'impure' character of the writing an awareness of and interest in the potency of the self-conscious narrative that continually opposes fiction. Nowhere however do we see Dickens directly investing his own authority in what Pearson calls a 'new self-consciousness' generated in *Dombey* (4), as in the authority of narrative. The capacities and limitations of self-consciousness in narrative remain only partially known; for whereas fiction is exposed and made vulnerable by contact with narrative (as Dick Swiveller was) narrative is qualified but at the same time protected by interrelation with the fictive (as Jarndyce and Bucket were).

Dickens' position only became financially secure after the publication and success of *Dombey and Son* (5); and just as this security offered what I suggested was a new confidence in providing us with Esther as a persona for the novel, so it offered the assurance necessary to test the nature and capacity of narrative. The figure of Dombey moves towards an examination of narrative by showing us the failure of authority; David Copperfield is finally a narrative figure who is close to Dickens' self.

The 'natural' faith of narrative is in its narrator, a faith which Dickens deeply distrusts. Even at the beginning of *David Copperfield* it is held very much in reserve. A complete faith in narrative would seem to indicate autobiography as its appropriate form; and while this novel is in some ways autobiographical it is by no means an autobiography. The details of its correspondence with the events of Dickens' life have been well documented (6); what concerns me here is the literary purpose of the novel, for it sets out to test what the narrative form can do, without necessarily accepting it. David's first words tell us as much:

Whether I shall turn out to be the hero of my own life,
or whether that station will be held by anybody else, these
pages must show. (7)

The novel is not a narrative but an account of narrative,
and a history of a narrative consciousness. It begins with a
childhood governed by the fictive, by fragmentation and by
instinct, and only traces its transformation into a narrative
sense as a rude awakening by a harsh reality whose terms then
become the subject of the novel. This narrative voice in the
novel, moreover, is not given real access to the life before its
inception, for such access would deny its true nature and
function. David's adult, narrating consciousness remembers it
instead as a different world, preceding the world it occupies,
and representing the distinct nature of the world of the child.
As this adult voice then tells us,

I think the memory of most of us can go farther back into
such times than many of us suppose; just as I believe the
power of observation in numbers of very young children
to be quite wonderful for its closeness and accuracy.
Indeed, I think that most grown men who are remarkable
in this respect, may with greater propriety be said not to
have lost the faculty, than to have acquired it; the rather,
as I generally observe such men to retain a certain
freshness, and gentleness, and capacity of being pleased,
which are also an inheritance they have preserved from
their childhood. (8)

Here, the adult knowledge of the world acknowledges the
potency of childhood; although not so much in its imagination,
which belongs to the world of fiction, as in its capacity for
observation, which is legitimately a narrative skill. In doing
so, narrative acknowledges its difference from fiction, and while
it confronts the inaccessibility of that world to narrative - the
childhood world remains a 'memory' - in doing so it confronts
a loss in growing up; a loss of what some men 'retain', "a
certain freshness, ... and capacity of being pleased".
These things remain the "inheritance" of adulthood, not
its substance; memory belongs to narrative, and immediately
begins to untangle what the vision of the child makes of experience. When David continues, "the first objects I can remember
as standing out by themselves from a confusion of things, are
my mother and Peggotty", and it was that 'confusion of things'
which provided the substance of Oliver's fictive childhood vision. But memory can acknowledge the meaning of confusion
to narrative, even though it cannot enter it; David tells us -
as narrative begins to disturb his childhood world in the figure
of Murdstone -

> I could observe, in little pieces, as it were; but as to
> making a net of a number of these pieces, and catching
> anybody in it, that was, as yet, beyond me. (9)

It is natural to the vision of fiction to see the world in little
pieces; the darkness at the beginning of *The Old Curiosity Shop*
allowed precisely that kind of fragmentary vision to Master
Humphrey, and we have seen how Esther restores it to *Bleak
House*. But such vision is a weakness to narrative, and while
it can recognise it - here in memory - and can even regret its
loss, it cannot itself make anything of it, other than as a state
of innocence.

It is very much in terms of innocence that it is seen here;
for the knowledge that the pieces make up is a trap, in which
David is about to be caught. It is a part of his innocence that
so far nobody ever has put the pieces together to catch him,
and a part of his innocence that David does not 'as yet' see the
point of putting them together himself to catch other people.

It is Mr Murdstone who catches David out, at the same time
forcing him into the action of a narrative world which deals,
not in little pieces, but in wholes;

> I say, David, to the young this is a world for action, and
> not for moping and droning in. It is especially so for a
> young boy of your disposition, which requires a great deal
> of correcting; and to which no greater service can be done
> than to force it to conform to the ways of the working
> world, and to bend it and to break it. (10)

This 'working world' then threatens to destroy David's
childhood, fictive self - the self we have glimpsed through the
recollection of David's own narrative - and to restrict it by
'correction'. Mr Murdstone offers the threat that narrative must
always hold out to fiction, of taking forcible control; a threat
we saw in *Oliver Twist* represented as much in Mr Brownlow
as in Sikes.

David does not exist to be protected - for that passivity
belongs to the fictive world - but in order to discover what
narrative can do to protect itself. As such, there is no Mr
Brownlow in *David Copperfield,* and Mr Murdstone does not
linger in the novel as a malevolent presence as Sikes does, but
translates his words directly into action; and that action is the
world of work and, for David, the wine warehouse. Once again,
the correspondence between wine warehouse and blacking factory is obvious. The 'autobiographical fragment' quoted by
Forster reproduces much of the eleventh chapter of *David
Copperfield* directly, where it relates to his condition as a child.
Both Dickens and David record that

for the Mercy of God, I might easily have been, for any care that was taken of me, a little robber or a little vagabond. (11)

Forster quotes Dickens, at the end of the 'fragment', writing that

I have never, until I now impart it to this paper, in any burst of confidence with anyone, my own wife not excepted, raised the curtain I then dropped, thank God (12)

and David Copperfield writes of this time in his life,

I never thought of anything about myself, distinctly. The two things clearest in my mind were, that a remoteness had come upon the old Blunderstone life - which seemed to lie in the haze of an immeasurable distance; and that a curtain had for ever fallen on my life at Murdstone and Grinby. I have lifted it for a moment, even in this narrative, with a reluctant hand, and dropped it gladly. (13)

The interrelation of autobiography and novel is obvious; what I am concerned with is the difference of the imaginations that inform the writing. In the 'fragment' Dickens' imagination is bound and restricted by the narrative that lifts the curtain that hides the past, whereas in the novel it is David's imagination that is so bound. Dickens himself is freed to show us what the narrative imagination does, and to show that remembering the past as a secret, upon which a curtain falls, is a part of the peculiar action of that imagination. In *David Copperfield*, then, Dickens is able to show us the life behind the curtain, the world beyond the reach of narrative recollection. Even David's narrative vision is able to admit this other world, as a partial loss of that vision in the innocent life of childhood:

When my thoughts go back, now, to that slow agony of my youth, I wonder how much of the histories I invented ... hangs like a mist of fancy over well-remembered facts! When I tread the old ground, I do not wonder that I seem to see and pity, going on before me, an innocent romantic boy, making his imaginative world out of such strange experiences and sordid things! (14)

This 'mist of fancy' lies beyond, and is something quite different from the 'facts' which are not obscured by it, but remain 'well-remembered'. David's narrative vision can only acknowledge this other world, and its "strange experiences and sordid things". The detail he gives, however, and which his narrative ultimately rejects as Dickens' own autobiographical vision did, takes us beyond the curtain, as a vision that does not belong to narrative. Narrative itself *emerges* - in the retrospective observations I have quoted has already emerged - from the world of 'strange experiences'. It is this emergence which is now Dickens' subject; as it could not have been in his own autobiography.

David finds the fictive innocence which his narrative remembers fondly, although as something different from itself, plunged into the life of suffering to which Mr Murdstone's harsh story condemns its victims; and as such we find ourselves temporarily in the fictive world which we saw in Dick Swiveller and in Esther could exist only at the price of suffering. While a part of David's story is told by his retrospect, and its narrative rhetoric of pain and pity, it has another, as yet still half fictive part at this point in the novel, which is told, not quite by David's voice, so much as by the Micawbers, who are the Swivellers of this novel.

The Micawbers' world is a very different place from the world of narrative, and the most important sign of its difference is the place in it of immediate comforts and attractions, and particularly of food. Where it is the chief anxiety of the narrative that in the Murdstone world David was "insufficiently and unsatisfactorily fed" (15) the Micawbers restore eating to what it was in the *Old Curiosity Shop,* and transform it from an animal necessity into an associative language. In the Micawbers, David's imagination becomes the social instinct that narrative rejects, so that David finds in the Micawbers what Oliver unexpectedly found in the underworld, and what Dickens found in Bob Fagin; a sense of friendliness and belonging, and the language that narrative excludes, of feeling. The Micawbers' sense of reality, and their ability to make a language, and so a comfort, out of hunger itself, brings congenial relationship in the midst of the discomfort which life in narrative has already shown itself to be.

David goes to Mr Micawber's house to find "a close chamber, stencilled all over with an ornament which my young imagination represented as a blue muffin" (16); and from this moment his imagination finds a home in the nourishment of the food which has appeared, oddly, but not unwelcomingly, on the wall. It is as if the room speaks to David itself, in offering a sign he can clearly understand; and what it says diminishes the fact that it is 'scantily furnished' by making it seem familiar. Food becomes a medium of communication (though not the only such medium) between both people and objects, and one person and another:

> Mr Micawber returned to the King's Bench when the case was over... The club received him with transport, and held an harmonic meeting that evening in his honour; while Mrs Micawber and I had a lamb's fry in private, surrounded by the sleeping family. (17)

The lamb's fry is the friendship of David and Mrs Micawber. Lamb, of course, is for the innocence of the occasion. Eating comes to represent perfectly the unlikely relationship of ten year old child to bankrupt's wife. Littleness is displaced by an imaginative life of things, where the world of objects suddenly and strangely comes alive and begins to speak. While we have heard this speech as the very structure and substance of *The Old Curiosity Shop,* which gave us a world of strange and grotesque, speaking objects, it is only here that we hear the speech of fiction, unprotected, and revealed to the narrative world of this novel in a mist, by the momentary lifting of the curtain. And although what is said is not 'factual' speech - what the lamb's fry says is not 'well-remembered' - it is felt nonetheless. A few paragraphs later, when Mrs Micawber breaks down into tears, Mr Micawber

> immediately burst into tears, and came away with me with his waistcoat full of the heads and tails of shrimps, of which he had been partaking. (18)

Mr Micawber's food here bespeaks his anxiety, both as to its degree (extreme - heads and tails) and to its kind (absurd - of shrimps).

The Micawbers' emotions are demonstrable in this way because they are immediate; they are physical, real things as they are encountered. After the assaults of creditors, for example,

> Mr Micawber would be transported with grief and mortification, even to the length ... of making motions at himself with a razor; but within half-an-hour afterwards, he would polish up his shoes with extraordinary pains, and go out humming a tune with a greater air of gentility than ever. Mrs Micawber was quite as elastic. I have known her to be thrown into fainting fits by the king's taxes at three o'clock, and to eat lamb-chops, breaded, and drink ale ... at four. (19)

Mr Micawber's feelings here are the creditior, his razor, shoe shining and his hummed tune in turn; while his wife's are the king's taxes and her lamb-chops.

While the Micawbers half live a fictive existence, however, they do so in a world which even they perceive as one of narrative, in which 'elasticity' is not so much irresponsibility as failed responsibility. Like Swiveller, they exist 'elastically', between fiction and narrative, but they show us the other side of Swiveller, and demonstrate that while his compromise protects fiction there is no such protection in compromise for narrative. They offer some protection to David's childhood, but they do so - as Bob Fagin did - at the expense of the retrospect of narrative, and humiliate David's adulthood by exposing its past (as they expose themselves) to suffering in a reality they do not attempt to control. Narrative must supply control for itself, and the novel now exists in order to discover what it must do in order to find its sense of authority. The Micawbers are in a sense David's revenge upon the adulthood of narrative, his way of learning Mr Murdstone's lessons for himself, rediscovering his childhood in them in order to leave it behind for himself. Just as he has been forced to enter the adult's world as a child, so he revisits the child's world among adults. We, and Dickens, see the attractiveness and comfort of the fictive world; but David sees only what Dickens himself knows - the knowledge that David releases him from, that fiction does not protect narrative, and that the suffering it offers is the price of its comforts.

David then determines, as Dickens did when he wrote his 'autobiographical fragment', to leave suffering firmly in the past, in the place he puts it when his narrative voice lets the curtain fall. The Micawbers have an interim usefulness to David's narrative; but there is always David's own narrative sense of things behind the compromises they make with reality. As they leave, at the end of David's association with them, Mrs Micawber sees this narrative truth about him as she "saw what a little creature I really was" (20). This sense of littleness pervades the whole of David's association with their own action, and it is a part of their own subjected and half fictive predicament that narrative continually moves them on, and so dispenses with them (as it does not dispense with David).

With the Micawbers gone, David "determined that the life was unendurable" (21), and performs his first narrative action of his own - and the one with which the rest of the novel really becomes preoccupied - and leaves the whole of his unfortunate childhood behind by leaving London for his Aunt Betsey's, at Dover.

Aunt Betsey is an important figure in this novel, and her conception in David's mind does seem to offer him the protection he needs, not so much for his narrative, but as a part of a narrative purpose and direction; for it is purpose and direction that are the ends and protection that narrative offers. Aunt Betsey seems to protect David in a curious way from the direct action of the world to which he has hitherto been subjected. His experiences on his journey to Dover are harsh and cruel ones; but the harshness and cruelty have been oddly transformed, and no longer seem to threaten as Mr Murdstone's cruelty threatened. David's story begins to look like the fairy story which it has often been suggested determines the course of his life, the story which in *Bleak House* is relinquished to a world of hope and faith as a way of imagining the impossibility of the unity of fiction and narrative from the foggy landscape of reality. There is as yet no fog in *David Copperfield*. The figures he encounters on his journey to Dover seem more like ogres and bad fairies than people. He meets, in rapid succession, two devils of Victorian social morality: a miserly pawnbroker and a vagrant thief. These speak the fairy-tale language of wicked giants:

> Oh, what do you want? Oh, my eyes and limbs, what do you want? Oh, my lungs and liver, what do you want? Oh, goroo! (22)

and then

> "Come here, when you're called," said the tinker, "or I'll rip your young body open." (23)

And the bad fairies are not limited to these characters; hunger, poverty, weakness and solitariness all have to be encountered on the road to Dover.

But while all of these threaten, they all do so from the controlled world of the literary imagination; David's narrative appears to offer the protection the writing has sought from its beginning in the *Sketches*. None offer the grim realism of the criminal world of Fagin and Sikes, or of the business world of Murdstone. While David begins to deal in action upon his own account, and finds in it hardship, he does not encounter the suffering of passivity inflicted upon Oliver in *Oliver Twist*, upon Dick Swiveller and Esther Summerson, and upon himself, in the earlier chapters of his own novel. David's narrative suddenly seems to turn action into Action, occurring in a controlled way which gives it a theatrical quality, participating in the content of the fairy tale.

This control however has a source which is not David's imagination; and that source would seem to be Aunt Betsey, for she is the way in which David continues his story, just as she was the way in which he conceived it. When David arrives at Dover, she very clearly emerges as the stage manager of his life. She acts quickly and professionally, first staging a denouement with Mr Murdstone, whose worldly action she is quite equal to, and then whisking David off to school in Canterbury before he quite knows what is happening to him.

Aunt Betsey seems to become the manager of the narrative, providing the control that makes action theatrical, but highly organised, providing the literariness that transforms the literal details of David's life into his story, and turns his narrative into a book. Her function as author is enforced by the fact that Mr Dick, David, and even Janet and the protegees -

> whom my aunt had taken into her service expressly to educate in a renouncement of mankind, and who had generally completed their abjuration by marrying the baker (24)

- are her second life: we are told in the opening chapter of the novel that she had been married to a husband younger than herself, who was very handsome, except in the sense of the homely adage, "handsome is, that handsome does" - for he was strongly suspected of having beaten Miss Betsey and even of having once, on a disputed question of supplies, made some hasty but determined arrangements to throw her out of a two pair of stairs window. These evidences of an incompatibility of temper induced Miss Betsey to pay him off, and effect a separation by mutual consent. (25)

Aunt Betsey seems to offer the authority of experience, and her authority to have a source very similar to that of the authority of *Bleak House,* coming out of the suffering we saw Esther undertaking to occupy.

Already, then, David's attempt to emerge from the fictive seems to depend upon the wisdom of the suffering of the past he wants to abandon. Aunt Betsey, moreover, has been important to the novel's fairy-tale imagination from its beginning; for we are told upon her departure at the end of the very first chapter that

She vanished like a discontented fairy; or like one of those supernatural beings, whom it was popularly supposed I was entitled to see; and never came back any more. (26)

Her wishes would seem to lie at the heart of the ideal that narrative has for the novel, transporting us out of the mundane world of a threatening and cruel reality into the magic world of fairy tales.

But the cause of her departure is very odd; for she leaves in offence when she discovers that David is not the human being she wants. As she tells his mother at the beginning of the chapter,

I intend to be her godmother, and I beg you'll call her Betsey Trotwood Copperfield. There must be no mistakes in life with *this* Betsey Trotwood. There must be no trifling with *her* affections, poor dear. She must be well brought up, and well guarded from reposing any foolish confidences where they are not deserved. I must make that *my* care. (27)

We begin to see that if Aunt Betsey represents the direction of the narrative, then that direction does not evade suffering, writing the individual out of what we have called the fictive world, but is actually informed by it. Aunt Betsey wants David to be a girl, firstly so that her own life can be made good by the protection of 'hers', and secondly so that 'she' might not inflict further suffering upon women such as herself. Aunt Betsey offers to re-educate childhood, and to bring David up, only upon these terms. When, upon his arrival at Dover, she relents, she asks him,

> Your sister, Betsey Trotwood, would have been as natural and rational a girl as ever breathed. You'll be worthy of her, won't you? (28)

And, of course, she renames him, although dropping 'Betsey' and calling him 'Trotwood' (29).

We see that something of a contradiction develops in Aunt Betsey's acceptance of the boy David. He has rejected the Murdstone world of work, the male world at whose hands Aunt Betsey suffered, which seeks to make a harsh coherence of the dreams of innocence, and to destroy the fragmentary world. But he has also come to Aunt Betsey, having really rejected the Micawbers (and of course their association with John Dickens), in search of that very coherence for himself, albeit in a more favourable form.

Aunt Betsey of course knows this when she asks him to be worthy of his sister; that she accepts him is an act of pure generosity, both to David and to her own past (a generosity which, as we later discover, is not simply invested in the past, for we find that she is still supporting the husband who deserted her).

To Aunt Betsey life does not have the simple and singular direction of a fairy tale, but is instead fraught with hidden divisions. While she presents reality to David as a writing of purpose and direction, exercising a quiet responsibility and never really seeming to lose control of the novel's action, this coherent self is her own contrivance. As she tells David,

> We must meet reverses boldly, and not suffer them to frighten us, my dear. We must learn to act the play out. (30)

The whole weight of her experience lies behind these words, and we see how much of what she presents to us as reality is dependant upon 'playing out' events which *in* reality seem contradictory and fragmentary.

This fragmentation, we realise, is the very substance of her own existence. Her decisiveness and purpose depend upon Mr Dick; she is separated from the man she secretly supports; her caution leads to the loss of most of her money; and while she is opposed to men she marries the maid to the baker. Her acceptance of David then is only another of these secret inconsequences, and while she offers the substance of his narrative, she achieves this function only by sheltering him from the world's incoherence. She gives him his story and makes a writer of him - a man with an autobiography - by witholding those forces which would disrupt the story, the forces of the fragmented, hostile and chaotic world which we saw above was the province of the fictive.

The world that Aunt Betsey produces for the novel, however, becomes very clearly a melodramatic one. While Aunt Betsey plays her 'game' with resignation and dignity, and with the complete self-discipline of meeting reverses boldly, what she creates for the novel, in the protective control of her experience, is a stage upon which not all of the novel's actors are professional and experienced. We saw that even upon the road to Dover the protection of having Aunt Betsey as its end made the reality of narrative curiously unreal. This unreality continues to dominate the action which unfolds under her authority, and is perpetrated by the novel's characters in the course of its development. Mr Wickfield, Dr Strong and his wife all join in the game with rather too much enthusiasm, and succumb at the crises of their lives to the melodramatic:

> I have preyed on my own morbid coward heart, and it has preyed on me. Sordid in my grief, sordid in my love, sordid in my miserable escape from the darker side of both, oh see the ruin I am, and hate me, shun me! (31)

cries Mr Wickfield in one of his more moving speeches. And Annie Strong answers her husband, at the end of what must be the longest speech in Dickens (so long that it needs to be extended three times, with "Let me say a little more!", "A little more! a very few words more!" and at the last gasp "Another word!"):

> Oh, hold me to your heart, my husband! Never cast me out! Do not think or speak of disparity between us, for there is none, except in all my many imperfections. Every succeeding year I have known this better, as I have esteemed you more and more. Oh, take me to your heart, my husband, for my love was founded on a rock, and it endures! (32)

These speeches have the near masochistic sentimentality of Victorian theatre, with its predilection for emotional humiliation as the denouement of the plot. They show us that it is not easy to exist in Aunt Betsey's world, and to play upon the stage she offers. As she knows, the price of narrative is the real feeling she keeps hidden in her suppressed and suffering self. Narrative, once made public, preserves no place for private feelings. These characters accept Aunt Betsey's terms without question, and the result is autobiographical exposure; the asssumption that these figures make is that life *has* the purpose David Copperfield seeks in Aunt Betsey, the strong moral direction of a journey towards a coherent and authoritative goodness. That they were exposed in the very space that she creates for David for such goodness is not due to any malignancy on her part, moreover, but to the nature of a world which will not allow them to authorise such moral, middle-class stories as publicly heroic actions. The close identification of autobiography and reality which this morality demands, and which these figures attempt to embrace, is precisely the identification which Aunt Betsey reserves in secrecy.

The Strongs and Mr Wickfield suffer in this way, from not having Aunt Betsey's self-consciousness; but the worst case is that of Little Emily, and the writing of melodrama reaches its highest pitch with Rosa Dartle's verbal flagellation of her in her fallen misery. "I have come to look at you," she tells her; and at this point mere words are not enough for Little Emily, and the narrative turns to mime:

> I could just see her, on her knees, with her head thrown back, her pale face looking upward, her hands wildly clasped and held out, and her hair streaming about her. (33)

This is the action of narrative, and what it is evidently in pursuit of is a correspondence with the tragic, in an attempt to make of the novel a classical stage. The supporting cast contributes to the effect; in the case of Little Emily, Mr Peggotty and Ham do their utmost to promote the tragedy (34). We see Mr Peggotty like a demented Lear,

> with his vest torn open, his hair wild, his face and lips quite white, and blood trickling down his bosom (it had sprung from his mouth, I think), looking fixedly at me (35)

- while Ham becomes at his end a ham Hamlet, paraphrasing the famous speech ("If it be now, 'tis not to come", V,II) with heartening good will:

> "Mas'r Davy," he said, cheerily grasping me by both hands, "if my time is come, 'tis come. If 'tan't, I'll bide it. Lord above bless you, and bless all! Mates, make me ready! I'm a-going off!" (36)

This world of melodrama is the outcome of an unselfconscious narrative, and an instinctive occupation of the stage Aunt Betsey offers. But David Copperfield, although an actor upon her stage, is also ostensibly the author of it, and is a very much more self-conscious figure, as indeed is Dickens; and this self-consciousness keeps him apart from her authorship.

Aunt Betsey provides, like Esther, a space upon which the world can write its narratives. Here, however, we see her from the perspective of the narrator, to whom the fact that her authority and the authority of narrative in turn is invested in her suffering in the world of fiction becomes highly problematic.

111

To the self-conscious writer, as David is, this space provides not a genuine opportunity for heroism, but for the 'game' of the novel, which must be played out as the second-time action of Aunt Betsey's self-consciousness. She has prepared her stage for a hero; but self-consciousness detaches him from the melodrama of what I have called Action, the action of the fairy tale.

In making a stage of the novel, Aunt Betsey offers to solve the narrative problems of *Oliver Twist* and Dick Swiveller, the refusal of life to resolve its fragmentary and self-divisive nature and become a fairy tale. At the same time, she removes the problems of authority and control we saw in Sikes and Brownlow, and in Murdstone. It seems now, in David's aunt, to be the function of the mother of the novel to produce the narrative from a kind of failure not available to its fathers; a failure which constitutes a complete breakdown of all that narrative demands, and an abandonment of an authority not informed by loss and suffering. This 'failure' is like Esther Summerson's, an acceptance of suffering, and only from it is the narrative authority of Aunt Betsey's stage produced, the result of a subjectedness and incoherence not previously admissible by narrative, as the substance of its opposite world of fiction.

When David enters upon his life with his aunt the division that I suggested above between narrative - the life of retrospect which then seemed unpropitious - and a 'fictive' existence with the Micawbers seems to be resolved with the realisation of his fairy-tale narrative. The unexpected identification of that narrative with Aunt Betsey's suffering knowledge however makes the resolution appear very much more problematic, for David pursues his narrative in the expectation that suffering will not be necessary but subject to its vision; in the expectation that narrative will be, not a game made possible by a second-time vision, but a reality visible from the first. This purity of narrative perspective begins, as he grows up, to appear impossible.

It is reality that fails David from the beginning. During a brief respite from school at the Creakles' he tells us,

> I almost believed that I had never been away; ... that Mr and Mrs Murdstone were such pictures, and would vanish when the fire got low; and that there was nothing real in all that I remembered, save my mother, Peggotty and I. (37)

The narrative is most true - to Dickens' own story - where it is most fictive; and here strives hardest for the fictive world, of "my mother, Peggotty and I", where it is hardest pressed by that truth. Life with Aunt Betsey is born of the disappointment David lives in his early life; of his mother's suffering, which is much like his aunt's, and of his own, which compelled

him to run away. As it progresses, the fairy tale which David's
first vision of life in Dover seemed to promise recedes. David
tells us, as he leaves Dr Strong's academy,

> I know that my juvenile experiences went for little or
> nothing then; and that life was more like a great fairy
> story, which I was just about to read, than anything else.
> (38)

This is the voice of David's own experience, and it sees
- as the figures discussed above do not - that Aunt Betsey's
world is a divided world; that the narrative of looking back,
the narrative she now provides, is very different from the
narrative of innocent anticipation which it is her concern to
protect, and which was David's own first consciousness and his
purpose in seeking out his aunt. We begin to realise that Aunt
Betsey does not provide writing with any easy grasp upon reality; and that the first consideration due to her generosity is
one of what it has itself cost her.

No writer then can exist self-consciously in her narrative
world; and here we see the beginning of David's own doubts.
"I know that my juvenile experiences went for little or nothing
then," he tells us, realising in retrospect that his vision of
growing up was an escapism; he sees 'now' the impossibility of
that easy unity of adult and child, and looks back to the past
with what we see is almost his aunt's own vision, remembering
it as a first life, and offering the present as a disappointed
second, as a life of shame and suffering. Only that past life,
Aunt Betsey has shown us, is real in the way that David at first
sought, and the price of writing a narrative is the dismissal of
dreams and fiction, and not, as David had childishly expected,
the future realisation of them.   So that, upon a visit to the
theatre, we are told,

> mingled reality and mystery of the whole show ... were
> so dazzling, and opened up such illimitable regions of de-
> light, that when I came out into the rainy street ... I felt
> as if I had come out from the clouds, where I had been
> leading a romantic life for ages, to a bawling, splashing,
> link-lighted, umbrella-struggling, hackney-coach-jostling,
> patten-clinking, muddy, miserable world. (39)

David here finds himself in Esther's foggy world, and finds
that the fairy tale is lost to it.   Clearly, the narrator in this
novel is too intelligent to accept the space offered by a fictive
narrative, and seeks to generate a narrative of its own; it does
not inhabit the world of Wickfield and the Strongs, or of little
Emily.   Theatre and the 'romantic life' of the theatrical world
is, as he sees, a long way from the reality outside - and here,
of course, in the city, it exists outside Aunt Betsey's protection
at Dover as well as beyond the 'clouds' from which David seems

113

to descend. In David, narrative leaves its stage and goes out to meet the world; and in doing so finds out the division, suffering and sheer ordinariness inherent in its conception.

David's maturing consciousness sees the responsibilities of the life he has written in anticipation of reality to reality itself. Effectively, in going to the theatre he discovers its audience; and in the same way in writing a middle-class drama - the story of Mr Wickfield, of Dr Strong and his wife, and of Little Emily and Steerforth - he meets the world that lies outside it, in spite of his aunt's attempts to keep that world hidden away.

Dickens, of course, is not David, but remains closer to Aunt Betsey. The disappointment that David finds in the nature of the narrative's stage is not Dickens' own, but the disappointment of the teller of a narrative; and much the same is true of the responsibility David now discovers as the responsibility of narrator, to do nothing less than confront and defeat the world at whose hands Aunt Betsey has suffered in order to assert the truth and freedom of his story. David finds that the task of autobiography is to provide a new coherence and unity for the world.

This is the task that self-conscious narrative finds that it must undertake: to reconcile stage and reality. It does so by attempting to produce the story of the self as the fairy-tale romance that seems missing from the world; so that although David leaves his past behind we never see him admit its dividedness. He considers the Micawbers in spite of his rejection of them, and tries in the course of his narrative to retain them within the story and provide a place for them. The place he finds, of course, is Australia, but the effort is there to make his narrative good for them as a universal truth.

From the beginning, however, the most potent source of this universal truth seems to be the 'romance' in which the ideals of the fictive meet the literal truths of reality in the shape of the opposite sex. The romantic visions of childhood and innocence did so, but existed in 'little pieces'; David failed to piece together Murdstone's threat to his mother and in the same way, in his innocent romance with Little Emily, his thoughts did not go beyond the attraction itself:

> As to any sense of inequality, or youthfulness, or other difficulties in our way, Little Em'ly and I had no such trouble, because we had no future. We made no more provision for growing older, than we did for growing younger. (40)

This rather prim retrospect looks back to a life innocent of even anticipation. "We had no future" sounds, in the language of looking back which the writing speaks, like a pessimism or even a nihilism, but it indicates the operation of a different kind of imagination altogether, the fictive, romantic imagination of immediate attraction.

This imagination, however, does seem to offer a story in Dora, where romance does make 'provision for growing older' by leading to marriage.

Once again, this begins very much as a matter of appetite and attraction. Until his marriage, David's romantic hunger is insatiable, and he uses all his resources of colour, dress and food by which to express its physical immediacy. When David goes to Mr Spenlow's for the first time,

> I don't remember who was there, except Dora. I have not the least idea what we had for dinner, besides Dora. My impression is, that I dined off Dora entirely. (41)

As to dress, David's 'passion' "makes me wear my silk handkerchief continually" (42) (although this relates to his infatuation at an earlier stage, for Miss Larkins) and

> If the boots I wore at that period could only be produced and compared with the natural size of my feet, they would show what the state of my heart was, in a most affecting manner. (43)

And, as to colour, Dora appears at her picnic "in a white chip bonnet and a dress of celestial blue" (44) and David buys her a ring "with its blue stones" (45) - white and blue, of course, signifying innocence and purity.

But when infatuation becomes marriage this world of appetites - the world of dreams, of spontaneity and irresponsibility - and the world of narrative collide, and bring a crisis to bear upon David. The fairy story which anticipation makes of marriage and narrative is disappointed by reality:

> It seemed such an extraordinary thing to have Dora always there. ... Sometimes of an evening, when I looked up from my writing, and saw her seated opposite, I would lean back in my chair, and think how queer it was that there we were, alone together as a matter of course - nobody's business any more - all the romance of our engagement put away upon a shelf, to rust - no one to please but one another - one another to please, for life. (46)

The vision of narrative tells us here that romance has been fulfilled and hunger satisfied; but suddenly that fulfilment does not seem a matter of social integration but of separation. Innocence views its own starvation through the looking-glass, as it were, and sees in hunger the companionship of dreams; such companionship disappears, as narrative concludes romance with the business of marriage, making 'mingled reality and mystery' a matter of past dreams. Marriage becomes an end of and separation from innocence, and David finds himself trapped in the world he wanted to leave behind. Marriage takes romance

115

back to mundane reality, and David finds himself still in the same in-between and compromised world as the one the Micawbers, and Dick Swiveller before them, occupied, having to deal with the economic facts of life, and finding romance - in Dora - a continual obstruction. David finds himself back in the wine warehouse, his romantic, fictive life with Dora returning to the everyday reality of mere necessity. Work interrupts both fairy tale and fiction, and shows that it cannot be banished by romance; and now it is discovered at the very heart of life, forming the relationship that was conceived as romance. "No one to please but one another" defines and contains happiness, and the narrative expectation it contains remains unreconciled by any fairy tale to the world of fiction. Happiness itself seems to be removed by its fulfilment, and fulfilment brings a new hunger for romance, for the continuation of the ideal story that was expected, but which now seems ended. David is returned to his earlier crisis; he needs a new narrative to write him out of an everyday continuity that now seems endless and, at the same time, cannot afford to reject life with Dora, and so admits his self-division. As with the Micawbers, he finds himself forced in between, so that he must both accept and reject life with Dora, bearing the division he feels within himself:

> The old unhappy loss or want of something had, I am conscious, some place in my heart; but not to the embitterment of my life. When I walked alone in the fine weather, and thought of the summer days when all the air had been filled with my boyish enchantment, I did miss something of the realisation of my dreams; but I thought it was the softened glory of the Past, which nothing could have thrown upon the present time. (47)

Past and present have become separated, and David finds that it is the responsibility of his own consciousness to hold them together, and himself to be the forcible realisation of the world's unity.

The immediate result of this self-division is an abstraction from the present which makes life seem unreal. Soon after his marriage David tells us

> We have a delightful evening, and are supremely happy; but I don't believe it yet. I can't collect myself. I can't check off my happiness as it takes place. I feel in a misty and unsettled kind of state; as if I had got up very early in the morning a week or two ago, and had never been to bed since. I can't make out when yesterday was. (48)

David finds that he no longer belongs to a story; "I can't collect myself," he tells us. At the same time, he no longer exists in little pieces, since he lives the story out, although he does not feel it. He finds himself neither a fragment of the world, and under its control, nor in control himself. Reality seems to exist as a narrative, but as one which seems to happen without him, and David finds himself unwillingly in the shadowy world of Esther's imagination.

This division is enforced in the novel in another way. David attempts to unite the world by experiencing narrative as romance - as attraction. From childhood, however, this romance of attraction has usurped narrative by proving itself incapable of choice, or of the moral perception central to narrative. The Micawbers were half-accepted in this incapacity, as Dora is accepted; but attractiveness also has a less benevolent force which makes its inability to choose highly problematic - as we saw in Nancy and Dick Swiveller. We saw that the immediacy of life with the Micawbers was born of the hardship inflicted by Mr Murdstone; and there is throughout the book a strong association of attraction, feeling and even enjoyment, and the world of suffering. It was so with Mr Creakle, who "had a delight in cutting at the boys, which was like the satisfaction of a craving appetite", and of whom David tells us,

> I don't watch his eye in idleness, but because I am morbidly attracted to it, in a dread desire to know what he will do next. (49)

The very vitality of Mr Creakle's paranoiac existence proves irresistible to David; and so does the figure who confirms his dividedness in the novel by confronting him with an alter ego, Uriah Heep:

> I saw him lying on his back, with his legs extending to I don't know where, gurglings taking place in his throat, stoppages in his nose, and his mouth open like a post office. He was so much worse in reality than in my distempered fancy, that afterwards I was attracted in very repulsion, and could not help wandering in and out every half-hour or so, and taking another look at him. (50)

We saw in Murdstone (who is another source of repulsion) that David sought to leave malevolent narrative behind; and now he does not recognise such a narrative in Uriah Heep. His romantic imagination still works in little pieces, and is unable to pass beyond the repulsion he feels to view the real narrative danger that Heep holds out. David's narrative will abstracts him from the actual story which, like his happiness with Dora, happens without him. Attraction and repulsion - which would govern an ideal narrative world - are irrelevant to the stories that David Copperfield's world tells, and he finds himself left out of them.

David refuses to admit the threat that divides his world, so that he does not succeed in leaving that threat behind with

Murdstone: Heep's kind of narrative merely repulses him. Uriah Heep, then, takes up and attempts to occupy (and for most of the novel succeeds in occupying) the stage that David leaves vacant. He does so with an outright determination which displays its origin as narrative as its source of power, where David hides his in his romance. 'Umbleness' is in a sense Uriah Heep's disguise; but it is also a declaration of his narrative aspirations, and of the linear way in which he sees the world, and it is one which David consistently, and as a matter of principle, refuses to recognise. Uriah Heep's designs are transparent, and David rejects them out of repulsion, not daring to admit their ends. We see this in what Uriah sees as his sexual competition with David over Agnes:

> I suppose you have sometimes plucked a pear before it was ripe?

he asks David after his first attempt to make Agnes marry him; and continues,

> I did that last night ... but it'll ripen yet! It only wants attending to. (51)

What matters to David is not so much the plot in what Uriah says as his comprehension of the words. Uriah knows that he threatens David, not directly, by his actions, but by insisting upon their recognition, so that he tells him a few chapters later,

> Oh, its very kind of you Copperfield .. and we all know what an amiable character yours is; but you know that the moment I spoke to you the other night, you knew what I meant. You know you knew what I meant, Copperfield. Don't deny it. (52)

Uriah forces David to see the nature of a narrative without ideals; he acts the play put with a vengeance, delighting in the identity of dissembler and unscrupulous cheat that the narrative of the stage world gives him. Oddly, he is the only character in the book to share Betsey's knowledge of the way that narrative works; but instead of using that knowledge to create a stage for himself, he shows us that the place for self-consciousness on this stage must be in villainy, and uses it to exploit the parts the other actors play. He is in a sense Aunt Betsey's true son, for he actually learns the lessons she half attempts to teach her protegees; he treats life as a game rather than as a fairy tale, and is well educated in the renouncement of mankind. Uriah never has a 'first time around' life, but lives life from the beginning as if for the second time, without Betsey's generosity which divides her between her narrative knowledge and her fictive sympathy. Uriah Heep exists to torture the fictive imagination - even his name seems to invite the repulsion which is David's romantic, half fictive response, beginning with a wriggle and ending in a Heep - by being made almost purely of and by narrative.

David suceeds in refusing to accept his part in the stage world, and in remaining in his romantic life, even, as I suggested above, at the price of self-division, until the time of Dora's death. It is this event, as a second attempt to preserve romantic life by leaving the past behind, that confirms David's place upon the stage, for only there, we are shown, can romance exist. Dora's death signals the failure of reality to supply romance. Barbara Hardy writes of Dickens that in the relationship between David and Dora he "is touching on a marvellous subject for a psychological novel, but only touching on it" and continues

> He chose to summarise, to evade, and then to cut the knot with Dora's death. Many a marital problem in Victorian fiction has been solved by the Providential death. (53)

But Dickens is one step ahead of his critic here; for again the point is that David is *not* Dickens. It is David who is writing this story, and it is David who 'cuts the knot', to choose the life of writing. Dora is killed by his hoped-for romance; but she is killed more exactly by the narrative of the stage which, it is now clear, is the only place in which romance will survive. We see this from the writing with which David seals her grave:

> I sit down by the fire, thinking with a blind remorse of all those secret feelings I have nourished since my marriage. I think of every little trifle between me and Dora, and feel the truth, that trifles make the sum of life. Ever rising from the sea of my remembrance, is the image of the dear child as I knew her first, graced by my young love, and by her own, with every fascination wherein such love is rich. Would it, indeed, have been better if we had loved each other as boy and girl, and forgotten it? Undisciplined heart, reply! (54)

David once again finds himself in the limbo which Esther thrives upon, of a narrative with a past but no future, of a fiction with an ideal which is a lost ideal. But at the same time we hear David's voice as a kind of rhetoric; and it is now time to see what narrative can do to fulfil its expectations, for David occupies his written world of loss while waiting for the narrative itself to bring him out of limbo.

It does so; for it is not long before we see that narrative provides action. It is at this point, when David's narrative seems exhausted in its efforts to see the world whole, and to grow up from childhood, that narrative takes over the novel, and shows its full potency; and at this point also that David begins to realise its true nature.

David goes to Yarmouth immediately after Dora's death, as if to turn his attention to the narrative which he has so long evaded, turning back towards the novel's wider stage. It does not disappoint him; for the storm it provides as the conclusion of the sub-plot involving Ham, Steerforth and Little Emily is a piece of cosmic stagecraft:

> It was a murky confusion - here and there blotted with a colour like the colour of the smoke from damp fuel - of flying clouds, tossed up into most remarkable heaps, suggesting greater heights in the clouds than there were depths below them to the bottom of the deepest hollows in the earth, through which the wild moon seemed to plunge headlong, as if, in a dread disturbance of the laws of nature, she had lost her way and were frightened. There had been a wind all day; and it was rising then, with an extraordinary great sound. (55)

David's bewilderment at this point is not the bewilderment of childhood, in which the world seems odd in its incoherence. This vision has a chaotic activity, and a massive energy; but it is not David's energy in the way that what Oliver saw was the energy of his childhood vision. This melodrama defeats self-consciousness and comes from a narrative which has continued without him, and carries him along with it. We are shown that David's feelings at first remain quite separate from it, as they remain separate from any other reality: when he arrives in Yarmouth,

> I was very much depressed in spirits; very solitary; and felt an uneasiness in Ham's not being there, disproportionate to the occasion. I was seriously affected, without knowing how much, by late events; and my long exposure to the fierce wind had confused me. There was that jumble in my thoughts and recollections, that I had lost the clear arrangement of time and distance. Thus, if I had gone out into the town, I should not have been surprised, I think, to encounter someone who I knew must be then in London. So to speak, there was in these respects a curious inattention in my mind. Yet it was busy, too, with all the remembrances the place naturally awakened; and they were particularly distinct and vivid. (56)

His bewilderment seems to be the bewilderment of dissociation - and not, like Oliver's, of a participation not understood. "I had lost the clear arrangement of time and distance," he tells us; the consciousness of loss, like Esther's at the end of *Bleak House*, again seems to be a kind of limbo, neither completely ignorant of the dimensions of narrative nor belonging to them. His solitude now is real isolation, having no recourse to the comforts of childhood loneliness which found companionship in the dream-world. There, his feelings were never 'disproportionate' to reality as they are here. David both knows and does not know; "I should not have been surprised, I think, to encounter someone who I knew must be then in London." And again this interim state of mind, neither reality nor imagination, finds itself invested in the past rather than the present the novel unfolds before him. The 'curious inattention' to real events is accompanied by "all the remembrances the place naturally awakened".

But the action of the novel now becomes inescapable, and begins to draw him out of this indeterminacy. David finds himself passively taking part in it, the observer of the hysterical parts that everybody around him plays:

> Joining these groups, I found bewailing women whose husbands were away in herring or oyster boats... Grizzled old sailors were among the people, shaking their heads, as they looked from water to sky, and muttering to one another; ship-owners, excited and uneasy; children, huddling together, and peering into older faces; even stout mariners, disturbed and anxious, levelling their glasses at the sea from behind places of shelter, as if they were surveying an enemy. (57)

But as the hysteria grows, David is still encased in his own solitude. "Something within me, faintly answering the storm without, tossed up the depths of my memory and made tumult in them" (58); so that, left alone to try to sleep, he finds himself gazing at nothing but his own reflection:

> I got up, several times, and looked out; but could see nothing, except the reflection in the window-panes of the faint candle I had left burning, and of my own haggard face looking in at me from the black void. (59)

The 'void' is reality itself; and it is also the narrative which has brought the world of the novel to this pitch. This is the turning point of Davids own mental condition, for he looks through the window towards the outer world, and sees only the inner, and himself. The window comes, as it does at the end of the book, to represent a way through to the whole of reality; and here it becomes what will in Dickens' last novel be an image for the confinement of narrative, a mirror which refuses the narrative unity with the outer, fictive world, and the vision which can see everything. David finds himself confined within his own narrating intelligence, controlled by his own will to control. He becomes the helpless spectator of his own story, and of his own loyalties, as Ham makes ready to attempt a rescue of the victims of the wreck, one of whom, of course, he discovers to be Steerforth:

> I was swept away, but not unkindly, to some distance
> where the people around me made me stay; urging, as I
> confusedly perceived, that he was bent on going, with help
> or without, and that I should endanger the precautions for
> his safety by troubling those with whom they rested. (60)

The 'Action' of the novel is beyond David, and the extent to which this is so is demonstrated by his final discovery of his former friend and hero. A fisherman

> led me to the shore. And on that part of it where she
> and I had looked for shells, two children - on that part
> of it where some lighter fragments of the old boat, blown
> down last night, had been scattered by the wind - among
> the ruins of the home he had wronged - I saw him lying
> with his head on his arm, as I had often seen him lie at
> school. (61)

This is in a sense the height of David's crisis between narrative and fictive. Even as David looks, the past and present are confused, and what he experiences is neither reality nor dream, neither the justice of the narrative in casting the sinner at his feet, nor the confused associative instinct of Oliver, which we see when he allows us to hear the last words of an earlier sinner, "What right have they to butcher me?" (62) David secretly knows too much to feel the killing of Steerforth as injustice, but refuses the guilt - of his own former attractions - of feeling it as justice.

Once again, however, the novel takes over his actions. Just as with Dora, the narrative provides in its action, the killing of Steerforth, its own judgement of him, which David must accept if he is to remain the narrator of the novel. He must accept the shame of 'Acting' against his own self-conscious spontaneous and half romantic sense, or relinquish his claim to write the story, passing it back to Heep and Aunt Betsey. The 'Action' which the narrative offers has now done its utmost.

And now the part he has so far refused begins to come to him. It begins with his last visit to Steerforth's house, for only here does he begin to take revenge upon his own mother's failed motherhood (63), and to act Aunt Betsey's play out. Miss Dartle, of course, speaks the words, but they belong to David as they have never done before. His first thought, after Steerforth's death, is to take the news to his mother;

> I knew that the care of it, and the hard duty of preparing
> his mother to receive it, could only rest with me; and I
> was anxious to discharge that duty as faithfully as I could.
> (64)

The real cruelty of the action lies in the 'duty'; and Miss Dartle only enforces the justice David acts out in performing it:

"I *will* speak!" she said, turning on me with her lightning eyes. "Be silent, you! Look at me, I say, proud mother of a proud false son! Moan for your nurture of him, moan for your loss of him, moan for mine!" (65)

Mrs Steerforth, with the rest of her kind, the narrative tells us, is at the root of the action that makes the world suffer, as the producer of the infidelity which brought both Murdstone and Aunt Betsey into David's life, and which brought the image of himself in Heep. And David never sounds more like Uriah Heep than here; "Oh, Miss Dartle, shame! Oh cruel!" (66), he interrupts her, as Dickens is unable to supress his delight in David's new role any longer. The exorcism of Steerforth is also the exorcism of David's secret loyalty to the glory of a past dominated by attraction, by Steerforth and by Dora. His acceptance of Miss Dartle's humiliation of both through Steerforth's mother is also to some extent the Heep-like acceptance of his own humiliation:

"A curse upon you!" she said, looking round at me, with a mingled expression of rage and grief. "It was in an evil hour that you ever came here! A curse upon you! Go!" (67)

With this dismissal, and with his own dismissal of the Micawbers, Mr Peggotty and Little Emily to Australia and of Uriah Heep to prison - as David finally plays the game and imposes a moral narrative upon him - David breaks off his attachment to the glory of the past, as Aunt Betsey hoped he would never have to, but at the same time knew he would. In doing so, Aunt Betsey is left behind, as David enters the limited world she provides, but which she herself stands outside of. In this world, life in the past is not changed, or integrated into the present; narrative ceases to attempt to build its fairy story in reality, and accepts the tale which Aunt Betsey's authorial intelligence has always offered, along with its second-time coherence:

The knowledge came upon me, not quickly, but little by little, and grain by grain. The desolate feeling with which I went abroad, deepened and widened hourly. At first it was a heavy sense of loss and sorrow, wherein I could distinguish little else. By imperceptible degrees, it became a hopeless consciousness of all that I had lost - love, friendship, interest; of all that had been shattered - my first trust, my first affection, the whole airy castle of my life; of all that remained - a ruined blank and waste, lying around me, unbroken, to the dark horizon. (68)

So David's own second-time vision is born - as Aunt Betsey again hoped it never would be. David describes this time as an awakening from a dream, and insofar as it is an awakening to a new life of narrative this is true. David leaves behind the world of dream and fiction in his knowledge of its loss, and wakes up to a world experienced for a second time. As he does so, narrative does finally escape the literal, mundane world of reality, and become literary; but it does so in an overwrought, artificial way. This second life is a lost life, and his new life of writing does not attain the common literariness of the fictive, but experiences life at second hand. We see as he celebrates in blank verse that the life of the narrative is adopted at the expense of the life of the imagination. That earlier life has become once and for all 'a ruined blank and waste'; and only with it condemned for ever to the past can David make this new beginning:

I came into the valley, as the evening sun was shining on the remote heights of snow, that closed in, like eternal clouds. The bases of the mountains forming the gorge in which the little village lay, were richly green; and high above this gentler vegetation, grew forests of dark fir, cleaving the wintry snow-drift, wedge like, and stemming the avalanche. Above these were range upon range of craggy steeps, grey rock, bright ice, and smooth verdure-specks of pasture, all gradually blending with the crowning snow. Dotted here and there on the mountain's side, each tiny dot a home, were lovely wooden cottages, so dwarfed by the towering heights that they appeared too small for toys. So did even the clustered village in the valley, with its wooden bridge across the stream, where the stream tumbled over broken rocks, and roared away among the trees. In the quiet air, there was a sound of distant singing - shepherd voices; but, as one bright evening cloud floated midway along the mountain's side, I could almost have believed it came from there, and was not earthly music. All at once, in this serenity, great Nature spoke to me; and soothed me to lay down my weary head upon the grass, and weep as I had not wept yet, since Dora died! (69)

Here, writing takes over experience. 'Great Nature' of course is the world of narrative which produced the storm as it now produces Wordsworthian tranquillity. Only now, however, does David fully join in with its action, hearing its voice as a rhythm which replaces a lost life of hopes and expectations. And now, with the past relinquished as a place of shame, and with his loyalties to it extinguished, writing seems to begin its fulfilment for him as a kind of paradise. Not only do its words provide a scenic vision: they provide a kind of love, when upon opening a 'packet of letters' David reads "the writing of Agnes"; and they provide an occupation:

> I worked early and late, patiently and hard. I wrote a Story, with a purpose growing, not remotely, out of my experience. (70)

It is only at this point that David can tell us, "this narrative is my written memory" (71), for only now is it true that the writing is the conscious activity of remembrance in words - the literal life of memory made plain by the second thought of writing.

Agnes is very much a part of this second thought; and the end of the novel belongs to her. As she first appeared to David in writing, so she continues to exist in the written world:

> When I read to Agnes what I wrote; when I saw her listening face; moving her to smiles or tears; and heard her cordial voice so earnest on the shadowy events of that imaginative world in which I lived; I thought what a fate mine might have been. (72)

It is as if David experiences his relationship with Agnes through writing, making her laugh and cry, and hearing her voice in it. The appetites and feelings of the dream-world are vanished entirely, along with the expectations that dreams had of narrative, that they should be realised in it. Reality itself, in its immediacy, has disappeared, and has been replaced by the consciousness that only the 'Narrative' is true. This Narrative, the narrative of fairy-tale, is a world of duty, of justice, and of formal relationship which exists as a 'mirror' image of reality, and which sees its own End as the true end: which has learned from the disappointment of dreams, and from the cruelty of the world's action, and has moved, as it were, inside itself. Narrative is a reflection of the world, refusing to do what the world of fiction and dreaming did, and pass through the glass and into the real world of action and deceit and cruelty, in which Narrative sees itself. That world brought about our dreams, but it did so with absolute immediacy, and dreaming in it produced in participation a kind of faith. The world of Action which reflects the action of reality, and refuses to pass through it, becomes a World withdrawn from the world. Its only companionship is in its own stagecraft; so that, while expectation no longer disappoints, it is no longer really expectation either. The novel becomes a 'written memory'; and from the point of 'awakening' knowledge is governed not so much by the perception of anticipation as by the recollection of retrospect. Upon *this* side of the looking glass we need no perception to tell us that the future exists indoors, and that to look forwards is to look backwards, and to look out is to look back in again. Little really changes from the night of the storm in Yarmouth when David looked out of his window and saw only himself. His bedroom has grown according to his knowledge of his loss, and his admission that he has lost everything makes the whole world his stage; but at the same time he has only revealed himself as the source of the novel's stagecraft. In doing so he gains control over his world - as he gains Agnes. But the knowledge of the Dream has been bought at the price of childhood, the price of knowing what lies beyond the Dream, in what, even on that night in Yarmouth, he could recognise as a 'void', the place in which the self exists on the other side of the glass, beyond dreaming.

Agnes exists indoors; and David's recurring image of her sees her standing in a window:

> I cannot call to mind where or when, in my childhood, I had seen a stained glass window in a church. Nor do I recollect its subject. But I know that when I saw her turn round, in the grave light of the old staircase, and wait for us, above, I thought of that window; and I associated something of its tranquil brightness with Agnes Whitfield ever afterwards. (73)

The association returns when David first remembers Agnes after Dora's death -

> And now, indeed, I began to think that in my old association of her with the stained-glass window in the church, a prophetic foreshadowing of what she would be to me ... had found a way into my mind. (74)

- and the image reappears at the end of the book, to symbolise their final reunion:

> We stood together in the same old-fashioned window at night, when the moon was shining; Agnes with her quiet eyes raised up to it; I following her glance. (75)

While Agnes is represented by what is an opening upon an outside world, she is not so much an opportunity for as a limitation upon vision. In her, the house of writing becomes constricted to its own indoor world. The principle in Agnes is much the same as that of the window in the church, by which she is symbolised; where we would normally expect to look outward, we see in the picture in the window the substance of the thought that has created the interior of the building; we become, as it were, surrounded by belief.

But while Agnes, like writing, makes a building of belief, she does not allow David to pass beyond - as, indeed, he no longer wants to do - and to experience life immediately; so that writing has come to replace the faith of dreaming, by inter-posing its own structure.

In accepting Agnes, David Copperfield understands life as narrative, as the reflection of his own life, as an indoor world. But the price of doing so is the understanding of life only as narrative, and of leaving dreams and fictions, and the realism which is the realism of innocence and amusement, in childhood. While David condemns himself to a second-time life, we see that narrative has failed him, as autobiography would have failed Dickens, for it has shut out the real life of imag-ination and left him in a shadow world. That shadow world is not like Esther's, where all is indeterminate, but one in which all is over-determined, and merely imitative. It becomes a place for recrimination and shame, where the written word displaces the loyalties of dream. In the David Copperfield that emerges at the end of this novel, narrative displaces fiction, and the indoor world of the writer excludes the wider world of fiction.

David then finds himself rejecting his aunt's generous vi-sion to live inside it, for he finds that a life of narrative cannot risk an experience of the whole world; while that world contains figures such as Aunt Betsey, it also contains Murdstone and Heep. Narrative finds itself forced to stage its own reality, its own justice and its own feeling, and to reject the reality that Aunt Betsey half-exists in. While she helps David to choose an indoor life with Agnes, that life - as she well knows - can do nothing for her, and exists by isolating itself from the knowledge and division we have seen in her.

Effectively, narrative fails in this novel; it fails to provide a vision of the world that is true beyond its own limitation, it fails to provide a generosity that can afford to care about the world outside itself, and it fails to make a better world for Aunt Betsey. More importantly, it seems to fail self-conscious intel-ligence. While we remain outside David, and at the end of the novel Dickens seems to stand closer to Aunt Betsey, as a writer like Esther, divided between fiction and narrative, we do so as an evasion of the limitation he has discovered in narrative. This novel was not prepared to find the terms of the narrative quite as stringent as they now appear, for it set out to test the constructive powers of narrative, and not to illustrate its limitation. *David Copperfield* is not quite a narrative novel; the abstention from fiction is not in *David Copperfield* suffi-ciently categorical, the understanding of narrative very much more complete at its ending than it was at its beginning. This novel leads us indoors, to a house-bound world, and discovers narrative as such a world. But it does so because David, and Dickens through him, still, here, seeks the unity which I sug-gested that a truly self-conscious narrative novel would have to abandon; and it will now be the writer's task to return David's confining intelligence to the outside world, the world we leave in *David Copperfield* in the hands of Aunt Betsey, and to place it in the landscape of reality, as we saw the fictive placed in Esther.

Footnotes

(1) See page 39 above.
(2) See 'Towards a Reading of Dombey and Son' in Gabriel Josipovici (Ed.), *The Modern English Novel*, 72.
(3) See Edgar Johnson, *Charles Dickens: his Tragedy and Triumph*, I, 45, or Christopher Hibbert, *The Making of Charles Dickens*, for typical examples of the view that Dickens' past must have dictated his writing; more recently, see Steven Marcus, *Dickens from Pickwick to Dombey*, 44, and Robert Newsom, *Dickens: On the Romantic Side of Familiar Things*, 92.
(4) See Gabriel Josipovici (Ed.), *The Modern English Novel*, 61.
(5) See 'Letter to D.M.Moir, 17 June 1855', in *The Letters of Charles Dickens*, Ed. Storey and Fielding, Vol. 5, p. 341, where Dickens writes that, "within these last three years or so ... I have got, by some few thousand pounds ... ahead of the world. Dombey has been the greatest success I have ever achieved." Reprinted in R.L.Patten, *Charles Dickens and his Publishers*, 196-7.
(6) See John Forster, *Life of Charles Dickens*, 12-13; Edgar Johnson, *Charles Dickens: his Tragedy and Triumph*, and also Owen Major, 'Into the Shadowy World' in *The Dickensian*, (1944), 15-18, p. 40.
(7) *David Copperfield*, 49.
(8) *David Copperfield*, 61.
(9) *David Copperfield*, 61.
(10) *David Copperfield*, 206.
(11) *David Copperfield*, 216; John Forster, *Life of Charles Dickens*, I, 49.
(12) John Forster, *Life of Charles Dickens*, I, 49.
(13) *David Copperfield*, 272.
(14) *David Copperfield*, 225.
(15) *David Copperfield*, 216.
(16) *David Copperfield*, 212.
(17) *David Copperfield*, 226.
(18) *David Copperfield*, 227.
(19) *David Copperfield*, 214.
(20) *David Copperfield*, 231.
(21) *David Copperfield*, 229.
(22) *David Copperfield*, 240.
(23) *David Copperfield*, 242.
(24) *David Copperfield*, 250.
(25) *David Copperfield*, 51.
(26) *David Copperfield*, 60.
(27) *David Copperfield*, 55.
(28) *David Copperfield*, 331.
(29) *David Copperfield*, 271.

(30) *David Copperfield*, 560.
(31) *David Copperfield*, 643.
(32) *David Copperfield*, 732.
(33) *David Copperfield*, 787.
(34) Q.D.Leavis approaches this view in "'Dickens and Tolstoy': the case for a serious view of *David Copperfield*" in F.R. and Q.D.Leavis, *Dickens the Novelist* (London 1970), but she concludes that he is writing "at two levels at once" and 'muddling' caricature and seriousness; see pages 78-80.
(35) *David Copperfield*, 513.
(36) *David Copperfield*, 864.
(37) *David Copperfield*, 165.
(38) *David Copperfield*, 330.
(39) *David Copperfield*, 344.
(40) *David Copperfield*, 87.
(41) *David Copperfield*, 452.
(42) *David Copperfield*, 326.
(43) *David Copperfield*, 458.
(44) *David Copperfield*, 542.
(45) *David Copperfield*, 550.
(46) *David Copperfield*, 701.
(47) *David Copperfield*, 713.
(48) *David Copperfield*, 695.
(49) *David Copperfield*, 142.
(50) *David Copperfield*, 144.
(51) *David Copperfield*, 645.
(52) *David Copperfield*, 683.
(53) See Barbara Hardy, *The Moral Art of Dickens*, 131.
(54) *David Copperfield*, 859.
(55) *David Copperfield*, 857.
(56) *David Copperfield*, 860.
(57) *David Copperfield*, 858.
(58) *David Copperfield*, 860.
(59) *David Copperfield*, 861.
(60) *David Copperfield*, 864.
(61) *David Copperfield*, 866.
(62) See page 34 above.
(63) Again, Q.D.Leavis anticipates this argument in her essay; see *Dickens the Novelist*, 105.
(64) *David Copperfield*, 867.
(65) *David Copperfield*, 871.
(66) *David Copperfield*, 871.
(67) *David Copperfield*, 873.
(68) *David Copperfield*, 886.
(69) *David Copperfield*, 887.
(70) *David Copperfield*, 889.
(71) *David Copperfield*, 889.
(72) *David Copperfield*, 931.
(73) *David Copperfield*, 280.
(74) *David Copperfield*, 839.
(75) *David Copperfield*, 937.

CHAPTER FIVE

The Novel as Narrative, II: Great Expectations

Autobiography, the story which offers a unity of fiction and narrative in the individual, is tested and discredited in *David Copperfield*. The novel represents a final attempt to produce a world without the detachment which we saw interfering with the earlier attempts at authorial assertiveness; this made the earlier narratives 'radically impure', and led us back into the fictive world, where the writer must be a persona of himself. In the emergence of Aunt Betsey as the novel's dominant voice this attempt to discover the pure, unqualified authority of narrative fails, for in her we see the novelist once again taking refuge in a persona who qualifies and accommodates his narrator.

In the novels that follow *David Copperfield* we see any such attempt at a narrative unity abandoned, and narrative remaining subject to the impurity of its coexistence with the fictive. We have seen that in *Bleak House* Dickens includes narrative within a fictive vision. In his other later work we find him concerned with the function of narrative and with the writing of what Pearson suggested was the consequence of the recognition of the limitation of narrative, and with what David Copperfield failed to write; with the self-conscious novel. Such a novel, I suggested in my second chapter (1), would necessarily attempt, not to include fiction, as David does (and as Dickens still in *David Copperfield* wishes that he could) but to abstain from it. What the self-conscious novel needs is what we have seen Dickens find for the fictive, a figure to combine the function of persona and narrator, but to do so in order to demonstrate the powers, not of fiction, but of narrative. This David, in his proximity to Dickens, could not. Just as Esther gave fiction a landscape in the real and imaginative world of the novel, so Dickens must now seek a figure he can place within a landscape for narrative, where the place of narrative can in turn be objectified as the imagination of fiction was objectified by the fog. David withholds such a landscape, for he exists too much within Dickens' personal past; instead, he shows us the artificial scenery of the stage world, the world indoors, which is the product of the wishful thinking of both David and Dickens.

While this world constitutes David's whole life, however, Dickens remains outside of David, and free to begin a realisation of what David Copperfield means to him.

In Dickens' next novel, Little Dorrit does not succeed in making this escape from the world. Instead, she shows us a world of prisons, and is a kind of prison herself. Instead of lightening the burden of existence as Krook did, by evaporating, Little Dorrit makes it heavier by the dogged solidity of her narrative intentions. She brings narrative back to the novel as domestic conscience, asserting that the values of domestic and social order, of careful housekeeping and sound economics, should govern the world in spite of their imaginative limitation, and doing so with a ferocious determination whose awful tenacity survives and conquers everything.

By imprisoning the narrative, however, Little Dorrit does begin to contain and confine a narrative voice which we have in turn seen is in any case contained and confined, and in this way moves us towards a sense of the location of narrative in herself, the child of the Marshalsea. In doing so she begins the most difficult of the realisations that the narrative part of Dickens' novel must make. For, in this novel, it is because of the divisive nature of the narrative itself, and not because of the individual, that the story (and Dickens' autobiography hidden in it) produces limitation. Narrative, this novel acknowledges, will change nothing; and after its heroine has achieved her happy ending she and her husband and fellow inmate, Arthur Clennam,

> went down quietly into the roaring streets, inseparable and blessed; and as they passed along in sunshine and shade, the arrogant and froward and the vain, fretted and chafed, and made their usual uproar. (2)

What Dickens knows, here, is what Aunt Betsey knew, but what David Copperfield, in his commitment to his own story, could not afford to admit: that no narrative purpose or intention can change the world. What it implicitly accepts is that the Marshalsea is as real to the end of the novel as it was to its beginning, and that nothing has been or can be written out of the lives of Little Dorrit or Arthur Clennam. In providing this acceptance the novel provides an acceptance of the past of the individual - of the blacking factory - and of the fact that the limitation of the narrative lies in what seemed to be its virtue, in its promise of a better world.

It is in this promise that this novel finds narrative wrong, and while it provides in Little Dorrit herself the figure that lies guiltily behind David Copperfield's hopes and actions, the figure of a sister that never was, it also shows - what again Aunt Betsey knew all along - that that guilt was as wrong as the expectation that produced it. Little Dorrit, and her forebear in Betsey Copperfield, is the figure narrative would have made of Dickens in its promise of a better world; and only now does that fact begin to be realised as characteristic of *narrative* and of the expectations behind narrative, rather than of a guilty past. It is here that the scepticism of autobiography endorsed by *David Copperfield* begins to turn finally into a full self-consciousness of narrative, although it is not yet ready to take its place within a landscape of reality.

Little Dorrit begins a process of realisation of what the failure of narrative means to the writer; and that process is continued and completed in *A Tale of Two Cities*.

As Edgar Johnson pointed out, this novel takes the figures of Little Dorrit and Aurthur Clennam further in their objectification of parts of the writer's self, making this novel a highly personal work. He quotes Dickens' Preface to the novel,

> I have so far verified what is said and done and suffered in these pages as that I have certainly done and suffered it all myself (3)

and continues

> The idea for the story had come to him while he was tearing himself apart as Richard Wardour in *The Frozen Deep*, and Sidney Carton's sacrifice of his life ... magnifies into chords of exultation, Wardour's death struggle among the ice floes of the arctic. Watching Dickens die every night ... was the fair and unattainable creature whom his imprisoning marriage rendered hopelessly remote ... During the months that followed, Dickens had thought of separation from Catherine as impossible, of his marriage as an iron-bound and stone-walled misery ... from which he could never escape. It is not strange that in the fantasy from which imagination is born he should dream of a prisoner bitterly immured for years and at last set free of a love serenely consummated, and a despairing love triumphantly rising to a height of noble surrender. These emotions were his; he had known and suffered them all. (4)

The purpose of the novel is not, however, this crude relief of real feelings in fiction. While these correspondences are important, Dickens' intentions in dealing with them operate at a much deeper level. The novel is concerned primarily with the relationship of narrative, writer and novel, and is a study of the dissociation begun in *Little Dorrit*. Each figure represents withdrawal and dissociation revealed within what have previously been the primary associative processes of narrative.

Mr Lorry seems at first to be the descendant of Pickwick and Brownlow, the man of generosity and sheer good feeling: but he has acquired a tactfulness here which undermines his usefulness to narrative. At the very beginning of the novel he asks Lucie to regard him as a "speaking machine" (5) and tells her her past as "the story of one of our customers" (6); his attempt to approach the subject of Dr Manette's obsessive shoemaking as 'blacksmith's work' may seem more annoying than absurd until we remember that this is precisely what Dickens did for his own past when he wrote *David Copperfield,* making the blacking factory into a wine warehouse. Mr Lorry's tact represents precisely the bourgeois fastidiousness of the transformation from shoe polish to wine bottles. The stories Mr Lorry tells are machines which are engineered as vehicles of dissociation; so that he becomes an important part of Dickens' feelings about himself and his writing. His tactful truth is also a truth about narrative, which - anticipating Mr Lorry's strategy - has come to be a form of dissociation. Mr Lorry takes the story of Little Dorrit one stage further in its self-consciousness, telling stories that are palpably *there* to fail. By telling us that stories are dissociative he also tells us that he himself has nothing to do with the novel, becoming a kind of anti-Pickwick and offering, not his protection, but his indifference.

Mr Lorry would in one of Dickens' earlier novels be the writer-protector of the action, and his dissociation, while ungenerous, seems born of a detachment from action. But, curiously in this novel, the other figures, from whom we would expect action, seem as dissociated and as convinced of the failures of their own stories as he is of his. Lucy, Manette and Darnay, the figures who would have been central to an earlier novel - interrelated as they are by the bonds of love, formal relationship, and a common past - fail to make any of these things, which previously seemed to be the values of narrative, matter to the story. Instead, the novel becomes the tale of the one man who seems to have no story and no past, of Sidney Carton. The narrative remains, and becomes identified with his choice of death, so rejecting the human ends of domestic stability and happiness, and of the working out of the past, the preoccupations of *David Copperfield,* from the substance of the narrative process.

Here, the guilt of the writer, which narrative seems to press in failing to provide a humanitarian reflection of the world, is dissolved in the realisation that narrative must fail in every ending but that of death itself. Narrative, with its values, is left behind with Carton at the end of the novel, to realise itself in a death of sacrifice; and in the process narrative reveals itself as an enactment from which the stories which end before death must be excluded. In showing itself to be a form of death, it demonstrates its failure for those human stories of domestic happiness and personal memory, and so absolves the writing from personal guilt; narrative, it now appears, is not an individual failure - the failure of a Dickens who could not afford to be David Copperfield and write an authoritative autobiography - but a general, collective failure which is at once both literary and cultural. Narrative fails to provide a better world that is at the same time a humanly possible world, and in showing that failure *A Tale of Two Cities* brings the ending of *Little Dorrit* to its absolute conclusion, rejecting the ending and so the process of narrative.

It is only at this point that Dickens is fully prepared to examine the meaning of failure, not in its implications for his personal self, but for his function as writer, and for narrative itself. By the end of *A Tale of Two Cities* Dickens has exorcised the ghost of the guilty autobiographical self, and of the 'pure' narrative without qualification, which haunted *David Copperfield*, and finally detaches his own intelligence from the intelligence of the authoritative narrative. By the end of this novel he is ready to return to the failures of that novel in an effort to confront the meaning of narrative, and of an existence in the writer's world. This, I shall argue, is the achievement of *Great Expectations*, to produce a self-conscious narrative novel.

This novel is very much a reworking of *David Copperfield*: so much so that Dickens wrote in a letter to Forster while the book was being planned,

> To be quite sure I had fallen into no unconscious repetition, I read David Copperfield again the other day... (7)

Great Expectations is from the beginning a work of self-confident virtuosity, taking up the uncertainties of the earlier novel and replacing them with a sense of direction. "Whether I shall turn out to be the hero of my own life, or whether that station will be held by anybody else, these pages must show" (8), we are told by David in the first sentence of his novel, as he goes on to "begin my life at the beginning of my life" (9). David Copperfield never really trusts the narrative that ultimately, as we have seen, betrays him, and begins at the beginning not because he feels himself identified with the narrative, but in order to perform the necessary function of narrator. Pip has no such doubts; and the beginning of *Great Expectations* could hardly be more different:

> My father's family name being Pirrip, and my christian name Philip, my infant tongue could make of both names nothing longer and more explicit than Pip. So, I called myself Pip, and came to be called Pip. (10)

Pip takes it for granted that he and the world in general which is to be encompassed by his story are identical, and so does what Dickens elsewhere remains reluctant to do, and initiates a world of the writer without qualification; a literal world where the substance of the novel is to be the substance of the life of the individual. David's story begins, "as I have been informed and believe"; and this belief is the belief of narrative, a belief which confines and limits David's consciousness, but one which the novel sets out to test. What it presents as David Copperfield's starting point, however, is the possibility that a belief in narrative might be a belief in the outside world and include a fictive, outer reality. When Pip plunges into "My first most vivid and broad impression of the identity of things" the act of narrative is unqualified, but it contains no such belief in the outside world, and so is a solitary act of belief in the letter, rather than the spirit, of the story he is about to write.

Pip does not exist, as David did, in order to test narrative, nor even to enforce some form of narrative life, but to show us the life that narrative produces for the individual who would undertake it as an authoritative - written - course of events.

Where David seeks to invent a narrative, Pip categorically invents himself *as* narrative; and, the greater his attempt to create a world beyond his own individuality, the greater is the weight we see placed upon his own shoulders. We have already seen that he invents his own name; and he goes on to invent a family:

> The shape of the letters on my father's tombstone gave me an odd idea that he was a square, stout, dark man, with curly black hair. From the character and turn of the description, "Also Georgiana Wife of the above", I drew a childish conclusion that my mother was freckled and sickly. To five little stone lozenges, each about a foot and a half long, which were arranged in a neat row beside their grave, and were sacred to the memory of five little brothers of mine - who gave up trying to get a living, exceedingly early in that universal struggle - I am indebted for a belief I religiously entertained that they had all been born with their hands in their trouser-pockets, and had never taken them out in this state of existence. (11)

We begin to see here that Pip's loneliness is the condition of his narrative, and that his story is born of and begins with bereavement. Already, Dickens' detachment from Pip dominates the novel, for while we see a peculiar coherence in what Pip thinks, and so narrates, we also see that it is generated by his own utter fragmentation from the outside world. By inventing his own name Pip loses any identity that might still be given him by the world he lives in, and, in the same way, by inventing his mother and father he relinquishes his real - albeit past - relationship to them. Narrative does not respect memory, we see, but extinguishes it, enforcing its own form of invented association. Narrative itself propels and invents Pip; it replaces Pip's relationship with reality with his story, and begins as the ending of any past life. So far as the narrative is concerned, the thoughts we hear in the first chapter of this novel are Pip's first thoughts, and he has no life before them, unlike David Copperfield, whose beginning exists only "as I have been informed and believe". Autobiography does not uncover but extinguishes the past of the writer, as we saw in the earlier novel which, without Aunt Betsey, would have condemned us to David's isolation at its ending, bereft of the generous inclusiveness which is half-fictive.

Without Betsey's protection, Pip becomes bound according to the literal nature of the narrative to his own thoughts and words, in a world that is at once produced by his consciousness and destructive of it. Narrative seems to promise everything to Pip, but really offers nothing; hidden behind the inclusiveness of the idea of the story is the reality of its solitariness.

We only now begin to see the narrator set in the wider world of the novels, which now represent Dickens' broader authorial intelligence, detached from narrative - as it was in *Bleak House* from commitment to fiction.

The effect that Pip's nature, and Dickens' detachment from it, produces in terms of the action of the novel is very odd indeed. On the one hand, everything seems associative and coherent; the action does not seem chaotic and arbitrary so much as to occur in direct response to the consciousness which relates and interprets it. But, at the same time, it is curiously limited to Pip.

Once the story has begun, everything that happens takes on the relation of narrative, and seems connected to what has happened already; but does so, not in terms of the wider world of the novel, but as an aspect of the privacy and solitude of Pip's world which seems unable to reach beyond the limitation of its own voice. We see this curious kind of division at work in the first chapter of the novel:

> My first most vivid and broad impression of the identity of things, seems to me to have been gained on a memorable raw afternoon towards evening. At such a time I found out for certain, that this bleak place overgrown with nettles was the churchyard; and that Philip Pirrip, late of this parish, and also Georgiana, wife of the above, were dead and buried; and that Alexander, Bartholomew, Abraham, Tobias and Roger, infant children of the aforesaid, were also dead and buried; and that the dark flat wilderness beyond the churchyard, intersected with dykes and mounds and gates, with scattered cattle feeding on it, was the marshes; and that the low leaden line beyond was the river; and that the distant savage lair from which the wind was rushing, was the sea; and that the small bundle of shivers growing afraid of it all and beginning to cry, was Pip.
>
> "Hold your noise!" cried a terrible voice, as a man started up from among the graves at the side of the church

porch. "Keep still, you little devil, or I'll cut your throat!" (12)

The mastery in this passage is that of Dickens' own ironical consciousness, which shows us how narrative works as the correlative of need, and conjures consequence out of the landscape it occupies. Pip's misery and loneliness are the introduction for the convict, as if he occupies the marshy space Pip creates for him. His first 'impression of the identity of things' in the marshes is also his first impression of his own solitude and lack of identity; narrative begins as the sense of loss which the convict appears both to fill and express. Pip's crying produces the command to stop, but at the same time is produced *by* it. His misery began, not necessarily on this "memorable raw afternoon" but "at such a time". What is acting here is not his memory but the memory of narrative, which extinguishes the precise course of real events by drawing them into the chain of association. The appearance of the convict confirms the existence of misery and solitude as narrative, just as that narrative in turn began in order to fulfil the need of which misery and solitude are the expression. Narrative then is revealed in the convict as a sense of guilt, and this guilt becomes the link between Pip's fear and the convict's appearance, writing his past into a story.

Pip's voice is a defensive one, and is defensive against solitude; but what it calls up in its associative impulse belongs to the marshland in which it places itself, and only confirms its solitariness. When Pip looks outwards to the world outside he sees nothing but the marsh, which in a sense is his version of the foggy world of *Bleak House,* a world of real but ordinary lives viewed not in the spirit of the truth (as through Esther and the fog) but literally and restrictively outside and resistant to the special life of narrative. Narrative begins to find itself, where it has never been before, located in a general landscape, which reflects its own ungenerous vision of things and provides it with what narrative must have, a horizontal, low and flat place to leave behind.

In the same way, when he seeks relationship with the world, and some identification of the people who occupy it, Pip finds the convict who, as we see, is a kind of human marsh himself,

A man who had been soaked in water, and smothered in mud, and lamed by stones, and cut by flints ...; who limped, and shivered, and glared and growled; and whose teeth chattered in his head as he seized me by the chin (13)

- and who brings Pip knowledge of what the marshes contain and mean. They become a world of animal realities, dominated by energy and terror. As he tells Pip,

There's a young man hid with me, in comparison with which young man I am an Angel. That young man has a secret way pecoolier to himself, of getting at a boy, and at his heart, and at his liver. It is in wain for a boy to attempt to hide himself from that young man. A boy may lock his door, may be warm in bed, may tuck himself up, may draw the clothes over his head, may think himself comfortable and safe, but that young man will softly creep and creep his way to him and tear him open. (14)

This phantom becomes the spirit of the marshes, and has two real faces. The first is that of Compeyson, the man behind Magwitch's own predicament - "hid with me" not literally, but as the enemy who has driven him both to criminal action at first, and then to his own escape; and the second is Pip's own enemy, Orlick, whom he sees as a part of the marsh, and who brings the fear the convict evokes out of the marshes, and into Pip's house. To both of these figures I will return; the point that I want to make here is that in each case the marshes become a death-like demon, and as Magwitch returns to his hiding-place he seems to half belong to this world of the dead:

As I saw him go ... he looked in my young eyes as if he were eluding the hands of the dead people, stretching up cautiously out of their graves, to get a twist upon his ankle and pull him in (15)

and then

I could faintly make out the only two black things in all the prospect that seemed to be standing upright; one of these was the beacon by which the sailors steered...; the other a gibbet, with some chains hanging to it which had once held a pirate. The man was limping on towards this latter, as if he were the pirate come to life, and come down, and going back to hook himself up again. (16)

Already, the marsh has become an image of a world Pip wants to leave, and his narrative has in it its initial identification of the world it wants to evade. This world is the world of Pip's own past, for the hands that reach out at the convict's ankles, "the dead people" in the graveyard, are in a sense Pip's family; the marsh land becomes a vision of an underworld from which the convict emerges to threaten, and into which he now returns.

This marshy world now becomes the landscape of the narrative, and in it the narrative imagination represents the world, not, as Esther did, concealed beneath a foggy indeterminacy, but instead as a flat, low place - David's muddy, miserable world - which is the world Pip now wants to write himself out of, just as David sought to write himself out of life under the direction of Murdstone. While David, however, saw the world he lived in divided - between life in the Murdstone world, and life at Dover with Aunt Betsey - Pip finds himself alone, and makes the division in himself. The appearance of the convict produces in him a secret self. As he tells us, "... I have often thought that few people know what secrecy there is in the young, under terror" so that "I am afraid to think what I might have done" (17). The marshes represent not just an external threat but another, private terror, an alter ego over which the narrating Pip is 'afraid to think' he might have had no control.

This fear is at once the source of Pip's written authority and its limitation. His narrative, writing voice is produced out of it, but is afraid to think of the secret world it seeks to leave and conceal: the world that Dickens' ironical vision of coherence in Pip makes of what we have previously known as the world of fiction.

I will return to the role that the fictive world plays in this novel later in my discussion. As yet, however, we have only seen the beginning of Pip's writing; it is necessary now to see how it develops the narrative world it has initiated, and is committed to.

The figure upon which Pip's narrative focuses is that of Miss Havisham.

Just as the beginning of Pip's story is a parody of David's loneliness and hardship, so the aim he conceives for his story parodies the purpose David conceives in his evasion of the world of his childhood. Miss Havisham is in a sense a version of Aunt Betsey; but where the latter is a divided figure, and half exists in the world of the reader, the former remains entirely undivided. In a novel which is concerned to show us the nature of the narrative voice, Miss Havisham gives us a vision of the life of the writing.

Miss Havisham shares Aunt Betsey's knowledge of reality, and of the disapppointment of innnocence which is at the root of the suffering that Betsey seeks to hide. This suffering, we saw, either destroys control or drives it indoors to Agnes. While Aunt Betsey gains her own authority for the novel, however, by recognising the futility of attempting to control the world, Miss Havisham has refused to make any such recognition.

Pip, of course, is sent to Miss Havisham, shortly after the convict episode, upon her whim, to amuse her:

> saw that everything within my view which ought to be white, had been white long ago, and had lost its lustre, and was faded and yellow. I saw that the bride within the bridal dress had withered like the dress, and like the flowers, and had no brightness left but the brightness of her sunken eyes. I saw that the dress had been put upon the rounded figure of a young woman, and that the figure upon which it now hung loose, had shrunk to skin and

bone. Once, I had been taken to see some ghastly waxwork at the fair, representing I know not what impossible personage lying in state. Once, I had been taken to one of our old marsh churches to see a skeleton in the ashes of a rich dress, that had been dug out of a vault under the church pavement. Now, waxwork and skeleton seemed to have dark eyes that moved and looked at me. (18)

Where Aunt Betsey half-resigns the story she once made for her life to a reality beyond her control, Miss Havisham has never let her story go, and lives out its ending. Where Aunt Betsey determined to accept the unwritten and chaotic world which ruined her life - and thereby saved it from complete destruction - Miss Havisham clings to events as they were once set down. Nothing chance impinges upon the objects in her room; in adhering to that once-happy sense of narrative she has made made life an ending. At the same time, however, she has retained a self-defeating kind of control over the events that are finished, remaining the author of an existence she once wrote for herself.

It is this sense of authorship in her which Pip immediately finds impressive. Like the waxwork and the skeleton, she is a kind of morbid artefact, presenting her life to us as a completed spectacle. In this, Pip sees the marshland churchyard oddly transformed from a sense of ordinariness and commonness into a home for his sense of himself. While he sees death in Miss Havisham, it seems a different kind of death to that of the universal graveyard of the marshes. Miss Havisham brings death indoors, and in privatising it seems to Pip to control it. In her, everything seems to have been completed, and to be set out forever:

I began to understand that everything in the room had stopped, like the watch and the clock, a long time ago. I noticed that Miss Havisham put down the jewel exactly on the spot from which she had taken it up. ...Without this arrest of everything, this standing still of all the pale decayed objects, not even the withered bridal-dress on the collapsed form could have looked so like grave-clothes, or the long veil so like a shroud. (19)

The last action of Miss Havisham's narrative was the last action of the real world for her, and in this way she shows us the real meaning of David's indoor world, achieving a final unity through the isolation he found to be the world of narrative. She shows us that truth to narrative is truth to its ending, and that autobiography ends as a curious kind of self-arrest. Miss Havisham's life is the book David wanted to write, and she is the true author of it.

In Miss Havisham, Pip quite literally sees his end. He has no interest in the marsh world which Miss Havisham seems to exclude, and he wants to share her story and enter her part of reality, the world where things are written and apparently permanent. What he does not see, of course, is what Esther showed us, that the retrospect of the narrative does not necessarily include its anticipation. Miss Havisham controls the past, and makes the world seem a place controllable by looking back; and Pip wants a place in that backward vision, not realising that its coherence does not defeat fragmentation, but exists alongside and is even subject to the chaotic and arbitrary.

Miss Havisham is only the projected end of Pip's story, the place where the narrative is to be finished. As with the convict his vision of her seems associative, and to offer him a kind of social inclusiveness, while what it in fact becomes is not so much a wider, outside world, as another aspect of the limitation of his own voice. His identification of her as the end of his story is also a separation from her; again, unlike David, he does not believe in her as a figure external to himself - as David believes in his aunt - but as an aspect of the narrative which he has conceived as a part of his own ego. We see Miss Havisham as the representative of his own authorship; and he in turn sees the content of the story she provides as Estella.

Estella, predictably, shows us what would have become of Aunt Betsey's protegees if the latter had remained in the writer's world - and not been allowed to marry the baker. Estella is the child of disappointment; but she is also the child of Miss Havisham's purpose and intention which as we have seen occupy the written world. In Estella, the world as Miss Havisham sets it down exists to be mistaken for reality. If the latter is the author of the work she has made of her life, then Estella does seem to be the present realisation of its content, bringing her retrospective vision into the real world. She is the embodiment of the knowledge of suffering, and such knowledge is the content of narrative, so that in her Pip sees the true content of his own story, a way of belonging to the story Miss Havisham looks back upon. Estella then represents Pip's direct relationship with the narrative world.

Even this relationship - indeed, we might say this relationship in particular - is subject to the limitation of Pip's voice to his own consciousness. Pip shows us that, in the written world of narrative, association is itself a form of suffering which takes the form of a continual disappointment.

Upon his first visit to Miss Havisham's, Estella is instructed to feed Pip:

> She came back, with some bread and meat and a little mug of beer. She put the mug down on the stones of the yard, and gave me the bread and meat without looking at me, as insolently as if I were a dog in disgrace. I was so

humiliated, hurt, spurned, offended, angry, sorry - I cannot hit upon the right name for the smart - God knows what its name was - that tears started to my eyes. (20)

The name of Pip's smart is the consciousness of commonness. Estella makes him feel like the animal he saw in the convict on the marshes, and as if he belongs to that marsh world which, we saw above, his narrative is conceived to evade. Estella seems to live at this point of the novel in the other world he sees ending in Miss Havisham, and from this point he aspires to that world, and to Estella, as the substance of his own story. It is here that we hear his first complaint against life with his sister, and with Joe:

I had known from the time when I could speak, that my sister, in her capricious and violent coercion, was unjust to me. I had cherished a profound conviction that her bringing me up by hand, gave her no right to bring me up by jerks. (21)

Pip's rejection of his sister is most important to this early part of the novel. If we remember the veneration in which David's sister was to be held by Aunt Betsey, we realise that Betsey's protection is precisely what Pip's sister has never had. She becomes the demon of the suffering that exposure to the harsh necessities of the world produces; while we hear of her sharp tongue, and of her bringing up by hand, she never treats Pip with any cruelty which is other than the cruelty of the world as she sees it, and as it has treated her. Estella becomes to Pip his Betsey Trotwood, the figure of the ideal sister and woman, replacing his sister's presence in his consciousness; and Estella, as Miss Havisham's protegee, is in a sense precisely that protected and cared-for figure the earlier novel sought.

She is also, however, the protegee of resentment. Her protection is actually born out of that very cruelty that Pip seeks to evade in her. Both in her adoption by Miss Havisham, and in her actual parentage, she belongs to the marshy world that destroys stories; and while she is presented as the content of narrative, the ideal sister Pip wants, the secret that is at the root of her nature is that narrative is as ordinary, and as common, as the world of the marshes, and can only exist alongside that world.

The irony in this is that Pip's narrative, in rebelling against a home life with the sister who seems to restrict aspiration, replaces her with a figure who is the representative of that very restrictedness, the child of the suffering he seems to reject. Pip's narrative punishes his sister for not providing the content it wants, through the resentment and violence it creates in Orlick, condemning her to a life of constant suffering as an invalid.

In Estella this cruel world which narrative would control becomes the very content of narrative. She is herself the child of cruelty, both in birth and in upbringing; in her, the suffering world takes its revenges upon narrative, showing that the content of the world is beyond control, and belongs to the marsh-world, the limitless, ordinary world in which it began, and which it wants to escape.

The difference that narrative seeks in Estella is effectively the removal of everything to a 'better' context, in her. Narrative puts everything, in Estella, into an ideal second-time world; and both Pip and Miss Havisham place their hopes in her. She is the second version of Miss Havisham's life; and when Pip in turn adopts her for his story she becomes the second version of his life, replacing his sister and his life at home. But what she shows us is the wider context of the novel in that in belonging, as we have seen, to the marshy world after all, the narrative is condemned to experience the disappearance of its ideals in placing them in her.

Pip suffers this disappearance; Miss Havisham herself seems to design it, but, as we shall see, she finds herself as limited by her design in her relation with Estella as Pip does and suffers similarly. Meanwhile, its consequences are stranger and more far-reaching than she herself realises, for in investing his story in Estella Pip does not merely suffer disappointment, but continual hints - and terrors - of a world he has lost. The first of these occurs upon Pip's first visit to Miss Havisham, and produces an incident which seems inexplicable. In the garden of the old brewery, Pip tells us,

> I could see ... that there was a track upon the green and yellow paths, as if someone sometimes walked there, and that Estella was walking away from me even then. But she seemed to be everywhere. For, when I yielded to the temptation presented by the casks, and began to walk on them, I saw *her* walking on them at the end of the yard of casks. She had her back towards me and held her pretty brown hair spread out in her two hands, and never looked round, and passed out of my view directly. So, in the brewery itself ... I saw her pass among the extinguished fires, and ascend some light iron stairs, and go out by a gallery high overhead, as if she were going out into the sky.
>
> It was in this place, and at this moment, that a strange thing happened to my fancy. I thought it a strange thing then, and I thought it a stranger thing long afterwards. I turned my eyes - a little dimmed by looking up at the frosty light - towards a great wooden beam in a low nook of the building near me on my right hand, and I saw a figure hanging there by the neck. A figure all in yellow white, with but one shoe to the foot; and it hung so, that I could see that the faded trimmings of the dress

THE NOVEL AS NARRATIVE, II

were like earthy paper, and that the face was Miss
Havisham's, with a movement going over the whole
countenance as if she were trying to call me. (22)

Pip has effectively excluded strange and dreamlike inci-
dents such as this in asserting the literal form of the narrative
as the substance of his vision; as indeed has Miss Havisham,
to whom Estella is a revenge upon narratives, and not intentionally part of the suffering and fictive world. The apparition
of Miss Havisham, then, which would have seemed integral to
Oliver's fictive imagination, is merely terrifying to Pip, and is
in a sense an aspect of that 'secret' self which Pip makes of
his alter ego in the marshes, as a manifestation of its (to narrative) deathly imagination.

Estella shows Pip's world of narrative what Miss Havisham
herself does not entirely understand, the suffering of the
marshy world that threatens and terrifies it. With "a movement
going over her whole countenance" we see Miss Havisham for a
moment racked with the feeling and suffering that Pip's narrative would exclude, in another world. Estella brings to the
story what is written in Miss Havisham's past, and represents
the secret life on the other side of narrative intention as well
as being the vehicle of resentment, which is again a suppressed
suffering.

Pip lives in the literal world of narrative, and simply does
not understand the fictive imagination where reality is presented, like this ghost, in the spirit of the truth. He finds
that the life he had before his narrative was conceived is lost
to him; and that, having left the world of the marshes, he
cannot return there. Apprenticed to Joe, he finds himself living
between two worlds, living an everyday life with a narrative
conscience:

Home had never been a very pleasant place to me, because
of my sister's temper. But, Joe had sanctified it, and I
had believed in it. ... I had believed in the forge, as
the glowing road to manhood and independence. Within a
single year, all this was changed. Now, it was all coarse
and common, and I would not have had Miss Havisham and
Estella see it on any account (23)

so that

I was haunted by the fear that she would, sooner or later,
find me out, with a blank face and hands, doing the
coarsest part of my work, and would exult over me and
despise me. (24)

The 'exultation' Pip projects in Estella here is in a perverse
way his own, a means of leaving behind his sister, Joe and the
forge even while he remains there. These feelings, the feelings

of narrative, replace the old feelings of Pip's home life, where, as he tells us - for we have only seen these feelings as they recede - he 'believed' in things as they were. Now, his resignation to the marsh life is his resignation to obscurity:

> I used to stand about in the churchyard on Sunday evening, when night was falling, comparing my own perspective with the windy marsh view, and making out some likeness between them by thinking how flat and low both were, and how on both there came an unknown way, and then the mist, and then the sea. (25)

It is not so much the prospect of death or ending that Pip fears here, as that of a 'flat' and 'low' oblivion; not so much the sea itself as the dark mist of the unknown way towards it. Once again, this is narrative's, and the writer's, vision of what we saw in *Bleak House* could be the fictive world. The river which is here an 'unknown way' is the same fog-bound story with which the earlier novel began; but here Pip views not a life within it, as Esther did, but (here an apparently impossible) escape from it. To narrative, the foggy world is a limbo, a meaningless, inactive and, not least, common place; and we are shown the landscape which lies beneath the fog, the marshland which (to Pip) denies the shadowy hope of the fictive.

Strangely, we find that even Pip is capable of experiencing this ordinariness as a kind of protection, as if for narrative self-contempt can become a half-fictive barrier between the self and the world. As with Dr Manette, the activity of blacksmith's work leads away from the narrative he has made of life, as an escape from the narrative meaning which was in turn conceived as an escape from the life he leads. In *Great Expectations,* Dickens shows us that while the two worlds of Pip's consciousness are mutually exclusive, they really belong together, and at this point in the novel the terrors and fears which have haunted Pip's narrative sense of himself cease as an ordinary life evades for a while the relentless course of the story.

When the story returns with Pip's fortune, this protection becomes unbearable to him. His will never ceases to be a narrative will, and once it is able it rejects home, and the figure who increasingly occupies that home, that of Joe.

With his sister's disablement, Joe, who from the beginning had 'sanctified' Pip's sense of home (26), becomes the voice of the marsh world, and as such directly opposes Pip's narrative sense in a way which, in offering protection, as we have seen, Pip finds more difficult to disown than his sister's bullying. Where Pip's sister presented merely a shrill and uncomfortable voice of hardship, Joe shows us that there is a strength and solidity which can endow the ordinary, unwritten world (Joe, of course, is illiterate, and so dissents directly from any narrative Pip might write for himself).

This strength becomes most apparent and most wrong to Pip when he does seem to succeed in leaving it behind, upon the apparent fulfilment of his expectations. In his illiteracy and apparent stupidity he seems to be beyond the scope of writing; but upon close examination we find that his words are only beyond the literal writing of narrative, and themselves belong wholly to that same world we saw the convict apearing from, and Estella disappearing to. When Pip asks him, in his 'improved position', whether it isn't "a pity now ... that you did not get on a little more, when we had our lessons here?" (27) Joe replies,

> Well, I don't know... I'm so awful dull, I'm only master of my own trade. It were always a pity as I was so awful dull; but its no more a pity now, than it was - this day twelvemonth - don't you see! (28)

Pip emphatically does *not* see; but the sense of story which his promotion confirms is not one that Joe can share. To Joe, nothing really changes in progression, so that what is 'a pity' now always was and always will be a pity. Pip's narrative consciousness is meaningless to him, as life at home now means nothing to Pip, being something he finally seems to have left behind.

With the resumption of progression, however, he loses that protection he rejects in Joe and in which even now he does not believe. The first sign of this new loneliness is the return of terror with the appearance of some convicts on a coach on the way to Miss Havisham's, and Pip's recognition of the man who had been Magwitch's messenger. At this point, Pip experiences "the revival for a few minutes of the terror of childhood" (29). But this terror is only a momentary loss of control of a condition which is now endemic to Pip's world, as he begins to realise the nature of the narrative world which, he sees, must replace his life with Joe for ever.

It becomes the prelude to his reunion with Estella, and to what is perhaps the oddest and most difficult part of the novel. As he tells us in Chapter 29, he goes to meet Estella as if to claim, finally, the content of the story we have seen him write for himself, supposing that Miss Havisham has "reserved it for me to restore the desolate house, admit the sunshine into the dark rooms, set the clocks a-going" and "do all the shining deeds of the young Knight of romance, and marry the Princess" (30).

This is still the fairy tale that Pip has imagined for himself from the beginning, and he makes the assumption which we saw that *Bleak House* refused to make (31), that the sleeping narratives of the foggy world *can* be awakened by a knightly hero. What we see happening in the course of his meeting with Estella is a process of disillusion; but this is not a disillusion with narrative but with everything *other* than narrative. As he tells us in his own retrospective, narrative voice,

> The unqualified truth is that, when I loved Estella with the love of a man, I loved her simply because I found her irresistible. Once for all; I know to my sorrow, often and often, if not always, that I loved her against reason, against promise, against peace, against hope, against happiness, against all discouragement that could be. Once for all; I loved her none the less because I knew it, and it had no more influence in restraining me, than if I had devoutly believed her to be human perfection. (32)

This faithlessness is the direct opposite of Miss Flite's fictive belief. Instead of placing his faith in the outside world in spite of the doubt of his own self, Pip places faith in himself, and in the narrative he has made, in spite of the lack of belief that that narrative has in the outside world. Insisting always upon his 'I', Pip maintains his narrative in spite of everything, just as Miss Flite - and through her Esther - maintained her fiction in spite of everything. The failure of Pip's belief in a world outside here is the failure we see in David, at the end of *David Copperfield:* except that, here, its faithlessness governs the whole narrative. We only realise its real meaning now, when it is challenged by the failure of the outside world. Pip's aspirations have seemed isolating and limiting, but only here do we begin to see the extent of their limitation.

Pip's continuing narrative makes self-presentation seem the function of narrative, and makes it apear to be an end in itself; and this is effectively the realisation he reaches in the passage above by resolving to write without faith.

A momentary panic began this realisation; Pip's faithlessness now controls such panic, and while it does not extinguish the possibility of further terror, of shock and disappointment, it is a sign of his preparation for anything that might become his story, for Pip now effectively possesses a readiness to believe in nothing but the images of the self, and to turn the world into the writing that can be the province of that first person vision. Pip here ceases to offer the real self that did half believe in the forge and in Joe, and offers instead the written individuality that reality demands if narrative is to be continued.

We see this self-presentation at work almost immediately: Pip finds that Estella

> was so much ... changed, ... in all things winning admiration had made such a wonderful advance, that I seemed to have made none. I fancied, as I looked at her, that I slipped hopelessly back into the coarse and common boy again. Oh the sense of distance and disparity that came upon me, and the inaccessibility that came about her. (33)

Already, Estella is made an image of Pip's love, and we see in her the ideal which narrative has previously only suggested to Pip. Pip ceases to see 'through' Estella, as he did before, and into the world of suffering, for his faithlessness allows him to believe only in his own vision. This vision makes what was previously general and universal, even in Pip's childish eyes, individual and singular. He sees only his own aspirations in Estella now, and nothing beyond them, and plays out the scene as her adorer.

At the same time, her previous disappearance becomes her private mystery, fastening the younger Pip's imagination upon Estella herself. Where he previously glimpsed the pain and sorrow of Miss Havisham, he now sees only the figure before him:

> What *was* it that was borne upon my mind when she stood still and looked attentively at me? ... I looked again, and though she was still looking at me, the suggestion was gone.
> What *was* it? (34)

- and then,

> In another moment we were in the brewery so long disused, and she pointed out to the high gallery where I had seen her going out on that same day, and told me she remembered to have been up there, and to have seen me standing scared below. As my eyes followed her white hand, again the same dim suggestion that I could not possibly grasp crossed me. My involuntary start occasioned her to lay her hand upon my arm. Instantly the ghost passed once more and was gone.
> What *was* it? (35)

It is extraordinary that Pip does not remember here the earlier apparition; narrative so dominates his consciousness now that his imagination can see only narratives in others, and those earlier glimpses of another world are lost to him. We shall return to the story he seeks in Estella; meanwhile, of course, Pip has taken up precisely the part that Miss Havisham wants the male world, the world at whose hands and through whose hypocrisy she suffered, to play. As she herself tells him, 'real love'

> is blind devotion, unquestioning self-humiliation, utter submission, trust and disbelief against yourself and against the whole world, giving up your whole heart and soul to the smiter - as I did. (36)

The course of the novel seems determined. She has herself no idea that the world of suffering could be glimpsed through Estella; the latter seems to her, at this point in the story, to be as written and finalised as her own fate. Miss Havisham is herself like Pip in believing only in the world of narrative, in spite of the fictive and innocent world she, like Pip, half occupied in her youth, before narrative.

Miss Havisham and Pip seem to have in common the content of the control they have chosen to exercise as the stories of their lives. Miss Havisham offers Estella as the content of a narrative she will tell, as it were, from its end; and Pip accepts Estella for the sake of that control, however malevolent it may turn out to be.

We have already seen that Estella's nature has seemed to offer a side that we have seen neither Pip nor Miss Havisham accept or understand, for she comes from the fictive world which is the correlative of both of their narratives, and is its child.

This gives her a power we have already seen in her as a child, to disrupt the story and to suggest the other world of real feelings which we have seen oddly invested in her. The change of heart that occurs in the middle of Pip's relations with Estella and Miss Havisham seems inexplicable; and, as with much else that seems strange in the novel, its source would seem to be Estella.

Firstly we hear Estella warning Pip in a rather different voice from the taunting one we have heard and know as a part of Miss Havisham's control. Pip himself depends as he has from the beginning upon this control - "she could not choose but obey Miss Havisham" - and accepts "that tone which expressed that our association was forced upon us" (37). But, as he tells us, "There were other times when she would come to a sudden check in this tone and in all her many tones, and would seem to pity me" (38):

> "Pip, Pip," she said one evening, coming to such a check, when we sat apart at a darkening window of the house in Richmond; "will you never take warning?" (39)

Clearly, Estella tries here to change the course of things by leading Pip away from the narrative Miss Havisham has decreed. She fails, of course, Pip referring us in his own narrative back to Miss Havisham's control, and continuing with the distinct and formal observation that

> My dread always was, that this knowledge on her part laid me under a heavy disadvantage with her pride, and made me the subject of a rebellious struggle in her bosom (40)

sounding, in this laboriously written prose, more like a civil servant than a lover.

Estella's second attempt to change the story is more successful. Having failed to lead Pip away from his written self, she turns to her adopted mother, and shows her what the literal vision of narrative means in reality.

As I suggested above, Miss Havisham is like Pip in that she knows only the narrative she attempts to bring about through Estella, and she wants, through her, to leave the world of suffering, her first life, behind in a perfected narrative in which she both revenges and controls. Like Pip, she rejects the 'home' life of the ordinary world which first deceived her, and does so without realising that it can have any importance to her. Unlike Pip, however, she has not determined to be completely faithless, for she has one faith left to her; and that faith is Estella.

In a world where all faith seems lost, this relation is the one means Estella finds of changing the narrative that is to destroy all relations. We hear that Miss Havisham is "dreadfully fond" (41) of Estella; when Pip's association with her is at its height he accompanies her to Satis House, where he witnesses, for the first time as he tells us, the following confrontation between them: "What would you have?" Estella asks:

"Love," replied the other.
"You have it."
"I have not," said Miss Havisham.
"Mother by adoption," retorted Estella, never departing from the easy grace of her attitude... "I have said that I owe everything to you. All I possess is freely yours. All that you have given me, is at your command to have again. Beyond that, I have nothing. And if you ask me to give you what you never gave me, my gratitude and duty cannot do impossibilities." (42)

Estella's words here are the opposite of her words to Pip; they are peculiarly formed and written. In them, Miss Havisham faces the last meaning of her story that remains to her, and the meaning of the story she has made for Pip, as nothing but another kind of loss. She finally begins to see Estella's life deprived of the feeling she still seeks herself, and finds herself left with the feeling she has written out of Estella. Miss Havisham finds that her faith to narrative, and to her own disappointed story, is that faithlessness in all else we have seen in Pip; it is no coincidence that Pip sees her late that night in a passage in the house, "going along it in a ghostly manner, making a low cry", "a most unearthly object" (43) by the light of her candle. She finds that narrative is not a way of continuing life, but of living without feeling, and this knowledge, which Pip showed us above, makes a ghost of the world she has made of Estella, destroying the 'literal' solidity of her narrative by showing her a world of the spirit.

Miss Havisham recognises Estella as the disappearance of the ideals of narrative (which are still, until this point, her own), into a world of commonness and suffering which has been missed for ever, along with the real feelings that accompany such suffering. Miss Havisham knows that she can never return to that first world of feelings; but here, through Estella, she effectively rediscovers it in the mirror of the written that Estella holds up to her.

What Estella achieves here is the release of Pip from Miss Havisham's narrative; but in holding up this mirror to narrative she also effectively sacrifices herself to the fictive life of suffering and ordinariness, by condemning herself to Bentley Drummle, with whom we see her at the end of the chapter. Pip himself reproaches her, here; "I have seen you give him looks and smiles this very night, such as you never give to - me":

> "Do you want me then," said Estella, turning suddenly with a fixed and serious, if not angry look, "to deceive and entrap you?"
> "Do you deceive and entrap him, Estella?"
> "Yes, and many others - all of them but you." (44)

From this point, Pip's narrative must exist on its own, in spite of Estella. She has effectively vanished from the narrative, and receded, generously, but against the will of narrative, into the common, everyday world; as we see, Pip does not give up his own story so easily, and through it he retains some hope of reclaiming her for his world.

First of all, however, we must turn to his relation with another aspect of the world he expects, with that part of the story which belongs specifically to Miss Havisham's control. The return of Magwitch is the other part of the major destruction of the narrative Pip has created for himself, at least in terms of its correspondence to the real world.

Magwitch returns like another ghost to a world already made miserable to Pip by the absence of Estella; alone at night, he hears a footstep on his stairway:

> What nervous folly made me start, and awfully connect it with the footsteps of my dead sister, matters not. It soon passed in a moment, and I listened again, and heard the footsteps stumble in coming on. (45)

Just as we saw the past return to Miss Havisham as a thing ghostly to narrative, so the past, returning here in Magwitch, conjures his sister's rejected world as a ghostly association in Pip's mind. His intuitive apprehension here is entirely accurate, as if he feels his narrative threatened by some other story. Certainly, this is what happens as Magwitch tells his - rival - tale:

> All the truth of my position came flashing upon me; and
> its disappointments, dangers, disgraces, consequences of
> all kinds, rushed in in such a multitude that I was borne
> down by them, and had to struggle for the breath I drew.
> (46)

Pip is here directly confronted with a story from the world
he left behind and, included within its marshy truth, he finds
himself floundering and drowning within it, his sense of himself
- his narrative sense - for the moment destroyed.   Magwitch
brings the marshes and the world of childhood and convicts into
Pip's own room in London, to the very core and centre of his
gentility; as he eats and drinks,

> I saw my convict on the marshes again.   It almost seemed
> to me as if he must stoop down presently, to file at his
> leg. (47)

The past seems to occupy the present after all, Pip finding
himself back where he began.   But Pip's sense of himself, and
of his own story, is all that he has, and he does not relinquish
it so easily.   Instead of accepting or welcoming the past in the
form of Magwitch he accustoms himself to it, planning to send
him back abroad, and rejecting any further money.
Magwitch becomes a version of Uriah Heep that must be
included within the content of the narrative.   Unlike David
Copperfield, Pip has no Aunt Betsey to take responsibility for
the outside world he represents: as he tells us, at the beginning,

> Words cannot tell what a sense I had ... of the dreadful
> mystery that he was to me.   When he fell asleep of an
> evening, I would sit and look at him, wondering what he
> had done... Once, I actually did start out of bed in the
> night..., hurriedly intending to leave him there with ev-
> erything else I possessed, and enlist for India, as a pri-
> vate soldier. (48)

Magwitch seems to be beyond Pip's 'telling'; while at the
same time he seems to have made Pip the subject of *his* story.
"I done it" (49), the convict tells him, having proprietorially
looked over his belongings, as if the realisation of all Pip's
hopes was a crime in itself, and laying waste to the comfort of
his life.
Pip only comes to terms with what happens to him in the
process of reasserting his own control.   It very quickly becomes
apparent that Magwitch has acted irresponsibly and rashly in
returning home, and in looking after him Pip manages to regain
some sense of his own authority.   Responsibility even becomes

a kind of affection by the time the convict makes his ill-fated bid for freedom; Pip tells us,

> Looking back at him, I thought of the first night of his return ... when I little supposed my heart could ever be as heavy and anxious at parting from him as it was now. (50)

Pip's concern here is also partly a relief; for, on the first night of his arrival, Magwitch threatened to take over completely. Here Pip's own voice has been re-established, and has survived the discovery of the source of his own fortune. Pip's faith in himself is restored, in terms of his own generosity of feeling; it has not become a faith in the convict, however, whom even as they row down the river Pip regards as a kind of alien being. In the boat, Magwitch "looked ... a natural part of the scene" (51), for even now it is to the marshy world that he belongs, and which sets him apart in Pip's eyes: as he tells us,

> It was remarkable (but perhaps the wretched life he had led accounted for it), that he was the least anxious of any of us. ...he was not disposed to be passive or resigned, as I understood it; but he had no notion of meeting chances half-way. (52)

That 'as I understood' provides Pip with the distance his narrative needs, restoring his own words to their proper place as the interpreter of Magwitch's 'dreadful mystery' - and making that mystery seem to be subordinate to Pip's interpretation.

Pip's control seems to be reaffirmed when he goes back to Miss Havisham with this new intelligence as to the source of his fortune:

> She turned her face to me for the first time since she had averted it, and to my amazement, I may even add my ter ror, dropped on her knees at my feet; with her hands raised to me in the manner in which, when her poor heart was young and fresh and whole, they must have been raised to Heaven from her mother's side.
>
> To see her white hair and her worn face, kneeling at my feet, gave me a shock through all my frame. I entreated her to rise, and got my arm about her to help her up; but she only pressed that hand of mine which was nearest to her grasp, and hung her head over it and wept. (53)

While this is hardly the narrative Pip wanted - he thought Miss Havisham was in a manner his mother, and controlled his story - it does not destroy or threaten his narrative sense but, again, merely places responsibility onto his own shoulders as an unexpected but not, to Pip, particularly hostile or incongruous reversal. As with Magwitch, Miss Havisham offers him the opportunity for a different kind of self-presentation to the one he expected; a self-presentation based in generosity and in magnanimity, in taking responsibility for the whole world himself, rather than in finding his life written out by others. He simply replaces the narrative he thought the world would give him with the narrative he writes for himself. The scene above is again as formal and written, as literal and limited by narrative, as his feeling for Magwitch, and the narrative depends upon the control it rediscovers in Miss Havisham's supplication. Pip's imagination deals in written, literal images rather than in the approximations of speech, and in relationships of responsibility and control, and not of passive sympathy. He appears to make himself the father and mother of the action of the novel in Magwitch and then in Miss Havisham by inverting their initial control over him.

The real test of this new control and responsibility however remains Estella; for in continuing his narrative Pip continues his attempt to bring Estella back within the action, over which it now appears that he has a new mastery. His unremitting concern since her desertion of him and her marriage has been to claim much the same voice of authority and responsibility for her as that which he has come to have over Magwitch and Miss Havisham. To this end, then, it has been his continual concern to make those glimpses of the fictive world that he had in her, into a part of his narrative understanding and responsibility. All his energy is now pressed into the identification of that mysterious 'something' he has recognised in Estella, for he is convinced that such an identification will give him much the same power over her as it did over the convict and her adopted mother, and so provide his narrative with the re-establishment it seeks.

He makes the connection which he believes he needs upon seeing Mr Jagger's housekeeper:

> I looked again at the hands and eyes of the housekeeper and thought of the inexplicable feeling that had come over me when I had last walked - not alone - in the ruined garden, and through the deserted brewery. I thought how the same feeling had come back when I saw a face looking at me, and a hand waving to me from a stage-coach window; and how it had come back and had flashed about me like lightning, when I had passed in a carriage - not alone - through a sudden glare of light in a dark street. I thought of how one link of association had helped identification in the theatre, and how such a link, wanting before, had been riveted for me now, when I had passed by a chance swift from Estella's eyes to the fingers with their knitting action, and the attentive eyes. And I felt

absolutely certain that this woman was Estella's mother. (54)

These 'links of association' still, as the connections of Pip's narrative, form the substance of the reality in which he believes. He is too fascinated with the narrative behind these connections to understand the associations they make. He does not see a world beyond his narrating self, but instead attempts to use the limited perception of narrative - as a means of control. He believes in nothing but the authorship of his own fate, and, even now, its capacity to include Estella's, and to control the world by understanding its interconnectedness.

He very rapidly discovers, however, that whatever else his discovery might be, it is not the story he hopes for, which will make a unity of the world. He does so through Jaggers, who is a figure much like Bucket, the arch-priest of the stories that exist in the real world, and, as a lawyer, the novel's representative of the justice Pip has always sought.

It is Jaggers, then, who continues Pip's story for him; continues, but does not finish it. As he says, of himself,

> Put the case that he lived in an atmosphere of evil, and that all he saw of children was, their being generated in great numbers, for certain destruction. Put the case that he habitually knew of their being imprisoned, whipped, transported, neglected, cast out, qualified in all ways for the hang man, and growing up to be hanged. Put the case that pretty nigh all the children he saw in his daily business life, he had reason to look upon as so much spawn, to develop into the fish that were to come to his net - to be prosecuted, defended, forsworn, made orphans, bedevilled somehow. (55)

This is the story that Pip seeks to uncover; the general, common world of the marshes, over which, it now appears, the fog of obscurity hangs just as it did in *Bleak House*. It is a general connection for the characters in the novel, for it is common to them all. It belongs directly to the convict Magwitch and his wife, and to Compeyson, who makes his living in this marshy world. It belongs to Pip, since as we have seen it is at the root of his own narrative sense, as the fear that impels him to narrate his life. It belongs to Miss Havisham, whom even wealth and status could not save from the deceit it holds out. It belongs doubly to Estella, whose fate it dictates both through Miss Havisham and through her initial plight as a homeless orphan. It belongs to Pip's sister, who struggled incessantly to rise above it, and to Orlick, whose violence and resentment it produces. It belongs even to Joe and Herbert, who must live with and in spite of the hostility and chaos it offers.

While this is the continuation of the common story Pip stumbles upon, it does not end or complete it, for Jaggers shows us that the marsh-world swallows endings and completeness in its own senselessness. In this world, as Jaggers tells Pip, narratives have no such common use:

> For whose sake would you reveal the secret? - For the father's? I think he would not be much better for the mother. For the mother's? I think if she had done the deed she would be safer where she was. For the daughter's? I think it would hardly serve her, to establish her parentage for the information of her husband, and to drag her back to disgrace, after an escape of twenty years, pretty secure to last for life. (56)

In the marsh-world there are no endings, and no final and happy resolutions. The narratives of this world are made of a confusion which is as bereft of endings as it is of beginnings.

Pip, however, is incapable of heeding this warning, and the novel shows us both what Jaggers' words mean and why Pip cannot comprehend or act upon them in the course of the next chapters.

Hitherto, Pip seems to have evaded the marsh-world, and created a world of his own responsibility. Jaggers' voice is precisely that; it threatens Pip's world with a limitation of its vision, but does not bring the marsh-reality back within the boundaries of Pip's life. Jaggers' word are a warning, and they warn of the mysterious summons Pip receives in the next chapter: "If you are not afraid to come to the old marshes ... you had better come" (57).

This is a direct challenge, and what it challenges is Pip's new-found authority and responsibility. Pip puts the matter to himself in terms of his responsibility for Magwitch: "in case any harm should befall him through my not going, how could I ever forgive myself!" (58) This however is merely the actual effect of the general burden he has taken upon himself, to bring his whole world within the province of his story.

Pip then returns finally to the marsh, and even as he arrives at the place feels its threat against himself:

> There was a melancholy wind, and the marshes were very dismal. A stranger would have found them insupportable, and even to me they were so oppressive that I hesitated, half-inclined to go back. But, I knew them, and could have found my way on a far darker night, and had no excuse for returning, being there. So having come there against my inclination, I went on against it. (59)

Already, it is the place that Pip finds disturbing, and opposed to his own sense of things, and already he finds its power defeating his own will.

The figure he goes to meet, of course, is Orlick. Orlick has been criticised, as has this whole episode, for a lack of realism and motive (60); but in fact he has had a large part in the nexus of associations that the marshes have come to represent for this novel. He belongs to all that Pip once tried to leave behind, as the equal - both he and the adopted Pip were apprentices at the forge - Pip sought to rise above, the man who seemed to Pip to belong above all others to the oppression of the landscape. We have already seen him start "up, from the gate, or from the rushes, or from the ooze (which was quite his stagnant way)". It has been in Orlick that Pip's narrative and his will to leave things behind has created the resentment of those left, and that resentment has of course already brought about his attack upon Pip's sister, which as I suggested above, and as Orlick himself now suggests to Pip, was in a sense Pip's own, as the violent expression of the disownment that narrative seeks. At the root of this disownment, of course, and inextricable from the 'oppression' Pip feels in the marshes, is that first apppearance of the convict; and Orlick is in a sense the final appearance of the "young man hid with me" (61), the evil and levelling cruelty of the marsh world.

Orlick returns as that childhood terror which had threatened everything; and whereas Pip has found every threat to his story capable of containment within the writing by which his world reaches a form of coherence in his own experience, the threat Orlick poses is unequivocal and final: "You're dead" (62). In him, the graveyard Pip has continually sought to escape returns with unavoidable force: as Pip tells us, "I felt that I had come to the brink of my grave" (63).

Narrative now faces the crisis it cannot overcome; a complete and final storylessness in the marshes. As Orlick tells Pip,

> I won't have a rag of you, I won't have a bone of you, left on earth! I'll put your body in the kiln - I'd carry two such to it on my shoulders - and, let people suppose what they may think of you, they shall never know nothing. (64)

This is the complete obliteration in the dark world that Pip has feared from the beginning, and it removes the one faith that his narrative has, in himself, and in what we now realise is his own immortality, the preservation of his 'I':

> The death before me was terrible, but far more terrible than death was the dread of being misremembered after death. And so quick were my thoughts, that I saw myself despised by unborn generations - Estella's children, and their children - while the wretch's words were yet upon his lips. (65)

This drowning in obscurity is of no use to narrative, but only shows a threat worse than death itself; the death of ordinariness that destroys Pip's story. Orlick does not simply offer to kill Pip, but to absorb him back into the marsh world, and thereby to kill the memory by which narrative has its life. We see this life in frantic activity now -

> In the excited and exalted state of my brain, I could not think of a place without seeing it, or of persons without seeing them. It is impossible to over-state the vividness of these images (66)

- but Pip's narrative sense has no answer to what it sees as "the tiger crouching to spring" (67). Pip, of course, is rescued; but his rescue does not re-establish his defeated story as the responsibility he thought himself to bear before the encounter with Orlick and the marshes. Instead, it reduces Pip's world to a series of small, fragmentary coherences - to the status of the marsh-world itself. His imagination remains the imagination of narrative; and shows us what happens to it where it is confronted with the confusion of a chaotic reality. As in facing the obscurity of death in Orlick, it ceases to produce a story, and produces a series of vivid pictures.

We have already been given the first of these by the time of the meeting with Orlick, as if the narrative has already been at work to produce resources for its own defence.

After his last visit to Miss Havisham, as "twilight was closing in" (68), Pip walks again in the ruined brewery, where he once again sees the apparition of the hanging figure, although here it is a 'fancy' and an 'impression' which "caused me to feel an indescribable awe" (69). We soon see that this 'awe' is invested not so much in the outside world as in Pip himself this time, however; for his own intuition now becomes the real import both of this vision and the consequent events. Upon the return of the ghost Pip returns to "assure myself that Miss Havisham was as safe and well as I had left her":

> I looked into the room... In the moment when I was withdrawing my head to go quietly away, I saw a great flame spring up. In the same moment I saw her running at me, with a whirl of fire blazing all about her, and soaring at least as many feet above her head as she was high. (70)

Pip's story can make no narrative of this spontaneous combustion; he fails to save her life, and at the same time prevents her death and consigns her to a painful decline, wrapped, we hear, in cotton wool. The confusion and chaos of reality takes over from narrative, and destroys its coherence. As with Orlick, this confusion only makes the picture brighter, as the memory that narrative clings to in the twilight world which it now occupies as the means to its vision. Here, as on the marshes with Orlick, daylight offers no respite, no reassertion of control or responsibility, and the narrative imagina-

tion finds itself having to exist between the confusion which
occupies the daylight world and the darkness which ends everything.   The written is sent, as David Copperfield found,
indoors, to a place which is sheltered from the real world, in
order to find a world that can still be written.

Miss Havisham is saved from the chaotic and remembered
by Pip's imagination as 'a great flame', the image standing for
the immortality Pip once sought for himself in narrative, as an
imitation of it.

We find Magwitch similarly preserved.   As Pip tells us of
his trial,

> The whole scene starts out again in the vivid colours of
> the moment, down to the drops of April rain on the win-
> dows of the court, glittering in the rays of the April sun.
> (71)

and as the death sentence is pronounced,

> The sun was striking in at the great windows of the court,
> through the glittering drops of rain upon the glass, and
> it made a broad shaft of light between the two-and-thirty
> and the Judge, linking both together, and perhaps re-
> minding some among the audience, how both were passing
> on, with absolute equality, to the greater Judgement that
> knoweth all things and cannot err. (72)

This scene becomes another symbol to Pip; this time, of
the justice which narrative has so palpably failed to work, as
Magwitch is consigned by the reality that has mistreated him
from his birth to the death he does not deserve.   Magwitch,
the judge and the courtroom audience all belong to the same
confused and chaotic world (an equality which in the narrative
omits the convict); judgement is saved, here, by bringing the
sun itself into the indoor world of the written to symbolise an
ending in which the narrative imitates the justice it seeks.

If immortality and justice are saved by these two pictures,
the narrative's most important symbol is its final one, for this
imitates nothing less than its own ending, and in it Pip saves
his own imagination from the chaotic world.

It is concerned, of course, with Estella, in whom Pip had
from the beginning seen his own special destiny.   Once again,
this final scene occurs in twilight, and is not so much a real
ending - hence Dickens' equivocation and flexibility about its
content - as the image of one.   Quite literally, it is an imitation
of *Paradise Lost* (73):

> I took her hand in mine, and we went out of the ruined
> place; and, as the morning mists had risen long ago when
> I had first left the forge, so, the evening mists were rising
> now, and in all the broad expanse of tranquil light they

showed to me, I saw no shadow of another parting from her. (74)

In presenting Pip and Estella as Adam and Eve, this image is hardly there to be believed; and belief is made the more difficult when we remember that it represents Dickens' own second thoughts. We may well agree with Forster, that the original ending, in which Pip only re-encounters Estella by chance in London, after she has suffered much and remarried, is "more consistent with the drift, as well as natural working out, of the tale" (75). At the same time, however, it remains true that the second ending reminds us of the nature of the novel, and of the artifice of the narrative which is the novel's real subject. Dickens shows us Pip's limitation in it more subtly than in the first ending, showing that reality lies beyond the writing of the narrator by confining him for ever within one final written image. Pip's whole life has in writing become an imitation of itself, bringing David's indoor world to its realisation, and at the same time showing us unequivocally the restriction of the grasp of narrative and narrator over human experience. This ending resolves nothing and answers no questions; the story, insofar as it sought to be the integration of narrator and reality, remains even now to be told - or simply, as Jaggers showed us, to continue. Pip seeks his own loneliness here, as a written individuality separated from a reality through which he has passed, it seems, with no effect upon anything but the home he left, and remains isolated from here; Joe and Biddy - whom Pip again missed as the woman who could have been his wife - can only imitate a life lost to the real world by calling their own son Pip.

Footnotes

(1) See page 40, above.
(2) *Little Dorrit*, 895.
(3) See Penguin edition of *A Tale of Two Cities*, 30; and Edgar Johnson, *Charles Dickens: his Tragedy and Triumph*, 972.
(4) Edgar Johnson, *Charles Dickens: his Tragedy and Triumph*, 972.
(5) *A Tale of Two Cities*, 54.
(6) *A Tale of Two Cities*, 54.
(7) John Forster, *Life of Charles Dickens*, III, 329.
(8) *David Copperfield*, 49.
(9) *David Copperfield*, 49.
(10) *Great Expectations*, 35.
(11) *Great Expectations*, 35.
(12) *Great Expectations*, 35-6.
(13) *Great Expectations*, 36.
(14) *Great Expectations*, 38.
(15) *Great Expectations*, 38.
(16) *Great Expectations*, 39.
(17) *Great Expectations*, 87.
(18) *Great Expectations*, 87.
(19) *Great Expectations*, 89-90.
(20) *Great Expectations*, 92.
(21) *Great Expectations*, 92.
(22) *Great Expectations*, 93.
(23) *Great Expectations*, 134.
(24) *Great Expectations*, 136.
(25) *Great Expectations*, 135.
(26) *Great Expectations*, 134.
(27) *Great Expectations*, 174.
(28) *Great Expectations*, 174.
(29) *Great Expectations*, 252.
(30) *Great Expectations*, 253.
(31) See page 74 above.
(32) *Great Expectations*, 253-4.
(33) *Great Expectations*, 256.
(34) *Great Expectations*, 259.
(35) *Great Expectations*, 259.
(36) *Great Expectations*, 261.
(37) *Great Expectations*, 319.
(38) *Great Expectations*, 319.
(39) *Great Expectations*, 319.
(40) *Great Expectations*, 319.
(41) *Great Expectations*, 320.
(42) *Great Expectations*, 322-3.
(43) *Great Expectations*, 325.
(44) *Great Expectations*, 329-30.

(45) *Great Expectations*, 332.
(46) *Great Expectations*, 336.
(47) *Great Expectations*, 340.
(48) *Great Expectations*, 353.
(49) *Great Expectations*, 339.
(50) *Great Expectations*, 392.
(51) *Great Expectations*, 447.
(52) *Great Expectations*, 447.
(53) *Great Expectations*, 410.
(54) *Great Expectations*, 403.
(55) *Great Expectations*, 424-5.
(56) *Great Expectations*, 426.
(57) *Great Expectations*, 430.
(58) *Great Expectations*, 431.
(59) See, for instance, H.M.Daleski, *Dickens and the Art of Analogy*, 242.
(60) *Great Expectations*, 432-3.
(61) *Great Expectations*, 38, and page 138 above.
(62) *Great Expectations*, 436.
(63) *Great Expectations*, 436.
(64) *Great Expectations*, 436.
(65) *Great Expectations*, 436.
(66) *Great Expectations*, 438.
(67) *Great Expectations*, 438.
(68) *Great Expectations*, 413.
(69) *Great Expectations*, 413.
(70) *Great Expectations*, 414.
(71) *Great Expectations*, 466.
(72) *Great Expectations*, 467.
(73) See Edgar Johnson, who quotes Milton, *Paradise Lost*, 646-9, in *Charles Dickens*, 994;

> "The world was all before them, where to choose
> Their place of rest, and Providence their guide;
> They, hand in hand, with wandering steps and slow,
> Through Eden took their solitary way."

(74) *Great Expectations*, 493.
(75) John Forster, *Life of Charles Dickens*, III, 336.

CHAPTER SIX

Our Mutual Friend and the Art of the Possible

We have now seen Dickens' intelligence producing an awareness of every capacity of the novel, and a full consciousness of the place and function of his own voice within it. We have seen that in both the fictive and narrative novel his voice is that detached one represented, not singly within the novel, but within the whole texture and composition, within what I have called the landscape, of its substance. This landscape is a larger and more potent source of energy and authority than any single voice in the novel could be. In the foggy world of *Bleak House* it offers fictive opportunity between the literal and the ideal. In the marshland of *Great Expectations* it shows us the same reality under the narrative intelligence, exposing the literal, narrative truth of Pip's autobiography, and uncovering the world that lay hidden in the earlier novel.

In each case, 'reality' turns out to be much the same; a formless world incapable of a single unity, but capable nevertheless of containing and even sustaining the two parts of what would, if it were fully coherent, be a fairy tale.

We have seen this world from the perspective of both fiction and narrative; but in each case those intelligences become limited to their own narrative worlds, and in each case we know that Dickens himself must know more. In *Bleak House* he must know what lies beyond Esther, in his own male intelligence which has determined to see the world whole in spite of his own authority, and the claims of that authority; in *Great Expectations*, he must know, as he knows in Esther, where Estella goes when she disappears from Pip's story (as she constantly does) and of what her female world consists. The question which would now appear to be the pressing one is whether the novel can be written in order to include both of these parts of the author's intelligence. Both *Bleak House* and *Great Expectations* come close in the landscapes they provide to achieving this imaginative inclusiveness - although they do not so much provide unity as a realisation of division; and indeed they seem to show us different aspects of, or ways of seeing, the same landscape. *Our Mutual Friend*, I want to argue, brings these opposing views together to achieve, not unity or the realisation of a fairy tale, but the novel at its most extensive and comprehensive, and to provide us with a landscape which includes and extends those of the earlier novels. *Our Mutual Friend* represents the realism of neither fiction nor narrative, but of a mature vision of the world between, and shows us the meaning of a world governed by accident.

This novel ceases to be concerned with a search for a figure to unite, or for a persona to characterise fiction and narrative, and turns instead to what lies between their two worlds - to the writing itself. "Seldom," James complained, "had we read a book so intensely *written* "(1), and if his complaint is unjustified, his observation is accurate. This novel is concerned directly with the way in which its text reflects the whole of the outside world, and with the way in which it is legitimately realistic, treating that world, and its own substance, as a landscape in which its disparate elements meet. We see this in its much-discussed imagery (2). In *Great Expectations* the world in which the narrative voice was set was characterised by the marshland; while in *Bleak House* the world in which the fictive perception was located was pictured in the shadowy world of the fog. *Our Mutual Friend* takes us to the place where fog and marsh meet. It is the place the marshy imagination feared, running out beyond its limits to the sea (3); and the place we discovered in the depth of Esther's foggy intelligence, its 'overcast and secret' heart which her narrators could not penetrate (4). And this place, of course, is the river.

From *The Old Curiosity Shop* and Master Humphrey's vision the river characterised narrative as "the stream of life that will not stop" (5), and at the same time held out an opportunity to fiction, as we see in *Bleak House* and in Master Humphrey's own observation that "drowning was not a hard death" (6). Unlike fog or marsh, the river offers a dualistic landscape, into which we can sink and rest, or with which we can run away and never be still. The river establishes an imagery between fiction and narrative, a current, like the writing, in which we alternately drown and progress. The river can be at once a fragmentary drowning world, and the progressive 'stream of life that will not stop'. No single sense of things will be adequate to a novel whose structure adopts the river as its imagery, and no universal role will allow us to sink or to swim in a landscape that exists in the middle of the novel's terms. In this landscape we see a place where life and death, coherence and fragmentation, chaos and order, fiction and narrative are not singly served (as they were in opposite ways by fog and marsh) but in which they meet, and in which they remain separate, but nevertheless do so in the course of encounter.

We see this in-between world extended not only into the novel's imagery and structure, but into its characterisation and humour as well. The river has aspects of both narrative structure and fictive imagination, and can be both a written image and a means of perception. The first chapter of the novel gives us two figures that enter these opposite worlds in Gaffer Hexam and in Lizzie. To Lizzie I will return; I want first of all to discuss Hexam and the novel's world of narrative.

Gaffer Hexam represents this world in its crudest and most imperceptive, and unselfconscious form; for he makes a living of drowning.

Hexam's ignorance is in this novel the worst of all ignorances, for he seeks to live upon one side of its reality, and to do so by pulling drowned men from the other. The work he does is almost profane, the crudest of all kinds of realism, heaving corpses bodily from the drowning world back into his own sordid business. He lives upon the surface of the river; but even at the beginning of the novel we see the mark of the river upon him:

> Allied to the bottom of the river rather than the surface, by reason of the slime and ooze with which it was covered, and its sodden state, this boat and the two figures in it obviously were doing something that they often did... Half savage as the man showed ... with such dress as he wore seeming to be made out of the mud that begrimed the boat, still there was business-like usage in his steady gaze. (7)

For Hexam, life is a living, a 'business-like usage'; and we see here that it is already a dead thing. He lives upon the thing that engulfs him with no knowledge of its nature, so that his 'business' meets death without knowing it as such in river and corpse alike. This ignorance, as an assertion that life is separate from the death that feeds it, is the ignorance of death - both unknowing and itself deathly. He is already half-absorbed by this death, which is the life that he denies, in a 'savagery' which expresses the brutality of the assumption that the only river with which he must deal is the narrow river - the narrative - of his own living. He says to his daughter when he accuses her of hating the river, "As if it wasn't your living! As if it wasn't meat and drink to you!" (8) To Hexam, the only river is his own. He looks at the river; but he fails to see into it. We are told at the end of this chapter,

> What he had in tow, lunged itself at him sometimes in an awful manner when the boat was checked, and sometimes seemed to try to wrench itself away, though for the most part it followed submissively. A neophyte might have fancied that the ripples passing over it were dreadfully like faint changes of expression on a sightless face; but Gaffer was no neophyte and had no fancies. (9)

If Hexam looked under the surface of the river he would see himself covered in 'slime' and 'ooze', and 'sodden', within it, as the novel sees the river in him; but he has not the imaginative power to pass beyond the narrative that is both his gain and his loss. His living makes a desert, a dust heap, of the river, a waste-land of mud and slime - and makes a small version of that desert in himself, and in his boat. 'Business' denies the life-in-death, the imaginative life that lies through the surface of the river; and at the same time it makes a truly dead thing of itself.

This dust heap of dead things does not simply belong to Hexam but is the imagery, the part of the river, that the novel uses for narratives, for the knowing world of ends and purposes. Dust, dirt and slime become the images of the dead world that pursues only itself, and this world extends beyond the course of the river into the city's world of business and usage. As with Hexam, the river exists at its centre, both metaphorically, as the writing's knowledge that dust and slime belong to the dead and drowned, and literally, for the city meets the river as the heart of its usage and trade. The dust, and the dust heaps, do not liberate narrative into a world of image and theme, but bring us back to the river which makes and drowns them.

The first point in the book at which we are shown a landscape away from the river takes us into the wasteland that the city has made of itself; as we follow Mr Wilfer home from the office we are taken across a desert-land:

> His home was in the Holloway region north of London, and then divided from it by fields and trees. Between Battle Bridge and that part of the Holloway district in which he dwelt, was a tract of suburban Sahara, where tile and bricks were burnt, bones were boiled, carpets were beat, rubbish was shot, dogs were fought, and dust was heaped by contractors. Skirting the border of this desert, by the way he took, when the light of its kiln-fires made lurid smears on the fog, R. Wilfer sighed and shook his head. (10)

This desert exists, not in the city itself, but in the space just beyond it; the space that we are told is occupied nominally by 'fields and trees'. Like the Gaffer's living, which looks into the river to see only that living in it, the city sees only its own business in the space around it, failing to see *into* the countryside, and to see something different from itself. That failure creates a dead landscape, a landscape of usage which fails to see the spaces between one world and another (this 'green belt' is another river) and instead sees only its own nature. In the process the landscape is wasted; but the reverse also happens - again, as with the Gaffer - and the city itself is revealed as a dead land, in its refusal to recognise anything but its own living.

Within the city itself, we see the landscape business makes of its own territory, as the place where this deadness is manufactured:

> It was not summer yet, but spring; and it was not gentle spring ethereally mild, as in Thompson's Seasons, but nipping spring with an easterly wind, as in Johnson's, Jackson's, Dickson's, Smith's and Jones's Seasons. The grating wind sawed rather than blew; and as it sawed, the sawdust whirled about the sawpit. Every street was a sawpit, and there were no top-sawyers; every passenger was an under-sawyer, with the sawdust blinding him and choking him. (11)

London is like a great factory, a sawmill, in which the wind is its machinery; and humanity its workmen. Spring brings only the working of the mill, as any other season will; the fact that it is spring only enforces the cruelty of a world that ignores what is natural. "April is the cruellest month" (12): as in Eliot's poem, the London spring brings not hope but betrayal:

> The wind sawed, and the sawdust whirled. The shrubs wrung their many hands, bemoaning that they had been over-persuaded by the sun to bud; the young leaves pined; the sparrows repented of their early marriages, like men and women; the colours of the rainbow were discernible, not in floral spring, but in the faces of the people whom it nibbled and pinched. And ever the wind sawed, and the sawdust whirled. (13)

The betrayal, moreover, is registered by the natural world before it is registered in human beings. It is the shrubs and the birds that do not belong to the factory; 'men and women' are the inmates of the mill, and have always repented of early marriages. It is this relegation of humanity from its good nature, from its natural sphere, that is so telling in this short passage. The faces of the people are not the faces of the 'floral spring' of nature but the factory faces of usage, and the 'rainbow' of colours becomes in those faces an awful spectre of the hope that God promised. The city offers the hope of machinery, the hope of business, and does not comfort but 'nibbles' and 'pinches'.

This factory world has a profound effect upon the book; it produces figures like Hexam and Riderhood, the nameless Inspector whose function it is to know the nameless places it contains and produces, the world of Podsnaps and Veneerings, and figures such as the usurer, Fledgeby, and the deceiver, Lammle. But this landscape does not dominate the novel as it dominated the worlds of Esther and Pip, in its covering of fog and in its human wasteland of marsh. What we are shown in these landscapes, as in Hexam's use of the river, is narrative's image for the world; and this hopeless humanity is not the whole of human life, but a life reflected in its 'living', a life with no knowledge of what, even here, at the very centre of the world of usage, lies upon the other side of itself. Even in this sawmill of existence the shrubs and the birds show us a way out of narrative ends into the imaginative world where feelings exist. The novel, even as it describes the factory, half-lives in another world, and, unable to attribute the feelings that are the imaginative world of the writing and the river to human life, gives them instead to the non-human things that become a way out of the world of business.

The world of usage comes to defeat itself, and, again, does so very much as Hexam does. He finds himself absorbed by the death of oblivion he has made of his own life; vitality is self-absorbed by living. Hexam dies as he has lived, by belonging to the surface of the river. At no time is he truly alive, and death makes little difference to his imaginative existence. At the end of the novel the 'winds' taunt him,

Why not speak, Father? Soaking into this filthy ground as you lie here, is your own shape. Did you never see such a shape soaked into your own boat? Speak, Father. Speak to us, the winds, the only listeners left to you! (14)

It is as if the earth absorbs Hexam, sucking him back into itself; and shows us where he has always belonged, to the waste-landscape of the business world. In this world of usage, death is no release, no freedom, but the working of a great machine that recycles corpses as Hexam himself recycled them for his living. The very earth becomes predatory upon human life, which is there only for the usage of the slime and the ooze, the rubbish that living makes upon the landscape.

The novel itself, however, has nothing to do with this inhuman cycle. Instead, it takes the part of the winds; and these are not the winds of the sawmill. They are the winds of a river which does not belong entirely to narrative, the voice of the place in which Hexam has drowned. They speak as the river speaks, taking the part of the writing; they offer what river and writing have offered, to speak and to listen, to be the mirror in which Hexam might see and converse with himself - although now they can only taunt with what might have been. They tell us now, what we saw in Hexam's own life, that his death has been the failure to sink and swim together, to control and to be controlled, to speak and to listen, to read and to write. His failure and his death are his nullification, for in his supposed control of his own destiny there is the control only of usage; so that we see narrative as 'living'; as a self-contained cycle where nothing can survive, and where nothing is but what is not.

What we rediscover here constituted a grave threat to Dickens' earlier writing, where narrative dominated the figure of the writer, even where it did not dominate writing itself. Pip's story evaded precisely this self-limitation for the novel by personifying narrative in a way we hardly see in Hexam or in the dust, in both of which Pip's narrative seems to be returned to a direct realism. But in this novel the writer has realised that the writing can find and indeed already is its own voice, as it was in both *Bleak House* and *Great Expectations*, in spite of the presence of author personae. At Hexam's death, this writing finds its voice in the wind: and, far from seeing the narratives of the city through the fog of injustice or as a part of the marshland of commonness, the wasteland which is revealed in it has a kind of self-contained clarity from which the writing is fully dissociated. No justice, no protection or distinction, is expected from the factory of life the city has produced; the writing has discovered itself as the true judgement both of its own function and of the life it seeks to represent.

This is a new confidence; but it is also the reawakening of some of the old confidences of Dickens' writing. Following Bradley Headstone and Charley Hexam to the place where his sister Lizzie lives, we are told that they

> got to the Surrey side of Westminster Bridge, and crossed the bridge, and made along the Middlesex shore towards Millbank. In this region are a certain little street called Church Street, and a certain little blind square called Smith Square, in the centre of which last retreat is a very hideous church with four towers at the four corners, generally resembling some petrified monster, frightful and gigantic, on its back with its legs in the air. They found a tree near by in the corner, and a blacksmith's forge, and a timber yard, and a dealer's in old iron. What a rusty portion of a boiler and a great iron wheel or so meant by lying half-buried in the dealer's fore-court, nobody seemed to know or to want to know. Like the Miller of questionable jollity in the song, They cared for Nobody, no not they, and Nobody cared for them. (15)

The writing seems restored to its old topographical confidence, bringing back Dickens' local knowledge of his city which was smothered by fog and marsh alike, and by the need to present himself. Like the early writing this passage collects objects rather than symbolises them - as we have seen narrative trying to do in Pip - rejecting the business vision of things, the vision of 'living', by refusing to *make* meaning of the world. We even see the shadow of the old ghost amongst the clutter, the blacksmith's forge which became the transposition of the blacking factory. Here, then, the writing again stands for the writer's vagrant voice - a voice like the river-wind - restoring it to its former Swivelleresque inclusiveness and dismissing the chaotic variety of the London scenery with a snatch from the music hall.

The difference in this late writing, however, is that the writing itself has become the Swiveller. It neither accepts nor rejects chaos, but puts it in its place with a scrap of folk-wisdom, "They cared for Nobody, no not they, and Nobody cared for them", which it is the writing's achievement to make sound like common knowledge. It does so by existing, like the river, between the narrative of the dusty world and the imagination of fiction, and by doing so takes its true place as a common act.

As such, this novel exists curiously between the characters that live among its pages, adopting no single mouthpiece for its thoughts and feelings. Dickens releases his writing, as it were, from himself. We have already seen the novel adopt the voice of the wind and of the music-hall; any speech which seems propitious can become the words of the book, and the act of writing becomes an in-between activity. It fastens upon that speech which, like the wind and the music-hall song, seems itself to exist in the in-between world, somewhere between the world of business and the world of imagination - of narrative and fiction.

Returning now to Lizzie, we find that the novel adopts its Swivelleresque stance in relation to her as much as to her father. She is the opposite of him, and it is immediately clear that it is her gift to see into things; she sees beneath the surface of the image to which her life is offered, and her response of horror (we see her watching the river like her father, but "in the intensity of her look there was a touch of horror" (16)) is the response of the fictive imagination to the business of narratives. Gaffer Hexam allows himself to be absorbed by the river; and it is this absorption that Lizzie fears, for her horror is of his lack of respect for and understanding of the separate energies of another world. Her own vision, her ability to see into the nature of things, can, however, when it is exercised upon her own account produce, not fear or horror, but a special kind of insight, which we see at work a few chapters later when she sees 'pictures' in the fire, telling her brother Charley his past and future. Lizzie shows us that she is able to recognise the transformation of things from death to life, and to see a special, imaginative power on the other side of the point at which the two worlds meet. Her pictures come in the 'glow' of the embers; when Charley goes to stir the fire she tells him,

Don't disturb it, Charley, or it'll all be in a blaze. It's that dull glow near it, coming and going, that I mean. (17)

The coals of the fire are both the root of 'business', the ground of England's prosperity, and the substance of the domestic hearth. Lizzie's life, the world of her imagination, is on the domestic side of the life in between that the fire re-

171

presents when it burns with this dull glow; it is the imagination of home-life that Pip rejected when he sought, not unlike Hexam, to make the narrative his 'living', and his own business. The fire comes to echo the river as a point at which business and imagination meet, and the writing finds itself with Lizzie, telling stories of past and present that are quite unliteral, but literary nevertheless. As Charley tells his sister, "Your library of books is the hollow down by the fire, I think" (18).

Lizzie exists, in the first place at least, in the fictive world of the novel, on the imaginative side of fire and river. Her vision is at the same time the passive and subjected vision of fiction which sees into the life of the world she lives in, and not the knowing and controlling vision of narrative. Her knowledge of the future is not 'written' but real, limited by the temporality of her own imagination. She is not like Esther or Pip, an authorial persona foreseeing the story, or knowing as fact; her knowledge and foresight are not written and secure, but they have nevertheless a fictive reality of their own, in the spirit of the truth.

This reality becomes another of the novel's rediscoveries, for, where Esther preserved suffering by personifying it and making a protective impulse of it, Lizzie returns us to the world before personae, to the vulnerability of passive life, and to Nancy. Her relationship to Charley and to her father has at its centre the same imaginative but passive wish to make life better that we saw in Nancy in her relation to Oliver and to Sikes. We see this relation, and the way it can exploit her, when she foretells the future to her brother. She tells Charley that the secret of his education will come to have "divided you from father, and from me", and continues,

> It is a great work to have cut you away from father's life, and to have made a new and good beginning. So there I am, Charley, left alone with father, keeping him as straight as I can, watching for more influence than I have, and hoping that through some fortunate chance, or when he is ill, or when - I don't know what - I may turn him to wish to do better things. (19)

What Lizzie does not see is as important as what she does see. Her imagination sees through the fire, as it sees through the river. She sees a better life for her father in the river that his business and living rejects, in the drowning of his activity; and she knows that such a change can come only in immersion, in illness, or even in what Charley has already forbidden her to mention when she tells him a few pages later, that if she would make her father

> believe that learning was a good thing, and that we might lead better lives, I should be amost content to die. (20)

("Don't talk stuff about dying, Liz" (21), is Charley's immediate response.) Death, Lizzie knows, is the only way her father will ever reach the imaginative world between the living and the dead.

What Lizzie does not know here, however, is that it is the only way that Charley will ever get there. It is made plain enough to us when he shows us that learning can be another kind of business, undertaken without imagination. Lizzie's perception in the fire is blind to this worldliness, and is very much a domestic life, for the hearth is at the heart of the home. Lizzie has her fictive imagination in the context of her Victorian woman's place, and as such is very much like Nancy, real and speaking because of her vulnerability; for she is just as likely to be drowned in the course of the narrative, at this stage, as Nancy was. The difference in Lizzie from the earlier novel, and the reason why she no longer needs the intentional passivity that in Esther was a protection for the fictive, is that her words are no longer personified as a way of speech for the writer. Lizzie's vulnerable and fictive, drowning imagination opposes the river's dead images which dominate the book's narratives, and brings life to a dead world in comforting her father and her brother. What the novel knows, however, is that she will do nothing for them; and just as it has no investment in narrative, so it has no direct investment in Lizzie's fictive imagination. What Lizzie must learn is much the same as what her father and brother must learn (although neither of course do so); the passage between the narrative world and another, in which the novel finds its true nature and intelligence. Rogue Riderhood shows us the only way in which Hexam might have achieved such a passage as the point at which he is literally half-drowned, and hangs between life and death. Of the 'rough fellows' that stand around him while he fights for his life, we are told, "Neither Riderhood in this world, nor Riderhood in the other, could draw tears from them; but a striving human soul between the two can do it easily"(22).

It is this Swivelleresque state between two worlds that the writing finds to be common ground; and we see it here in the river, in the wind and in the fire in which Lizzie has her fictive existence.

This life in-between then rediscovers the fictive world of Nancy just as it rediscovers the harsh narrative that threatens her in Sikes; and this rediscovery goes further, for in Lizzie's friend and ally, Jenny Wren, we find ourselves returned to the wholly fictive world of *The Old Curiosity Shop*, for Jenny is curiously both Nell and Quilp together. Like Nell, she is neither adult nor child; while of "very tender years indeed" (23) she has in her drunkard father the "troublesome bad child" (24) that Nell had in her grandfather. At the same time, she is her own contrary. As we are told in the second chapter of Book Two, she has, 'happily for her', a dream of being courted and married by 'Him'; having dealt with her drunken father she

becomes preoccupied, as she tells Lizzie, by "what I would do
to Him, if he should turn out to be a drunkard" (25), and
continues, when Lizzie objects, "Oh, but he won't",

> I shall try to take care of it beforehand, but he might
> deceive me. Oh, my dear, all of these fellows with their
> tricks and manners do deceive! ... And if so, I tell you
> what I think I'd do. When he was asleep, I'd make a spoon
> red hot, and I'd have some boiling liquor in a saucepan,
> and I'd take it out hissing, and I'd open his mouth with
> the other hand - or perhaps he'd sleep with his mouth
> already open - and I'd pour it down his throat, and blister
> it, and choke him. (26)

Here, Nell suddenly seems to be taken over by Quilp's
imagination, as if the novel now acknowledges their existence
in the same fantasy world. For, once again, it now has no
investment in the world of fiction, and no interest in distinguishing the fictions of good and evil. Nell and Quilp seem
objectified, and where in the earlier novel narrative wanted to
make a waxwork doll of Nell, it now half succeeds in Jenny
Wren, who has a bad back and queer legs, and is a dwarf and
a doll's dressmaker.

What does interest the novel, however, is the revisiting
of her world, and the knowledge of its difference from narrative. The writing is now the Swiveller, and what it delights
in is Jenny's encounter with narrative, when narrative finds
her merely incomprehensible. We see this incomprehension at
its most forcible when she meets Fledgeby - perhaps the most
extreme of all the novel's encounters. Fledgeby represents the
world of the business and usage of narrative at its most brutal,
and at what might in an earlier novel have been its most dangerous, for his is not the brutality of mere stupidity. Like
Hexam, he is the product of the factory world and we are told,
"His youthful fire was all composed of sparks from the
grindstone" (27); but, unlike Hexam, he presents us with the
intelligence and consciousness that the factory can produce.
He is a later form of the previously highly problematic figure
of Uriah Heep, and his knowledge is the knowledge of bad
stories that has always threatened the good story of the novel.
As we see in the encounter with Lammle in Chapter 5, book 2,
he presents us with a form of self-consciousness that belongs
to the literal imagination of narrative, and opposes the authority
of the river writer;

> "What did you think of Georgiana?" asked Mr Lammle.
> "Why, I'll tell you," said Fledgeby, very deliberately.
> "Do, my boy."
> "You misunderstand me," said Fledgeby. "I don't
> mean I'll tell you that. I mean I'll tell you something else."
> "Tell me anything old fellow!"

"Ah, but you misunderstand me again," said Fledgeby. "I mean I'll tell you nothing." (28)

Fledgeby lets Lammle know "something" here, but in doing so conveys that his meaning is "something else": he says what he wants to say by saying nothing. His speech is there for show; he displays it as a trader would display goods, waiting for Lammle to pay. To Fledgeby, speech is merely a part of the business world that exists for show, and as such he understands the way that it functions very well; he tells us as much when he says to Lammle, of the dinner at the Podsnaps' the evening before,

> I am not calculated to show to advantage under that sort of circumstances. I know very well you two did show to advantage, and managed capitally. But don't you on that account come talking to me as if I was your doll and your puppet, because I am not. (29)

These words usurp social speech, as they usurp the social function of the dinner party, contaminating its language. To Fledgeby, 'show' is not merely the external appearance of things, but the whole business. The display absorbs the whole of his energy, as it absorbs the whole of Lammle's: it is 'calculated' and 'managed'; and its rewards are 'advantage' and 'capital'. The whole show is under the control, not of Fledgeby or of Lammle, but of these words. Although these two are less crudely ignorant than Hexam, they are defeated by the same trap, for they are themselves controlled by the language they use to control others, just as Hexam is by his own world of usage.

We see the new freedom of this novel at work when this corrupted factory and city speech is encountered by the fictive world it cannot see in itself. When Fledgeby disturbs Jenny Wren in the rooftops garden over the Jew, Riah's shop, Jenny tells him: "We are thankful to come here for rest, sir", explaining, "It's the quiet and the air":

> "The quiet!" repeated Fledgeby, with a contemptuous turn of the head towards the City's roar. "And the air!" with a "Poof!" at the smoke.
> "Ah!" said Jenny. "But it's so high. And you see the clouds rushing in above the narrow streets, not minding them, and you see the golden arrows pointing at the mountains in the sky from which the wind comes, and you feel as if you were dead."
> ..."How do you feel when you are dead?" asked Fledgeby, much perplexed.
> "Oh, so tranquil!" cried the little creature, smiling. "Oh, so peaceful and so thoughtful! And you hear the people who are alive, crying and working, and calling to

one another down in the close streets, and you seem to
pity them so! And such a chain has fallen from you, and
such a strange good sorrowful happiness comes upon you!"
(30)

This encounter is something of a tour-de-force; fiction and
narrative meet, while the novel, in between, registers their
difference. Neither are seen to be directly involved in the
novel's action, for, taking place upon the rooftops, their encounter is almost physically removed from the novel. The
writing reclaims for itself both the imagination that Jenny represents, which previously died out of the course of the novel,
of an unprotected fantasy world, and at the same time the language that Fledgeby corrupts. The writing embraces both Nell
and Quilp and the world of Sikes; and here the impossible
happens, and they are brought momentarily together, and shown
to be mutually exclusive. Fledgeby cannot enter Jenny's world
of drowning imagination, while she cannot participate in the
business of the city. The rooftop garden becomes another in-
between place, where two worlds meet and exchange.

The exchange here, of course, is marginal, and the meeting of these two extremes little more than a demonstration of
the writing's new confidence in its own middle place. Not all
of the meetings it brings about, however, are so cursory and
ultimately insignificant. We have seen the world of narrative
in the novel only at its crudest, and its world of fiction at its
extreme. Although the world of Hexam, Riderhood, Fledgeby,
the world of dust and dirt, is incapable of meeting the world
of imagination in any meaningful way, just as Jenny's fictive
world, limited by its necessary precariousness and disability
cannot meet the world of business, elsewhere the novel finds
its figures more capable of using the space it provides for the
meeting of narrative and fiction, of authority and imagination,
and these encounters become its chief concern.

We saw that Lizzie, in reproducing Nancy's subjected female and working-class imagination, occupied the fictive world,
and that where *Oliver Twist* was concerned only with what could
be done to her, and protection seemed to be the responsibility
of the novel, *Our Mutual Friend* is very much concerned with
what she can do for herself, with the way that she can interact
with the narratives the world offers, and in which narrative
can in turn interact with her. Again, the writing offers itself
as a middle ground, and, while it is one Jenny Wren cannot use,
Lizzie is not incapable of meeting the narratives of the world
in it.

The ground of this meeting is the ground of Jenny's fantasies, the encounter with 'Him', the romantic story which as
Jenny tells us provides a man as either the god or devil of a
future existence. While the angelic and demonic seem to belong
to her nature, 'His' remains the all important identity of the
narrative she will herself never meet, and an important part of

THE ART OF THE POSSIBLE

the novel now centres upon what 'He' might in reality be like,
and upon the kinds of narrative that might be capable of meeting
Lizzie's fiction.

We have already seen that her father's world of 'usage' is
not capable of doing so; and that her brother's aspirant intelligence similarly rejects imagination. Two very different figures
engaged in the active world of the novel - in its narrative
business - seem willing to approach her world, however. The
first of these is closely related to Charley in being his
schoolmaster, Bradley Headstone.

Bradley Headstone is very clearly and openly the narrator
of his world; a man who finds the world to be the way that
David Copperfield feared it would be at its beginning, but finds
himself grown up in that world. Where David tests the language
narrative offers, Headstone invests himself in it, exchanging
the flexibility of a childhood self-consciousness for the inflexi-
bility of an adult vision. Pip shows us the defeat of the writer;
and Headstone shows us how the writing ego proceeds after
defeat, approaching Lizzie in the self-justification, the proof,
of its control over reality. Headstone refuses to recognise the
difference of her world from his own; so far as he is concerned,
she is merely inferior by education, his own self-improvement.
While his narrative is not dogmatically hostile to feeling or imagination, and desperately wants Lizzie's feeling to assent to
his own, the awful mistake that Headstone makes is the refusal
to distinguish between feeling and speech; and the mistake is
the more dreadful for the fact that it is made simply by believing
too much in the reality of things. He stands for and embodies
the values of Victorian middle-class society; for progress, for
education, for self-improvement and for self-enlightenment.
Those things are to him what his feelings are; they are his
passion, his life, and his love, so completely does he absorb
what seems to him to be the order of things within his own
nature. What he says is what he means; so that he refuses to
distinguish between his own meaning and the meaning of the
world, assuming that the difference between what he was and
what he is - which is to him a great virtue and good - is a
communicable and so common good. He effectively believes in
and practises his own individual language as a common language,
and asserts that language in his dealings and conflicts with
others. He tells Eugene Wrayburn,

You reproach me with my origin... you cast insinuations
at my bringing-up. But I tell you, sir, I have worked
my way onward, out of both and in spite of both, and I
have a right to be considered a better man than you, with
better reasons for being proud. (31)

That 'better' is at the root of Headstone's language, and
in it his speech, feeling and belief are united. But he finds

177

that unity of self destroyed even in the process of its expression:

> "Oh, what a misfortune is mine," cried Bradley, breaking off to wipe the perspiration from his face as he shook from head to foot, "that I cannot so control myself as to appear a stronger creature than this, when a man who has not felt in all his life what I have felt in a day can so command himself!" He said it in a very agony, and even followed it with an errant motion of his hands as if he could have torn himself. (32)

Progress has only made of Headstone a kind of sophisticated Hexam, and has failed to lead him from the savagery which is at the heart of the world of usage. He finds himself caught in an identical trap to the one that absorbs Hexam: social progression is his river, and he makes his 'living' out of it. Just like Hexam, he is incapable of seeing a world beneath its surface. Where Hexam's failure is a failure of ignorance to enter the world of imagination, however, Headstone's failure is the failure of knowledge and consciousness: and where Hexam's savagery is that of an animal, Headstone's is the failure of a human being, the failure of power and control. Where Hexam is used by use, Headstone is compelled by his own compulsion, finding that those things that seem to offer social control and a way of dealing with the human world - his feelings and passions - somehow dehumanise and make a monster of him. He finds himself dissociated and devalued by what he sees as and fully believes to be his associative powers and genuine, proper and common values. He calls himself a 'creature' while seeing Eugene as a 'man', and stands, a mere animal even in his own eyes, sweating and violently restless, as a result of what he knows to be his very self-control, internalising what he believes to be external and common values even as he places his faith in them.

Moreover, there is nothing that he can himself do about his predicament, for his faith is his living, and it is his constant surprise and frustration, but never his expectation, that it is not everybody else's. Headstone's consciousness seeks the unity of the literary and the literary in the way that Pip's would have done had it not been sensitised by constant defeat, and is incapable of knowing that feeling must often remain silent, and unspoken. Pip represents Dickens' relinquishment of unity, while Headstone shows us what its full assertion must mean for the individual.

Headstone only discovers meaning in the assertion of that unity for himself, remaining convinced of his 'better' way of living, and unable to see the other side of himself. As he tells Lizzie,

It seems egotistical to begin by saying so much about myself ... but whatever I say to you seems, even in my own
ears, below what I want to say, and different from what
I want to say. I can't help it. So it is. You are the ruin
of me. (33)

These words, of course, are an appeal; and what they seek
- or rather demand - is that Lizzie should step through the
looking-glass of the words that reflect Headstone's self-esteem,
his "confidence", "resources" and "government" of himself as
he says, as merely "egotistical" and "below what I want to say"
(34), and assent to them as common values. He wants Lizzie
to join him, to save him from joining her: an outcome which goes
to the root of his fears, since Lizzie is herself a part of precisely that humble origin he evades in himself. The egotism of
this is very nearly sublime, the attempt at honesty becoming
an assertion of control, not over an abstract reality, but over
Lizzie herself. His language must be common language, or it
is nothing; it may seem 'low', but it will be heightened by
assent.

It is a compulsion which Lizzie must and does refuse; and
her refusal leaves Headstone with the true nature of his words,
as self-compulsion. Because of his belief that the words he
speaks must come from somewhere other than himself - and so
are a language - he finds himself controlled through them by a
power which is that of his own ego:

I must try to give expression to what is in my mind: it
shall and must be spoken (35)

he tells Lizzie. 'It', he feels, is tangibly there, a reality outside himself, when it is really only him. His torture is that
while its 'must' compels him, it has no power whatever over
Lizzie, or over anybody else; and his "I can't help it" is not
the register of an unearthly power, but of his own impotence.

Bradley Headstone then shows himself capable of approaching Lizzie only as a reassurance for his own world, and
as an assertion of his own narrative control. He demands in
doing so that the fictive shall be controlled by narrative,
showing himself to belong to the world of usage and offering
Lizzie no middle ground in which her fictive existence can en-
gage. His approach to her is a demand that she relinquish her
own nature in his.

The other approach to Lizzie's world of fiction seems at
first to be more promising. Eugene Wrayburn becomes
Headstone's great enemy and adversary, and seems to take an
opposite way, for where the latter assumes that his language
is a common one, Wrayburn makes the contrary assumption that
no language is a common one. Eugene sees in silence the kind
of potency that Headstone wanted so desperately for his speech,
and where Headstone stands for the impotence of the open mo-

rality of narrative, insisting as Pip found he could not upon himself as its centre and source, Eugene opposes such narrative. "It's not easy for me to talk to you," Lizzie tells him, "for you see all the consequences of what I say, as soon as I say it" (36). This power of interpretation is not undertaken by appealing to the social significance of individual responsibility, which Headstone finds to be mere egotism, but by Eugene's refusal to acknowledge any responsibility at all, his assent to whatever seems to happen without interference. Eugene sees all experience in little pieces; but his vision is not, like David Copperfield's, a sign of his innocence but of his disbelief in the unity of life. This, Lizzie finds, makes him impossible to talk to, for he does not, like Bradley, see only one end, but all ends: he *expects* reality to disappoint, and in a curious way makes narratives of incoherence. His power, and his perception which give his grasp upon the reality, are born of a faith in faithlessness, in the incoherence of the world, and in the devaluation of his stories, amid which he nurtures his own, secret narrative, born out of narrative's failures. This secret he guards fiercely. When Mortimer Lightwood challenges him, early in the book, with 'withholding something' and asks him whether it is true, Eugene replies,

> Upon my soul, I don't know. I know less about myself than about most other people in the world, and I don't know. (37)

Eugene knows about other narratives what he won't know about himself - that they fail. He refuses to see any such failure in the secret of himself, unlike Headstone, who constantly confronts the brick wall of his own story. As Eugene later says, when the object of his distraction has been settled as Lizzie,

> I don't design anything. I have no design whatever. I am incapable of designs. If I conceived a design, I should speedily abandon it, exhausted by the operation. (38)

This silence is against the feelings that 'designs' admit; in so being it produces a problem, for while what it fears on the one hand is Headstone's failure, it fears on the other the feelings themselves, wanting a secret story without their exposure. In this second instance, Wrayburn is against the best intentions of narrative, to be responsible and open, as Headstone is not; and is not unlike Fledgeby in his refusal to put anything into words. Eugene moves towards a 'wrong' narrative, the narrative of exploitation and cruelty, and of a threat which offers real danger to Lizzie, where Headstone's story was at least 'right' in expressing its direction and needs. When Lightwood, speaking for the schoolmaster morality, tells

THE ART OF THE POSSIBLE

him to "Look on to the end", which is the duty of narrative, it is to the responsibility of so doing that Eugene objects:

> Ah! See now! That's exactly what I am incapable of do-ing... When we were at school together, I got up my les-sons at the last moment, day by day and bit by bit; now we are out in life together, I get up my lessons in the same way. In the present task I have not got beyond this: - I am bent on finding Lizzie, and I mean to find her... I ask you - for information - what does that mean? When I have found her I may ask you - also for information - what do I mean now? But it would be premature at this stage, and it's not the character of my mind. (39)

Eugene here sets open narrative upon the side of the schoolmaster, and sets himself against the plot that 'gets up its lessons' in advance. He refuses the language which is narrative and moral responsibility, for he sees no opportunity within it - whether that opportunity is to include or to reject the world of feeling. Narrative sits around the Podsnaps' dinner table - in the Podsnaps, in the Veneerings (and aspirantly in Headstone) - and when Eugene finds himself there, he declines to participate.

Condemnation of Eugene is rendered difficult in this social context, for it is clear that his reticence is self-protective from the devaluation of feeling that speech becomes in the world of Podsnappery. At the same time, however, reticence is the privilege of his position at the table, and his silence in the passage quoted above does not relinquish the control that moves him consistently towards a position which will be the direct exploitation of the relative positions of himself and Lizzie, and so produce another direct exploitation of fiction by narrative. The novel becomes curiously divided in its attitude towards him, for while reticence copes properly with the false values and false narratives of 'society', its reserve also refuses to protect the feeling of fiction by denying its own secret ends. The following is typical of the novel's external observation of the character:

> So much of what was fantastically true to his own know-ledge of this utterly careless Eugene, mingled with the answer, that Mortimer could not receive it as a mere eva-sion. (40)

Here, the novel equivocates between condemnation and qualified approval, for it is impossible to know what lies within Eugene's silence. Headstone betrays his nature, and condemns himself; but while we cannot see this self-betrayal in Eugene, we cannot believe in his authority as a constructive social value either.

Neither Headstone nor Wrayburn then seems to offer to approach the world of fiction and to relinquish narrative in the hope of finding an in-between life; and in neither does Lizzie as yet find the opportunity she needs to act in her own, different way, by meeting them there. Her only response to these approaches, which seem to belong securely to the self-defeating world of narrative she has seen in her father and is growing to understand in Charley, can be to reject them.

To these three figures I will return; but first of all it is necessary to pay closer attention to what we have called 'narrative' and 'fiction' in this novel, for in having no commitment to either the writing shows the 'real' nature of each. Headstone, Wrayburn, Jenny and Lizzie all have as their inner ideal the meeting of fictive and narrative, and the finding of the in-between world where authority and vulnerability are brought together; but what we now begin to realise is that such an encounter is horribly difficult to achieve. Jenny shows us that fantasy is born out of the necessity of an isolation that the writing now knows it can do nothing for, as is Lizzie's emotional imagination; and at the same time, nothing can be done to relieve the male identities of Headstone and Wrayburn of the isolation of their respective narratives, for narrative, too, lies oddly beyond the common grasp and language of writing. All the writing can do here is to wait upon coincidence.

It is this dependence upon the chances of life in between that creates the structure of the book, and which dictates the odd contrast of its other part. This contrast has frequently been criticised as error. Kincaid, for example, notes, "I think that the reader is forced to pay for the increasingly moving Wrayburn-Hexam plot with the increasingly silly Wilfer-Harmon plot" (41) and quotes Taylor Stoehr's suggestion that "the novel is really one half of a great novel" (42).

But the 'Wrayburn-Hexam' relation is not really a 'plot' in the sense of its being narrative at all; as we have seen, the writing *refuses* to plot. The accompanying 'Wilfer-Harmon' story is not an artistic error, but shows us why the writing depends upon chance.

This second part of the book is the only place that we really find a narrative, where narrative produces a language; the story of 'the man from Somewhere' is the story of the whole novel, the plot that is on everybody's lips, and the common and only property of its public wisdom. Lightwood and Wrayburn, Hexam and Riderhood, the dinner table of the Podsnaps and Veneerings and the public at large all tell it; and in a world where other languages seem private and dissociative it is hardly surprising that the notoriety which provides common ground should take up so much of the novel's attention.

The nature of this story, moreover, and the way that it is treated, accord entirely with the writing's occupation of a middle ground. It is essentially the story of John Harmon, of course; his father, we learn, was the 'Golden Dustman', the man who made a fortune of the dust which, we saw, was the image the river gave to the world of business. It is entirely apt that the only common language the figures of the novel find is constructed by his Will. It is this, and the furore it creates, which fills an emptiness of common speech, and provides an order that the dusty world can embrace.

The Golden Dustman, then, becomes the novel's narrator; and the story he sets out is his son's, that he shall return from abroad, from exile from his father, to inherit the dust conditionally upon marrying Bella Wilfer. Should Harmon die, or refuse the marriage, the dust will pass to Mr Boffin, his foreman.

The novel itself asks no questions of this narrative; it places it as we see among the dust to which it consigns its other progressions, as a language which merely confirms the world's void of languages. John Harmon, however, takes up what in an earlier novel might have been the writer's part, to dissent from and question it. Since he enters upon his story missing, assumed drowned, he is granted anonymity which it appears can be used to test and control the narrative which is then to be his. He is not unlike Dickens as we saw him at the beginning of *David Copperfield* in holding back from the autobiography the world seems to offer in order to explore its possibilities and limitations; but unlike Dickens he is utterly committed to the story which *he* wants to narrate. His reticence is a competition with his father for control of a world which he sees as his story, where Dickens' reticence was to discover whether the world *could* be his story.

Where Headstone and Wrayburn represent two egotisms of narrative, Harmon represents a third, and perhaps the worst. For where, in the first two, identity is problematic and obstructs feeling, in Harmon it is almost a religion. He believes, as the others do not, not in the love which is at the heart of both Headstone's impotence and Wrayburn's silence, but in the *bringing about* of love, in the control which is narrative. His consciousness is dominated by narrative, so that his 'death' achieves, not a meeting with Jenny Wren's dead world of fiction, but the after-life Pip wanted so badly as the end of narrative: as he tells us,

> Dead, I have found the true friends of my lifetime still as true, as tender and as faithful as when I was alive, and making my memory an incentive to good actions done in my name. Dead, I have found them when they might have slighted my name, and passed greedily over my grave to ease and wealth, lingering by the way, like single-hearted children, to recall their love for me when I was a poor frightened child. Dead, I have heard from the woman who would have been my wife if I had lived, the revolting truth that I should have purchased her, caring nothing for me, as a Sultan buys a slave.
>
> What would I have? If the dead could know, or do know, how the living use them, who among the hosts of

dead has found a more disinterested fidelity on earth than
I? Is that not enough for me? If I had come back, these
noble creatures would have welcomed me, wept over me,
given up everything to me with joy. I did not come back,
and they have passed unspoiled into my place. Let them
rest in it, and let Bella rest in hers. (43)

That Harmon finds death so successful as a strategy is
due simply to the fact that he is *not* dead; unlike Pip, he evades
the fear of mismemory that real death offers to narrative. That
Harmon is not properly immersed in the river of things becomes
clear here. Unlike the novel's own voice he exists between the
two worlds of life and death in an artificial way, calling what
continues to be his life, his death; he is not even like Aunt
Betsey, living a 'second time around' existence, for his first
life is palpably not over. Memory, and the awareness of memory, belongs to the world of narratives, and to the world of
the living, and Harmon's concern for his place in the world as
a 'dead' man is still a concern for the world of the living. He
makes no passage between the two worlds, but finds himself -
insofar as he wishes to preserve his position as author of events
- living in a world he cannot enter, and this exclusion becomes
the price of a happy ending.
Harmon's 'death' is an image of what we saw at the beginning of this chapter was a division of 'writer' and 'writing',
and in him Dickens shows us what he discovered in *David
Copperfield*, that no strategy of separation is capable of
avoiding this division if what it seeks in the novel is a world
that the writer can comfortably occupy at its ending (absence
being the only proof of that world); separation only becomes
an affirmation of his commitment *to* the world. "If I had come
back"; these words present us with Harmon's dilemma, for while
in one sense he is still missing, in another he is already and
inextricably returned, and indeed was never absent. Harmon
shows us that the narrator cannot pass through the looking
glass into fiction, unifying experience, where writing represents
a personal interest, and a personal fate. The writing of
Harmon's story is not the river that exists between fiction and
narrative, but another version of the narrative that represents
the writer's absorption in himself. John Harmon's interest is
in this control of his own fate; but the outcome of that interest
is that, even 'dead', his imagination is controlled by interest
itself, and the writing that is his is appropriated by him.
The result that is produced is the appropriation of the
other figures in his story - for all his agonising over their
happiness without him - to his own. Mr Boffin seems to become
a part of the machinery of this tale, which by the end of the
novel appears to work perfectly: at the climax of this narrative,
where all is revealed to Bella, "By a master-stroke of arrangement, the inexhaustible baby here appeared at the door, sus-

pended in mid-air by invisible agency" (44). And Bella, too, is absorbed; when she assents to Harmon's proposal of marriage,

> Bella responded, "Yes, I *am* yours if you think me worth taking!" And after that, seemed to shrink to next to nothing in the clasp of his arms, partly because it was such a strong one on his part, and partly because there was such a yielding to it on hers. (45)

The narrative Harmon proposes thus comes true, and his control seems justified, having brought about one of those changes of heart of which narrative is so fond as the revelation of its underlying omniscience. That it does so depends heavily upon the other factors in it. The first of these is Bella herself, for Harmon does not really change her. From the beginning, his inheritance claims Bella for his narrative, and even in her change of heart, it is in that narrative world that she remains. We see this even in the way that the change in her consciousness occurs:

> "What he said was very sensible, I am sure, and very true, I am sure. It is only what I often say to myself. Don't I like it then? No, I don't like it, and though he is my liberal benefactor, I disparage him for it. Then pray," said Bella, sternly putting the question to herself in the looking-glass as usual, "what do you mean by this, you inconsistent little Beast?"
> The looking glass preserving a discreet ministerial silence when thus called upon for explanation, Bella went to bed... (46)

Here, as elsewhere, Bella seems curiously one-dimensional. She sees herself reflected in Mr Boffin as she sees herself reflected in her mirror, and once again these reflective media offer the values of writing as an intermediary, interpretative place. But Bella is never allowed to see through the looking glass; she only sees herself reflected in it. Her nature is entirely unlike Lizzie's for it exists in the narrative world of mere observation, without the fictive dimension of imagination. Because Bella has been claimed by narrative and by expectation, in having them forced upon her, she is unable to recognise writing, and the places in which writing exists, as an in-between world, a place of refuge - a fictive world - but instead finds stories, and her own story among them, as a place only for the exposure and commitment of narrative.

Bella's greed and her wilfulness are a kind of romantic expectation of the outside world that is at all times controlled by that world. John Harmon only redirects it into marriage, preserving narrative at all cost. What makes Bella so flat a figure in relation to Lizzie is the fact that her allegiance to narrative makes her at all times personal to John Harmon, and to his story. Her charm and her declarations are constantly controlled by the hidden fidelity she must have to the figure who has made her consciousness, both in its initial greed and in its subsequent self-realisation. Just as Harmon is a living dead man, so Bella is a widow whose husband is curiously present, hidden, as it were, in the surface of the mirror through which he will never allow her to pass, and through which he has never passed himself. What Harmon discovers in Bella is not the liberation of the other world that both Headstone and Wrayburn seek in Lizzie, but only what is after all his own narrative, the same story that he himself lives out, told by his father, and accepted by Bella.

The second, and most important, factor in Harmon's apparent success is represented by Mr Boffin and also by Mr Venus, for it is these figures who construct his narrative for him by pretending to be what they are not. This pretence - particularly in Mr Boffin - has often been criticised as an absurdly clumsy machinery for the narrative; but this is precisely the point, for, once again, the novel has no investment in what they do for narrative. It is they themselves that matter to the novel, for both are placed in the position that it recognises as its own, in the middle of things. They echo the judgement made by the writing by showing us how unconvincing the interference in narrative to produce a happy ending must be. In both Mr Venus and Mr Boffin fiction and narrative meet. Mr Venus is caught between the dustheap of his business and his unlikely love affair with Pleasant Riderhood, and we see the Swiveller at work in his eventual compromise; as he tells Wegg, Pleasant's objection to his business is overcome when he ask her,

> whether if, after marriage, I confined myself to the articulation of men, children, and the lower animals, it might not relieve the lady's mind of her feeling respecting being - as a lady - regarded in a bony light. (47)

Unlike Wegg, Mr Venus does not belong entirely to the dusty world, and his success here is to humanise his own business with a dignity that makes even the dust heaps respect human feeling. Mr Boffin's position, meanwhile, is not dissimilar. As the manager and then the owner of the dust he remains a half-fictive figure both in his home life (he concurs entirely when Mrs Boffin remarks, "Lor, how many matters *are* matters of feeling" (48) asserting, as Kincaid remarks, "the key comic doctrine, the primacy of feelings" (49)) and in his innocence. We see most forcibly in his dealings with Webb the vulnerability of his illiterate simplicity to Wegg's sharp narrative consciousness. At the same time, we see his narrative intellect overcome by his imagination: Mr Boffin, we are told at the end of Wegg's first reading,

186

soon laid down his unfinished pipe, and had ever since
sat intently staring with his eyes and mind at the enormi-
ties of the Romans (50)

and was "so severely punished that he could hardly wish his
literary friend Good-night" (51). It is Boffin, of course, who
is 'literary' here, and recognises the imagination of the literary
world as a stunning reality. This, of course, is very largely
the gift of his innocence; and it is Mr Boffin's innocence which
has often been found so difficult in his complicity with John
Harmon. When he joins in with narrative he does so more
convincingly than the narrative itself might have required,
producing at the point where real feelings meet the artifices of
narrative a confusion in which the story finds itself taken over
by the power of those good feelings; and this produces a great
deal of mystification. Mr Boffin plays the game of narrative,
but does so with the real feeling which has no place in it. He
does what the novel would do, and makes the most of a life
in-between the imagination which left him vulnerable and the
narrative which seems to exploit, or at least to control. Boffin
very oddly comes to dominate the Wilfer-Harmon plot, which is
left with a happiness that seems mere rhetoric in comparison to
the warmth of his own speech. He brings inspiration to a
narrative in which it is sorely needed; as he tells us himself
in Book 4, Chapter 13,

> When John said, if he had been so happy as to win your
> affections and possess your heart, it come into my head
> to turn round upon him with "Win her affections and pos-
> sess her heart! Mew says the cat, Quack quack says the
> duck, and Bow-wow-wow says the dog." I couldn't tell
> you how it come into my head or where from, but it had
> so much the sound of a rasper that I own to you it as-
> tonished myself. I was awful nigh bursting out a laughing
> though, when it made John stare! (52)

Narrative, in Mr Boffin's hands, comes as if from nowhere,
and takes over Harmon's story, discrediting the language of the
Will as Venus discredits it in Wegg, and replacing it with his
own spontaneous speech. What is important here is that it is
he, and not Harmon, in whom the novel has its interest, whatever the interest of the narrative. He exposes the weakness
of Harmon's end, and the emptiness of its language, and gives
his happiness the feeling that seems so sadly missing from the
dreary rhetoric of his marriage, when "O there are days in this
life, worth life and worth death. And O what a bright old song
it is, that O 'tis love, 'tis love, 'tis love, that makes the world
go round!" (53) It is the Boffins who re-stage this marriage
at the end of the book with its proper feelings.

While Mr Boffin's good nature, however, exists between fiction and narrative, it does not exist between Bella and John Harmon. Their happiness is Boffin's happiness; their life remains the self-absorbed life of narrative. Bella and Harmon do not so much meet each other, as are themselves met by Mr Boffin's imagination. We do not find a middle ground in their relationship so much as in what Boffin does for it, and their happiness depends upon his peripheral involvement and is displaced there. Narrative cannot control this happiness, we see; it rests instead with the chance encounter of narrative with the fictive imagination.

Returning now to the novel's other chief concern, that of Lizzie, Headstone and Wrayburn, the isolation in which we left these figures does at least seem to promise more than the dead and unhappy associations of narrative. Their very isolation seems to leave a space for the kind of interaction that was impossible between Bella and Harmon, even if that interaction must come about without control, and by chance. At the same time, while such relationship is difficult, all three figures seek a marriage in a world different from Harmon's, a world in which fiction misses narrative and narrative fiction, in which authority misses vulnerability and vulnerability misses authority; a world in which a middle ground is *sought*. Whereas in the story of Harmon and Bella there is no room for the operation of the 'in-between' vision, the kind of irony which refuses control of either fiction or narrative, here, in the relation of these figures, we see that there is a kind of void in which no figure is capable of asserting a fictive or narrative voice as an authoritative vision. None of these figures, it becomes clear, is capable of emerging alone as the dominant force of this part of the plot, for each is governed by a crisis of feeling and action. Lizzie finds herself confined by feeling; Eugene and Bradley by opposite kinds of action, the first by the limitation of silence and the second by the limitation of speech.

Each, moreover, finds him- or herself the object of the narrative or fictive wills of the others. Lizzie becomes an object of home (which both Bradley and Eugene seek); Bradley of middle-class aspiration (which Lizzie rejects); and Eugene of middle-class detachment and ennui (which Lizzie distrusts).

While narrative in each case however finds itself incapable of moving towards fiction, it does find in its opposing form an effigy of the world it hates. In Eugene this produces merely bored contempt; in Bradley Headstone it produces violence. This violence then becomes the medium of the novel's in-between vision, the middle ground in which what happens is accidental and beyond control. It is the equivalent in human relationship to the image of the river, existing *between* individual and social responsibility, having neither the authority of narrative, in the blindness of its passion, nor the innocence or incoherence of fiction in its clear purpose. This passion is the exasperation of the middle class world, the only *active* feeling we see remaining to the middle classes, and the blind impulsion of the resentment of its expectations against a world which can impose a structure of expectation without a structure of fulfilment. This, we see, is the accidental energy of the middle-world which exists outside any narrative control, and at the same time beyond any imaginative acceptance, as what Nietzsche might have called the conclusion of a social order 'against itself' (54), as the consequence of the disparity and separation of the fictions and narratives it contains. Bella and Harmon became trapped in the similarity of their ends; now, the opposition of the ends of Bradley and Eugene begins to offer the possibility of a freedom. Bradley cannot plot to make Lizzie love him, but he can plot to overthrow what already exists in his own world, and to destroy Eugene's silent consciousness. If his narrative cannot control fiction, then at least it will seem to assert its authority in the world of narrative, where that world seems to oppose feelings.

In a sense, Bradley's attack upon Eugene is then the expression of his love for Lizzie, and of his own will to move where he cannot, towards her world. At the same time, the attack takes Eugene where he has no will to go; and confronts him with the failure of his secrecy, bringing his knowledge of other narratives, that they *must* fail, into his own, and releasing him from the terrible self-absorption that a survival in secrecy has become. The two figures are brought together by narrative, in the violence engendered by their different kinds of self-obsession, the one craving authority and the other a hiding place, as the outcome of the opposite activities of a male search for the imagination of feeling. The following is the climax of this interaction - for, as we will see, it ceases to be a narrative:

> The rippling of the river seemed to cause a correspondent stir in Eugene's uneasy reflections. He would have laid them asleep if he could, but they were in movement, like the stream, and all tending one way with a strong current. As the ripple under the moon broke unexpectedly now and then, and palely flashed in a new shape and with a new sound, so parts of his thoughts started, unbidden, from the rest, and revealed their wickedness. "Out of the question to marry her," said Eugene, "and out of the question to leave her. The crisis!"
> He had sauntered far enough. Before turning to retrace his steps, he stopped upon the margin, to look down at the reflected night. In an instant, with a dreadful crash, the reflected night turned crooked, flames shot jaggedly across the air, and the moon and the stars came bursting from the sky. (55)

This is the point at which Eugene's silence becomes the spoken lie it hides, and it is at this point that chance takes over.

The choice, of course, is impossible; but here Headstone saves him from choice. Once again, we see the action from the perspective of the writing, which finds its own intermediary; and once again it finds it in the river. The river produces a 'reflection', a 'correspondent stir', which functions as a moral, narrative sense. Functioning for a moment like a mirror, it produces the judgement upon Eugene that we have never quite had access to, revealing 'wickedness'. For a moment, we see the river as the relentless force that Master Humphrey feared; as the force that Eugene fears in feeling, the force that Headstone embraces and assents to, "all tending one way". Headstone only becomes the tool of this mighty stream of tendency, in punishing Eugene for the lie that is finally spoken.

Immediately, the river changes: "In an instant, with a dreadful crash, the reflected night turned crooked, ... and the moon and the stars came bursting from the sky." There is in this change precisely the dualistic generosity which we have previously seen the river offer, for it does not simply swallow Eugene into its terrible surface. We see again here that it has another dimension; that reflection only betrays the depths that lie within it. "I'll send you to the moon, I'll send you to the stars," Orlick tells Pip; and Pip, rather like Harmon, can only think of how he will be remembered. Here, the moon and the stars become a reality, another world, and in the instant of the violence that the 'movement' of the river has done to Eugene's will to sleep we have passed through its surface, away from memory and reflection, to glimpse another world, the dream world of death that is the reality of silence. The river becomes our passage between two worlds, as it becomes Eugene's, and as it never was Harmon's.

This immersion in the world of fiction provides Lizzie with her opportunity to act. She pulls Eugene, half-alive, from the river just as her father pulled corpses, and in doing so finds a kind of equality with Eugene in which both acknowledge an existence both on and through the river's surface. The 'Word' Eugene is able to find in marriage is entirely unlike the word that John Harmon uses to marry Bella, for it is born of this equality, the half-immersion of Lizzie and Eugene together creating a real language which exists in between the worlds of silence and lies, just as each character has come to do. Headstone, meanwhile, having murdered in the guise of the once-drowned Riderhoood, finds the river his resting place, the place of peace and of sleep, and dies, as he resolves, the death that Master Humphrey told us was 'easiest and best', in his evasion of the 'movement' of things that eventually threatened to destroy him as he had attempted to use it to destroy Eugene. Thus Headstone, too, passes through the surface of things; and while, like Hexam, there is no in-between place for him, he persists, in a sense, in the man his violent integrity makes of Eugene; so that Twemlow's final tribute is a tribute to Headstone as well.

Twemlow's voice, ending the novel, has a dual function. First, it reminds us of the part of the novel which has been of real importance; mediated by Mortimer, Twemlow's 'Voice' has the authority at least of a tired but persistent decency, and recognises a strength in Eugene with which Harmon was unable to provide us:

> "I say," resumes Twemlow, "if such feelings on the part of this gentleman, induced this gentleman to marry this lady, I think he is the greater gentleman for the action, and makes her the greater lady. I beg to say, that when I use the word, gentleman, I use it in the sense in which the degree may be attained by any man." (56)

The second function of this judgement lies in the character of Twemlow himself, reminding us that if the writing has a voice, it does not belong to the narrative, and neither to the world of imagination and innocence. Twemlow has had no part in the story, while he has at the same time experienced too much for his bewilderment to be in any sense fictive. Curiously, the ending comes between the two endings we might have expected; the 'happy ending' of the novel's narratives has been achieved in the previous chapter, and its life is over. "Nobody's business any more" (57), David Copperfield's complaint after his marriage, might be the complaint of narrative, and of John and Bella Harmon, here. At the same time, the nemesis of the dinner-table, and the fall of the Veneerings, is yet to come. Twemlow's tired tribute provides another place for the novel's in-between vision, for it comes from what is apparently the periphery of things. Writing here refuses to glorify or sustain itself by ending, and in doing so preserves what it has discovered in its course, an accidental world which has discovered the 'Word' Eugene seeks by refusing to pursue it into either the world of imagination or the world of beginnings and endings, remaining strictly in between the fiction and the narrative of the novel.

In this ending Dickens' voice ceases to offer or to require a specific authority, and ceases, too, to find that authority must be sacrificed. His voice has instead been located throughout the novel, as a knowledge and understanding of the meaning of every part of the reality it represents, and with no direct investment in any single aspect. Dickens withdraws from both narrative and fiction, and allows them to take their own place in the landscape of the novel, to do what they can to bring about coherence. The interaction they provide does produce, finally, a kind of unity, which is the unity of reality. It is accidental, precarious, but, in the detachment which is the chance that Dickens is himself prepared to take in order to bring it about, it is possible.

Footnotes

(1) See Henry James, *The House of Fiction*, Ed.   Leon Edel (1957), 254.

(2) See for instance H.M.Daleski, *Dickens and the Art of Analogy*, 271-2; A.O.J.Cockshut, *The Imagination of Charles Dickens*, 170, 175.

(3) See page 146, above.

(4) See page 86, above.

(5) *The Old Curiosity Shop*, 43, and page 42 above.

(6) *The Old Curiosity Shop*, 44, and page 42 above.

(7) *Our Mutual Friend*, 44.

(8) *Our Mutual Friend*, 45.

(9) *Our Mutual Friend*, 47.

(10) *Our Mutual Friend*, 76.

(11) *Our Mutual Friend*, 191.

(12) *The Wasteland*, I, 'The Burial of the Dead', 1-2.   The wasteland imagery has been well documented.   In the draft of the poem, Eliot quoted from *Our Mutual Friend* for its title, "He do the Police in Different Voices".   See *'The Wasteland': a facsimile and transcript of the Original Drafts*, Ed. Valerie Eliot (1971), 5, and Note 125.   For further discussion of the correspondences with the poem see Edgar Johnson, *Charles Dickens: his Tragedy and Triumph*, 1043

(13) *Our Mutual Friend*, 191.

(14) *Our Mutual Friend*, 222.

(15) *Our Mutual Friend*, 271.

(16) *Our Mutual Friend*, 43.

(17) *Our Mutual Friend*, 71.

(18) *Our Mutual Friend*, 73.

(19) *Our Mutual Friend*, 73.

(20) *Our Mutual Friend*, 70.

(21) *Our Mutual Friend*, 71.

(22) *Our Mutual Friend*, 504.

(23) *Our Mutual Friend*, 283.

(24) *Our Mutual Friend*, 283.

(25) *Our Mutual Friend*, 294.

(26) *Our Mutual Friend*, 294.

(27) *Our Mutual Friend*, 321.

(28) *Our Mutual Friend*, 321.

(29) *Our Mutual Friend*, 323.

(30) *Our Mutual Friend*, 333-4.

(31) *Our Mutual Friend*, 346.

(32) *Our Mutual Friend*, 345.

(33) *Our Mutual Friend*, 452.

(34) *Our Mutual Friend*, 452.

(35) *Our Mutual Friend*, 453.

(36) *Our Mutual Friend*, 288.

(37) *Our Mutual Friend*, 338.
(38) *Our Mutual Friend*, 348.
(39) *Our Mutual Friend*, 600.
(40) *Our Mutual Friend*, 339.
(41) J.R.Kincaid, *Dickens and the Rhetoric of Laughter*, 228.
(42) See Taylor Stoehr, *The Dreamer's Stance*, (New York 1965), 203-5; J.R.Kincaid, *Dickens and the Rhetoric of Laughter*, 228.
(43) *Our Mutual Friend*, 429.
(44) *Our Mutual Friend*, 841.
(45) *Our Mutual Friend*, 671.
(46) *Our Mutual Friend*, 527.
(47) *Our Mutual Friend*, 853.
(48) *Our Mutual Friend*, 389.
(49) J.R.Kincaid, *Dickens and the Rhetoric of Laughter*, 245.
(50) *Our Mutual Friend*, 104.
(51) *Our Mutual Friend*, 104.
(52) *Our Mutual Friend*, 848.
(53) *Our Mutual Friend*, 738.
(54) See *The Genealogy of Morals*, Trans. Samuel, Ed. Levy (London 1910), 209.
(55) *Our Mutual Friend*, 766.
(56) *Our Mutual Friend*, 891.
(57) See *David Copperfield*, 701, and page 115 above.

Primary Works

Thomas Carlyle   *Selected Writings*, Ed. Alan Sherston (Penguin, Harmondsworth, 1971).

S. T. Coleridge   *Biographia Literaria*, Ed. George Watson (Dent, London, 1975).

S. T. Coleridge   *Poems*, Ed. John Beer (Dent, London, 1963).

S. T. Coleridge   *The Friend* (Bell, London, 1904).

De Quincey   *The Confessions of an English Opium Eater*, Ed. John E. Jordan (Routledge and Kegan Paul, London, 1973).

Charles Dickens   *American Notes and Pictures from Italy*, Library Edition (Chapman and Hall, London, 1874).

Charles Dickens   *A Tale of Two Cities*, Ed. George Woodcock (Penguin, Harmondsworth, 1970).

Charles Dickens   *Barnaby Rudge*, Ed. Gordon Spence (Penguin, Harmondsworth, 1973).

Charles Dickens   *Bleak House*, Ed. Norman Page (Penguin, Harmondsworth, 1971).

Charles Dickens	*David Copperfield*, Ed. Trevor Blount (Penguin, Harmondsworth, 1966).
Charles Dickens	*Dombey and Son*, Ed. Peter Fairclough (Penguin, Harmondsworth, 1970).
Charles Dickens	*Great Expectations*, Ed. Angus Calder (Penguin, Harmondsworth, 1965).
Charles Dickens	*Hard Times*, Ed. David Craig (Penguin, Harmondsworth, 1970).
Charles Dickens	*Little Dorrit*, Ed. John Holloway (Penguin, Harmondsworth, 1970).
Charles Dickens	*London Crimes*, Ed. Nadya Aisenberg (Rowan Tree Press, Massachusetts, 1982).
Charles Dickens	*Martin Chuzzlewit*, Ed. P. N. Furbank (Penguin, Harmondsworth, 1970).
Charles Dickens	*Miscellaneous Papers*, Additional Volume to Library Edition (Chapman and Hall, London, 1908).
Charles Dickens	*Nicholas Nickleby*, Ed. Michael Slater (Penguin, Harmondsworth, 1978).
Charles Dickens	*Oliver Twist*, Ed. Peter Fairclough (Penguin, Harmondsworth, 1966).
Charles Dickens	*Our Mutual Friend*, Ed. Stephen Gill (Penguin, Harmondsworth, 1970).
Charles Dickens	*Pickwick Papers*, Ed. Robert L. Patten (Penguin, Harmondsworth, 1972).
Charles Dickens	*Selected Short Fiction*, Ed. Deborah A. Thomas (Penguin, Harmondsworth, 1976).

Charles Dickens   *Sketches by Boz*, Library Edition (Chapman and Hall, London, 1874).

Charles Dickens   *The Christmas Books*, 2 Vols., Ed. Michael Slater (Penguin, Harmondsworth, 1971).

Charles Dickens   *The Mystery of Edwin Drood*, Ed. Arthur J. Cox (Penguin, Harmondsworth, 1974).

Charles Dickens   *The Old Curiosity Shop*, Ed. Angus Easson (Penguin, Harmondsworth, 1972).

Charles Dickens   *The Uncollected Writings from Household Words 1850-1859*, Ed. Harry Stone, 2 Vols. (Allen Lane, Bloomington and London, 1969).

Charles Dickens   *The Uncommercial Traveller*, Library Edition (Chapman and Hall, London, 1875).

The Letters of Charles Dickens: Ed. Madeline House and Graham Storey, The Pilgrim Edition, Vol. I (Clarendon Press, Oxford, 1965).

The Letters of Charles Dickens: Ed. Madeline House and Graham Storey, The Pilgrim Edition, Vol. II (Clarendon Press, Oxford, 1969).

The Letters of Charles Dickens: Ed. Madeline House, Graham Storey and Kathleen Tillotson, The Pilgrim Edition, Vol. III (Clarendon Press, Oxford, 1974).

The Letters of Charles Dickens: Ed. Kathleen Tillotson, The Pilgrim Edition, Vol. IV (Clarendon Press, Oxford, 1977).

The Letters of Charles Dickens: Ed. Graham Storey and K. J. Fielding, The Pilgrim Edition, Vol. V (Clarendon Press, Oxford, 1981).

T. S. Eliot   *Complete Poems and Plays* (Faber and Faber, London, 1969).

SELECT BIBLIOGRAPHY

T. S. Eliot   *The Wasteland: a Facsimile and
                            Transcript*, Ed. Valerie Eliot
                            (Faber and Faber, London,
                            1971).

William Hazlitt   *The Plain Speaker* (Dent, London,
                            1928).

William Hazlitt   *Selected Writings*, Ed. Ronald
                            Blythe (Penguin, Harmondsworth,
                            1970).

Henry James   *The House of Fiction*, Ed. Leon
                            Edel (Rupert Hart-Davis, Lon-
                            don, 1957).

D. H. Lawrence   *Study of Thomas Hardy*, re-
                            printed in *Pheonix* (Heinemann,
                            London, 1961).

William Wordsworth   *Poetical Works*, Ed. Hutchinson,
                            Revised De Selincourt, Oxford
                            Standard Authors (Oxford Uni-
                            versity Press, Oxford, 1936).

William Wordsworth   *The Prelude*, Ed. Jonathon
                            Wordsworth, M. H. Abrams, and
                            Stephen Gill, Norton Critical
                            Editions (Norton, New York and
                            London, 1979).

Secondary Works

Robert Altick   *The English Common Reader*
                            (University of Chicago Press,
                            Chicago, 1957).

M. Bakhtin   *The Dialogic Imagination* (Uni-
                            versity of Texas Press, Austin,
                            1981).

John Bayley   *The Uses of Division* (Chatto and
                            Windus, London, 1976).

George Bornstein (Ed.)   *Romantic and Modern* (University
                            of Pittsburgh Press, Pittsburgh,
                            1977).

G. L. Brook — *The Language of Dickens* (Andre Deutsch, London, 1970)

Marilyn Butler — *Romantics, Rebels and Reactionaries* (Oxford University Press, Oxford, 1981).

John Carey — *The Violent Effigy* (Faber and Faber, London, 1973).

Louis Cazamian — *The Development of English Humour* (Duke University Press, North Carolina, 1952).

Kellow Chesney — *The Victorian Underworld* (Pelican, Harmondsworth, 1972).

G. K. Chesterton — *Appreciation and Criticisms of the Works of Charles Dickens* (Dent, London, 1933).

A. O. J. Cockshut — *The Imagination of Charles Dickens* (Collins, London, 1961).

Philip Collins (Ed.) — *Dickens: the Critical Heritage* (Routledge and Kegan Paul, New York, 1971).

Philip Collins (Ed.) — *Dickens: Interviews and Recollections,* 2 Vols. (Macmillan, London, 1981).

H. M. Daleski — *Dickens and the Art of Analogy* (Faber and Faber, London, 1970).

Davies and Beatty (Eds.) — *Literature of the Romantic Period 1750-1850* (Liverpool University Press, Liverpool, 1976).

Dyos and Wolff (Eds.) — *The Victorian City* (Routledge and Kegan Paul, London, 1973).

A. E. Dyson (Ed.) — *Dickens, Modern Judgements* (Macmillan, London, 1968).

A. E. Dyson — *The Inimitable Dickens* (Macmillan, London, 1970).

SELECT BIBLIOGRAPHY

George H. Ford — *Dickens and his Reader* (Princetown University Press, Princetown, 1955).

Ford and Lane (Eds.) — *The Dickens Critics* (Cornell University Press, New York, 1961).

John Forster — *Life of Charles Dickens* (Chapman and Hall, London, 1872).

Northrop Frye — 'Dickens and the Comedy of Humours', *Experience in the Novel*, Ed. Roy Harvey Pearce (Columbia University Press, New York, 1968), pp.49-81.

Gross and Pearson (Eds.) — *Dickens and the Twentieth Century* (Routledge and Kegan Paul, London, 1962).

Barbara Hardy — *The Moral Art of Dickens* (Athlone Press, London, 1979).

Christopher Hibbert — *The Making of Charles Dickens* (Longmans, London, 1967).

H. W. Hill — 'Books that Dickens Read', *The Dickensian*, 45 (1943-4), pp.81-90, pp.201-207.

Susan R. Horton — *The Reader in the Dickens World* (Macmillan, London, 1981)

Hulin and Coustillas (Eds.) — *Victorian Writers and the City* (Universite de Lille, Lille, 1979).

Humphrey House — *The Dickens World* (Oxford Paperbacks, London, 1960).

Louis James — *Fiction for the Working Man, 1830-50* (Oxford University Press, London, 1963).

Derek Jarrett — *England in the Age of Hogarth* (Hart-Davis, MacGibbon, London, 1974).

Edgar Johnson — *Charles Dickens: His Tragedy and Triumph*, 2 Vols. (Gollancz, London, 1953).

P. J. Keating	*The Working Classes in Victorian Fiction* (Routledge and Kegan Paul, London, 1971).
Arnold Kettle	*An Introduction to the English Novel*, 2 Vols. (Hutchinson, London, 1971).
J. R. Kincaid	*Dickens and the Rhetoric of Laughter* (Clarendon Press, Oxford, 1971).
Suzanne Langer	*Feeling and Form* (Routledge and Kegan Paul, London, 1953).
Coral Lansbury	'Dickens' Romanticism Domesticated', *Dickens Studies Newsletter*, 3 (1972), pp.36-46.
F. R. and Q. D. Leavis	*Dickens the Novelist* (Chatto and Windus, London, 1970).
Maynard Mack	*The Garden and the City* (University of Toronto Press, Toronto, 1965).
J. Hillis Miller	*Charles Dickens: the World of his Novels* (Cambridge, Mass., 1958).
Sylvere Monod	*Dickens the Novelist* (University of Oklahoma Press, Oklahoma, 1968).
S. J. Newman	*Dickens at Play* (Macmillan, London, 1981).
Robert Newsom	*Dickens: on the Romantic Side of Familiar Things* (Columbia University Press, New York, 1977).
Friedrich Nietzsche	*The Genealogy of Morals*, Trans. H. Samuel, Ed. O. Levy (Foulis, London, 1910).
J. C. Olmsted (Ed.)	*A Victorian Art of Fiction* (Garland, New York, 1979).
Orel and Worth (Eds.)	'The Nineteenth Century Writer and His Audience', *University of Kansas Studies*, 40.

George Orwell — 'Charles Dickens', *Dickens, Dali and Others: Studies in Popular Culture* (Harcourt, Bruce and World, New York, 1963), pp. 1-75.

D. J. Palmer — *Comedy: Developments in Criticism,* Casebook Series (Macmillan, London, 1984).

R. B. Partlow Jr. (Ed.) — *Dickens the Craftsman* (Southern Illinois University Press, Carbondale London and Amsterdam, 1970).

R. L. Patten — *Charles Dickens and his Publishers* (Clarendon Press, Oxford, 1978).

Martin Price (Ed.) — *Dickens: A Collection of Critical Essays* (Prentice-Hall, New Jersey, 1967).

Raphael Samuel — *East End Underworld* (Routledge and Kegan Paul, London, 1981).

Scholes and Kellogg (Eds.) — *The Nature of Narrative* (Oxford University Press, New York, 1968).

F. S. Schwarzbach — *Dickens and the City* (Athlone Press, London, 1979).

P. J. M. Scott — *Reality and Comic Confidence in Dickens* (Macmillan, London, 1979).

David Simpson — *Irony and Authority in Romantic Poetry* (Macmillan, London, 1979).

Michael Slater — *Dickens and Women* (Dent, London, 1983).

Taylor Stoehr — *Dickens: the Dreamer's Stance* (Cornell University Press, Ithaca, New York, 1965).

Harvey Peter Sucksmith — *The Narrative Art of Dickens* (Clarendon Press, Oxford, 1970).

SELECT BIBLIOGRAPHY

Deborah A. Thomas

Dickens and the Short Story (Batsford, London, 1982).

Kathleen Tillotson

Novels of the 1840s (Clarendon, Oxford, 1954).

Dorothy Van Ghent

'The Dickens World: A View From Todgers' ', *Sewanee Review,* lviii (1950), pp.419-38.

Ian Watt

The Rise of the Novel (Chatto and Windus, London, 1957).

Alexander Welsh

The City of Dickens (Clarendon Press, Oxford, 1971).

Raymond Williams

Culture and Society (Chatto and Windus, London, 1958).

Raymond Williams

The Country and the City (Chatto and Windus, London, 1973).

I have used the following abbreviations where appropriate: (SB) for *Sketches by Boz*, (PP) for *Pickwick Papers*, (OT) for *Oliver Twist*, (OCS) for *The Old Curiosity Shop*, (NN) for *Nicholas Nickleby*, (MC) for *Martin Chuzzlewit*, (DS) for *Dombey and Son*, (DC) for *David Copperfield*, (BH) for *Bleak House*, (LD) for *Little Dorrit*, (TTC) for *A Tale of Two Cities*, (GE) for *Great Expectations*, and (OMF) for *Our Mutual Friend*.

Fog 72, 73, 75, 79, 85, 93, 106, 112, 131, 138, 146, 165
Fogg, Mr (PP) 16
Food 57, 104-105
Forster, John 1n., 70n., 100n., 102-103, 136
Frozen Deep, The 133

Garlands, the (OCS) 65
Golden Dustman, the (OMF) 182-183
Great Expectations 135-161, 164, 170
Guppy, Mr (OMF) 86, 92-93, 94-95

'Hackney Coach Stands' (SB) 11
Hamlet 111
Hardy, Barbara *The Moral Art of Dickens* 1n., 119
Harmon, John (OMF) 182-188, 190, 191
Havisham, Miss (GE) 140-142, 147, 149, 150-151, 154-155, 156, 159
Hawdon, Captain (BH) 86, 90, 91, 92
Headstone, Bradley (OMF) 177-179, 181, 182, 183, 188-189
Heep, Uriah (DC) 56, 117-118, 122, 123, 127, 153, 174
Hexam, Charley (OMF) 171-173, 177, 182
Hexam, Gaffer (OMF) 166-167, 168, 169, 171, 174, 178, 182
Hexam, Lizzie (OMF) 166, 171-173, 174, 176-180, 181, 182, 185, 186, 188-190
Hibbert, Christopher 100n.
Hillis Miller, J. 1n.
Hirsch, E.D. 2
Hogarth, Mary 59
'Horatio Sparkins' (SB) 15
Hortense (BH) 85
'Hospital Patient, The' (SB) 13
House, M. 70n.
Household Words 9
Humphrey, Master (OCS) 41-47, 48, 49, 50, 51-52, 60-61, 71, 72, 96, 99, 102, 165, 190

Illness 42, 78, 80
Inspector, Mr (OMF) 168
Intuitionism 2, 3, 5

Jaggers, Mr (GE) 155, 156, 157, 161
James, Henry 165
Janet (DC) 107
Jarley, Mrs (OCS) 53, 62
Jarndyce, Mr (BH) 77, 81-83, 87, 88, 100
Jiniwin, Mrs (OCS) 59
Jo (BH) 86, 91-92
Joe (GE) 145, 146, 147, 148, 156, 161
Joe, Mrs (GE) 143, 152, 156
Johnson, Edgar 1n., 70n., 100n., 133
Josipovici, Gabriel 1n., 99n., 100n.